AMERICAN GRAND STRATEGY
IN THE AGE OF TRUMP

AMERICAN GRAND STRATEGY

IN THE AGE OF

TRUMP

HAL BRANDS

BROOKINGS INSTITUTION PRESS
Washington, D.C.

The Brookings Institution is a private nonprofit organization devoted to research, education, and publication on important issues of domestic and foreign policy. Its principal purpose is to bring the highest quality independent research and analysis to bear on current and emerging policy problems. Interpretations or conclusions in Brookings publications should be understood to be solely those of the authors.

Library of Congress Cataloging-in-Publication data are available.
ISBN 978-0-8157-3278-5 (cloth : alk. paper)
ISBN 978-0-8157-3279-2 (ebook)

9 8 7 6 5 4 3 2 1

Typeset in Minion Pro

Composition by Westchester Publishing Services

Contents

Preface and Acknowledgments

We live in a time of disruption, uncertainty, and contention in American grand strategy. The election of Donald Trump in November 2016 raised profound questions about America's global role—not just about how the day-to-day chaos of Trump's presidency would affect Washington's many foreign relationships, but about what the rise of a leader whose campaign rhetoric rejected so many long-standing tenets of U.S. foreign policy might indicate about the future of America's approach to the world. Nor is Trump the only source of debate and disquiet in American grand strategy today. For regardless of who triumphed in the 2016 presidential election, the United States would have had to confront numerous fundamental questions about how it has addressed the international environment in the recent past—and how it will do so in the years to come.

Has America really blundered about quixotically on the global stage since the end of the Cold War, or has its grand strategy actually been fairly sensible and effective? Did the Obama administration leave a disastrous legacy of U.S. retreat and metastasizing international chaos, or did it execute a shrewd approach that maximized U.S. power for the long term? What would happen if the United States radically pulled back from the world in the face of a more difficult geopolitical panorama, as many leading international relations scholars advocate? Is the tradition of American internationalism politically sustainable in light of the rise of Donald Trump? What might a more nationalistic grand strategy look like, whether in the age of Trump or after, and what might its effects be for the United States and the international system? How much military power is necessary to sustain the ambitious grand strategy—and relatively benign international order—to which America has become accustomed, at a time when the geopolitical threats to that strategy are more severe than at any time in a generation? All of these issues are being debated—often heatedly—today, because all are crucial to understanding the recent trajectory and future prospects of American grand strategy in a changing world.

The goal of this book is to begin making sense of these issues, and thereby to provide a firmer intellectual foundation from which to address the dilemmas and uncertainties of America's global role. I have no intention, in publishing this collection of essays, of seeking to fully keep up with the foreign policy headlines of the Trump presidency, a job that is difficult in any administration and utterly hopeless in this one. My primary intent, rather, is to analyze the broader contours of American grand strategy in the present moment, and to work through some of the deeper questions and bigger debates surrounding U.S. foreign relations today—two tasks that are vital both to understanding the Trump era and to getting grand strategy right.

"Grand strategy" is itself a contested concept, of course. Here as elsewhere, I define grand strategy simply as the integrated set of concepts that gives purpose and direction to a country's dealings with the world. A grand strategy consists of considered assessments of the global environment, a country's highest interests and goals within that environment, the most important threats to those interests and opportunities for advancing them, and—not least—the ways that limited resources can be allocated across competing priorities and issues. This intellectual calculus, in turn, shapes policy—the everyday operations, endeavors, and initiatives through which a country interacts with the world. Grand strategy, then, is the intellectual framework that connects means to ends, ideas to action, at the highest level of national affairs; it is a country's guiding conception of where it wants to go and how it seeks to get there. In concerning itself with U.S. grand strategy, this book thus focuses on the overarching, first-order questions about America's purpose and policies in the global environment.

When it comes to American grand strategy today, charting the path ahead first requires looking backward, at the record of U.S. global engagement since the Cold War. The conventional wisdom on this subject is that American grand strategy took a radical turn once the superpower conflict ended, that this change led Washington from disaster to disaster over the subsequent quarter century, and that the fading of U.S. dominance has now left Washington with little choice but to accept a far more circumscribed role in global affairs. As I argue in chapter 1, the conventional wisdom is wrong. There was no radical break after the Cold War; U.S. officials simply adapted a successful post–World War II grand strategy to the more favorable conditions of a one-superpower world. This strategy was far from quixotic or counterproductive; it helped create a global environment that was—by any reasonable historical standard—remarkably stable and advantageous to American interests. And while American primacy is under real pressure today, Washington retains a formidable and unmatched position in the international hierarchy, and so it should not abandon but rather recalibrate and recapitalize a post–Cold War strategy that has fared pretty well. Adaption at the margins may not be sexy, but it best suits U.S. interests in an age of increasingly contested American primacy.

Yet what would happen if the United States were to undertake a more thoroughgoing geopolitical retrenchment? This is the course advocated by many leading international relations scholars—and also, at times, by Donald Trump during his run for the White House in 2016. By pulling back from U.S. overseas commitments and dramatically reducing U.S. global activism, proponents of this "offshore balancing" strategy contend, America can actually enjoy greater security and influence at drastically reduced costs. As I argue in chapter 2, however, there is no such thing as a free lunch where global security and U.S. interests are concerned. If implemented, offshore balancing would probably invite significantly increased violence and instability in key regions from Europe to East Asia, while undercutting American influence and compromising key policy objectives such as counterterrorism and nuclear nonproliferation. In the near term, Washington might save some money by pursuing radical retrenchment, but in doing so it would usher in a far more dangerous world—one in which America might well face vastly greater long-term costs.

Chapters 1 and 2 thus address ongoing debates about post–Cold War grand strategy and its alternatives. Chapter 3 examines another key debate, about Barack Obama's statecraft. During his presidency and after, Obama's supporters argued that he pursued a wise grand strategy focused on positioning the country to succeed in "the long game." His detractors countered that Obama's legacy was one of weakness and retreat, or simply that he lacked any coherent strategy whatsoever. In truth, the story was more complicated than either side allowed. Obama indeed had a coherent grand strategy, aimed at perpetuating American primacy and the post–Cold War order—but doing so at reduced military costs, through enhanced engagement with adversaries, and by shifting America's geographical focus to reflect long-term geostrategic trends. In practice, that strategy did help recalibrate U.S. global engagement after the overextension of the Bush years, and it informed numerous policies that were more constructive than not in their effects. Unfortunately, however, Obama's statecraft strategy also revealed deep dilemmas—from the limits of light-footprint military intervention to the double-edged nature of diplomacy with adversaries—at the heart of recent U.S. grand strategy, and it led many observers to wonder whether he had avoided the mistakes of his predecessor only to commit the opposite mistakes himself. Obama ultimately left an ambiguous record, both the positive and negative aspects of which profoundly shaped the world his successor inherited.

Obama's successor, of course, was Donald Trump, and so the following two chapters grapple with what Trump's rise means for both the historical patterns and the medium-term future of American grand strategy. Chapter 4 asks whether the election of Trump—who campaigned on a sharply anti-internationalist platform emphasizing hostility to U.S. alliances, free trade, and other long-standing pillars of American global engagement—was simply a political aberration, or whether it means that the post–World War II tradition of U.S. internationalism is now politically dead. The answer, here as elsewhere, is not as obvious as it may seem. Postelection hyperbole notwithstanding, Trump's rise does not signal the collapse of American internationalism, because public support for key aspects of that tradition remains fairly strong—and because the tradition itself has proved quite resilient over time. Yet Trump's ascendancy has nonetheless revealed deeper, long-building strains within American internationalism—strains that he skillfully exploited in 2016. It is too early, then, to pronounce American internationalism politically dead, but that tradition is indeed suffering from accumulated maladies that will have to be addressed if it is to endure.

If one accepts that American internationalism is facing a crisis, then how might U.S. policy change—not today or tomorrow, but in the coming four years, eight years, or even longer? Chapter 5 answers that question by offering two models of what a more nationalistic grand strategy might look like during the Trump presidency or after. The first model is "Fortress America," a hard-line, neo-isolationist strategy that would deliberately undermine the existing global order in search of unilateral (and ultimately ephemeral) advantage. This model is troubling but not entirely implausible; one could trace its basic outlines in many of Trump's campaign promises from 2016. Fortunately, there is also a second, less destructive, model. Under this approach, Washington would not deconstruct an international system that has, on balance, served it well. But it would focus on redistributing burdens, securing more advantageous deals and arrangements with U.S. partners and allies, and strengthening America's national position within the existing system—much as Richard Nixon did during an earlier period of global upheaval and domestic discontent. Indeed, whereas Fortress America is likely to lead to a more disordered world and the end of the American superpower as we know it, this "better nationalism" might actually help shore up an internationalist tradition that, for all its successes, is in need of bolstering.

If America is to continue playing anything like its current role in upholding the international order, how much military power will it need? For as chapter 6 points out, the hard-power backbone of recent U.S. grand strategy has been unrivaled military primacy, and that primacy is now being challenged to a dangerous degree. The security threats that Washington confronts have become both more severe and more numerous than at any time since the Cold War. Meanwhile, deep and prolonged budget cuts have significantly eroded American might. The United States still has the world's strongest military by far, but today it nonetheless risks sliding into strategic insolvency—a condition in which commitments exceed capabilities and the stabilizing effects of American primacy begin to wane. In these circumstances, U.S. policymakers may be tempted to retrench geopolitically, or simply to accept greater risk to their various global commitments. Yet a superior option would be to undertake a concerted military expansion similar to the Carter-Reagan buildup of the late Cold War—an approach that would be expensive and politically difficult, no doubt, but one that need not be as economically onerous as often assumed, and one that offers the best chance of sustaining a highly favorable global order.

Chapters 1 through 6 therefore deal with some of the most pressing big-picture debates, challenges, and uncertainties in American grand strategy. Yet in the age of Trump, the sad fact of the matter is that one of the greatest sources of uncertainty in today's international order is the behavior of the United States. And so I conclude this book, in chapter 7, by offering a necessarily provisional assessment of American grand strategy and its consequences through the first year of the Trump presidency. The picture that emerges is of an administration that has not proven as radical in its policies as Trump's campaign rhetoric or tweets might have led one to expect— but that has nonetheless managed, through both its initiatives and its mannerisms, to compromise many of the qualities that have made U.S. statecraft so successful in the past. The president claims to be making America great again. But in reality, the Trump presidency seems likely to diminish the American superpower, while also exacerbating the disruptive tendencies at work in global affairs.

Altogether, if there is a single theme that runs through this book, it is that an engaged and assertive American grand strategy has generally had a constructive impact on the world and on U.S. well-being, and that the dramatic grand strategic departures that have often been proposed in recent years—whether by scholars or America First politicians—are profoundly misguided. Yet it is undeniable that America's existing grand strategy faces serious and growing problems, from the erosion of U.S. military primacy, to the weakening political foundations of American internationalism, to the damage being caused by the Trump administration's own policies, and that nontrivial adjustments will therefore be needed to keep a good thing going. In the end, readers may or may not agree with this assessment; they may accept or reject my answers to the various questions this volume addresses. But my hope is that, at minimum, these essays will stimulate constructive debate about American grand strategy in an age of upheaval.

As usual, I have accumulated a large number of debts in completing this work. Helpful comments and input on the various chapters were provided by, among others, James Baker, Robert Berschinski, Alex Bick, Eliot Cohen, Colin Dueck, Antulio Echevarria, Charles Edel, Eric Edelman, David Epstein, Miriam Estrin, Ryan Evans, Peter Feaver, John Gaddis, Adam Garfinkle, Francis Gavin, Francis Hoffman, Melvyn Leffler, Alexander Lennon, Peter Lewis, Alan Luxenberg, Kelly Magsamen, Thomas Mahnken, John Maurer, Andrew May, Steven Metz, Vali Nasr, Michael Noonan, Mira Rapp-Hooper, Mary Sarotte, Kori Schake, and Thomas Wright. I am especially grateful to Eric Edelman, who kindly permitted me to republish here a revised version of an article that we originally wrote together.

The process of writing this book spanned my tenure at two wonderful institutions, the Duke Sanford School of Public Policy and the Johns Hopkins School of Advanced International Studies. I am profoundly thankful to both institutions for the vibrant intellectual climates they provided. I also thank my editor, Bill Finan of Brookings Institution Press, for helping to conceive this project and bring it to fruition. And, as always, my deepest debt is owed to my family. Emily, Henry, Annabelle, and Dolly are the greatest possible inspirations for my work; I am equally grateful for the fact that they do, occasionally, manage to drag me away from it.

As this book consists of essays published previously and then revised for this volume, a final acknowledgment goes to the journals and magazines in which these pieces first appeared. Chapter 1 was originally published as "U.S. Grand Strategy: Not So Bad After All," *American Interest* 12, no. 3 (January/February 2017), pp. 6–17. Chapter 2 was originally published as "Barack Obama and the Dilemmas of American Grand Strategy," *Washington Quarterly* 39, no. 4 (Winter 2017), pp. 101–25. Chapter 3 was originally published as "Fools Rush Out? The Flawed Logic of Offshore Balancing," *Washington Quarterly* 38, no. 2 (Summer 2015), pp. 7–28. Chapter 4 was originally published as "Is American Internationalism Dead? Reading the National Mood in the Age of Trump," *War on the Rocks*, May 2017. Chapter 5 was originally published as "U.S. Grand Strategy in an Age of Nationalism: Fortress America and Its Alternatives," *Washington Quarterly* 40, no. 1 (Spring 2017), pp. 73–94. Chapter 6 was originally coauthored with Eric Edelman and published as "The Crisis of American Military Primacy and the Search for Strategic Solvency," *Parameters* 46, no. 4 (Winter 2016/2017), pp. 26–42. Where applicable, I thank the editors of these journals and magazines for granting me permission to republish these pieces here.

ONE

THE PRETTY SUCCESSFUL SUPERPOWER

The post–Cold War era has now lasted over a quarter century—longer than the period between the world wars and more than half as long as the Cold War itself. This period, moreover, has been no quiet or restful time in American grand strategy. The United States did not withdraw from the world after the Soviet collapse, or even become a more "normal" country, as some observers advocated at the time. Rather, it recommitted itself to pursuing a globalism every bit as ambitious and energetic as during the bipolar era. Today, at a time when the international order is often thought to be reaching a new inflection point, when the debate over America's global role is more heated than at any time since the early 1990s, and when the political rise and presidency of Donald Trump have injected great uncertainty into U.S. policy, it is worth considering what insights the experience of the post–Cold War era has to offer.

Unfortunately, discussions of America's post–Cold War grand strategy are afflicted by three misconceptions that have become conventional wisdom among critics of U.S. foreign policy. The first is that, with the end of the Cold War, America broke dramatically with its previous grand strategic tradition and undertook a radically new approach to the world. The second is that America's post–Cold War grand strategy has been ineffective and even quixotic—that Washington has essentially squandered the position of preeminence it attained with the Soviet collapse. The third is that this period of U.S. primacy is now over, and that American leaders have no choice but to retrench fundamentally as a result.[1]

All three ideas are more myth than reality; they obscure more than they illuminate. The United States did not embrace a radically new grand strategy after the Cold War; it simply adapted its long-standing post–World War II grand strategy to a new era of American dominance. That endeavor was hardly fruitless or self-defeating; on balance, it has helped ensure that the post–Cold War system has been far more stable, more liberal, and more congenial to U.S. interests than many leading observers predicted as that era began. Finally, although Washington currently faces more—and more pressing—challenges to its international superiority than at any time since 1991, it is premature to conclude that the age of American primacy has passed. The time has not come for radical retrenchment of the sort proposed by many leading academics and championed in Trump's campaign rhetoric. The proper course, rather, is to do what is necessary to sustain the grand strategy that America has pursued, more or less successfully, over the past quarter century.

NOT SO RADICAL

We often think of the end of the Cold War as a fundamental point of departure in America's approach to the world.[2] Yet the grand strategy that successive administrations pursued after 1991 is best seen as the logical extension of an approach that originated decades before, following World War II. For U.S. officials, World War II demonstrated the basic interdependence of the world environment and the corresponding need to define national security in broad, indeed global, terms. Accordingly, the postwar decades saw a sustained American activism designed to mold the external environment—to construct an overarching international order congenial to America's security as well as to its liberal values.

To this end, and throughout the postwar era, American officials consistently promoted an open, liberal economy that would foster U.S. and global prosperity, and they sought to preserve a peaceful international environment in which democracy and human rights could flourish. They worked to create stability and security in key regions from Europe to the Middle East to East Asia, to bind key countries in these areas to the United States both geopolitically and economically, and to prevent any hostile power from dominating these regions either by force or otherwise. They strove to maintain an overall global balance of power that favored America and its Western allies, and to contain and ultimately roll back the influence of aggressive authoritarian states that threatened these various objectives. In support of this basic design, U.S. policymakers undertook a range of global commitments, from security guarantees and forward military deployments to leadership of international trade pacts and institutions. These commitments were unprecedented in U.S. history, and they were designed to project American influence into key regions and issues around the world. During the Cold War, these endeavors helped to foster a thriving international order in the noncommunist world, and to contain—and ultimately defeat—the rival order Moscow sought to create in the socialist bloc.[3]

When the Cold War ended, then, U.S. officials did not have to go back to the drawing board or chart a radical new course in America's approach to the world. They needed, rather, simply to adapt the country's successful postwar grand strategy to a new age of U.S.

and Western supremacy. The United States emerged from the Cold War with clear military, economic, and diplomatic primacy, and at the head of a Western coalition that commanded a vast majority of global power. In these circumstances, Washington effectively doubled down on the core objectives—and many of the specific initiatives—that comprised its postwar statecraft.

The long-standing goal of maintaining favorable balances of power both globally and within key regions, for instance, became one of locking in the remarkable U.S. and Western overmatch that the Soviet collapse had produced. The goal of fostering an environment in which democracy could flourish evolved to include more actively and directly promoting democratic institutions in countries around the globe. The goal of creating a robust liberal economy in the noncommunist world became one of promoting ever-deeper integration in the "first world," while spreading market concepts and institutions into the former second and third worlds. And the goal of containing and ultimately defeating the Soviet Union became one of preventing any new threat—international terrorism, nuclear proliferation, the actions of aggressive "rogue states," or the potential resurgence of tensions within key geopolitical regions such as Europe or East Asia—from rising to the level of the former Soviet menace or otherwise bringing the good times to an end.

In sum, America's post–Cold War grand strategy might best be characterized as one of preserving the geopolitical primacy that America's postwar statecraft had helped deliver, deepening and extending the liberal order that had taken hold in the West during the superpower competition, and suppressing those dangers, whether extant or prospective, that threatened to disrupt such a benign international environment. This strategy was first explicitly spelled out in the Pentagon's 1992 Defense Planning Guidance, a document specifically intended to chart America's course for decades to come. And despite the hysteria at the time, stimulated by the leak of an early version of the document, recent scholarship has emphasized that this approach was subsequently adopted—with some variation in focus, tone, and emphasis—by every post–Cold War administration that followed.[4]

This strategy, moreover, was pursued by concrete means and initiatives that represented continuity as much as change. For a quarter century, every post–Cold War administration remained committed to maintaining America's globe-straddling military posture, so as to deter or defeat emerging challenges and provide the hard-power backbone of the unipolar international order. Similarly, every post–Cold War administration preserved and even extended America's Cold War–era alliances and security commitments, in order to lock in stability and U.S. influence in key regions, to hedge against the reemergence of hostile great powers, and to provide a security envelope to enable additional countries (in eastern Europe, for example) to integrate into the liberal order. In fact, the first four post–Cold War leaders—George H. W. Bush, Bill Clinton, George W. Bush, and Barack Obama—all presided over successive expansions of NATO while affirming U.S. guarantees in other regions as well.

With respect to the global economy, each of these administrations pursued international economic integration through the institutionalization of liberal economic practices, the liberalization of global currency and capital flows, and the pursuit of free trade agreements, from NAFTA in the early 1990s to the Trans-Pacific Partnership under Obama. And all of these administrations continued to contain and confront aggressive actors that threatened the smooth functioning of the international system, from Saddam Hussein's Iraq to a perpetually provocative North Korea, through a mixture of economic, diplomatic, and military means. Finally, even in those cases where U.S. policy did become more assertive following the Cold War—as in the case of promoting democracy—that policy followed essential precedents set by Cold War–era initiatives from the Marshall Plan to the encouragement of liberal political reforms by the Carter and Reagan administrations.[5] American statecraft from the early 1990s onward did not break sharply with the past; it simply built upon the foundations laid by a successful, multidecade postwar grand strategy.

Of course, none of this is to say that there was *no* change in American strategy after the Cold War or that there was perfect consistency across post–Cold War administrations. The U.S. government did certainly take on some new endeavors in the unipolar era, perhaps the most notable being the practice of humanitarian military intervention—which had generally been deemed an unaffordable luxury during the Cold War—in countries ranging from Somalia to Libya. After 9/11, moreover, the *assertiveness* with which the United States pursued many of its goals—from democracy promotion to counterterrorism and counterproliferation—jumped significantly, as manifested most clearly in the invasion of Iraq. And from George H. W. Bush to Barack Obama, U.S. presidential administrations differed on many things, from their rhetorical styles to their approaches to using military force.

Yet focusing on these differences obscures the basic continuity of purpose running through U.S. post–Cold War grand strategy, as well as the extent to which that grand strategy and many of its specific manifestations have been rooted in the broader tradition of postwar statecraft. In 1950, the authors of NSC-68 stated that efforts "to foster a world environment in which the American system can survive and flourish" constituted "a policy which we would probably pursue even if there were no Soviet threat."[6] The trajectory of American grand strategy after the Cold War, as well as during it, illustrates the truth of this statement.

NOT SO BAD AFTER ALL

A second myth regarding America's post–Cold War grand strategy is that this strategy has proved quixotic and even "disastrous"—

that Washington has wasted its remarkable primacy by tilting at geopolitical windmills.[7] The same critique was often made by Donald Trump on his road to the White House in 2016.[8] This verdict, of course, is influenced heavily by America's long wars in Iraq and Afghanistan, embroilments that consumed much American power but produced unsatisfying and, on occasion, remarkably counterproductive outcomes. And in the post–Cold War period, as in any other, it is easy to identify mistakes of omission and commission, failures of conception and implementation, examples of hubris and consequent blowback. From the humiliating failure of U.S. intervention in Somalia in 1993 to the fallout from an initially successful intervention in Libya in 2011, there is plenty to lament and criticize.

But if self-criticism is generally an admirable quality—and Americans are practiced from of old with the jeremiad—there is also a more positive, and more accurate, way of viewing the past quarter century. And that is to note that, for all its travails, American strategy has played a central role in making the post–Cold War international system more stable, more liberal, and more favorable to U.S. interests and ideals than it would otherwise have been—and certainly in bringing about a more benign international environment than many expert observers expected when the post–Cold War period began. Just as it is now widely accepted that America's Cold War grand strategy was broadly successful despite the myriad frustrations and failures that occurred along the way (a catastrophically counterproductive war in Vietnam being the most significant), it is clear that, when it comes to shaping the international system, the overall record of America's post–Cold War engagement has been fairly impressive.

To grasp this point, go back to some of the most prominent forecasts about the future of international politics made just after the Cold War's end. There were certainly some sunny predictions, Francis Fukuyama's "end of history" thesis being the most prominent.[9] But there were also some very dark and pessimistic ones.

Most leading international relations theorists initially believed, for example, that the unipolarity America enjoyed following the superpower conflict was inherently unsustainable—that it would promptly cause renewed great-power balancing and the rise of countervailing coalitions.[10] Many such observers—and also policy-makers from around the world—worried that the end of the Cold War would lead not to a stable, liberal peace, but to vicious, multipolar instability. The argument was, in essence, that bipolarity had suppressed sources of violence and anarchy in international affairs; its collapse would unleash a flurry of destabilizing influences. A revanchist Japan and Germany, the emergence of febrile security competitions in Europe and East Asia, rampant nuclear proliferation and aggressive behavior in the world's key strategic theaters: these were among the pernicious phenomena that leading analysts expected to materialize after bipolarity's demise. "We will soon miss the Cold War," John Mearsheimer famously warned. "The prospect of major crises, even wars . . . is likely to increase dramatically now that the Cold War is receding into history."[11]

Yet whatever the imperfections of the post–Cold War era (and there have been many), what is striking is that these dogs mostly did not bark. By most meaningful historical comparisons, the quarter century after the Cold War was a time of relative international peace, stability, and liberal progress. Until recently, for instance, great-power tensions remained remarkably low-key compared to the Cold War or to any period dating back to the Concert of Europe. Regions such as East Asia and Europe have been mostly free of interstate conflict, and German or Japanese revanchism has been conspicuously absent. Nuclear proliferation, both extant (North Korea) and prospective (Iran), remains a serious concern, but on the whole it has advanced much more slowly than many predicted. Several countries actually gave up their nuclear weapons or weapons programs in the early and mid-1990s, and the proliferation spirals that were feared in key regions have yet to materialize.

Meanwhile, democracy continued its advance after the Cold War, with the number of electoral democracies growing from 76 in 1990 to about 120 in the early 2000s.[12] Economic integration and the spread of free markets continued apace, and global living standards continued to rise in the aggregate, even as the gains of that prosperity were shared unequally. Not least, predictions of a rapid return to unstable multipolarity proved mistaken. Instead, the United States retained a vast economic and military lead over any competitor through the end of the millennium and beyond, and many of the world's second- and third-tier powers generally chose to cast their lots with rather than against it.[13] There remained opposition to American power, of course, some of it murderously violent, and some of it partially generated by America's own policies. And from mass-casualty terrorism to ethnic violence, there also remained significant sources of tension and conflict. But relative to what many expected—and certainly relative to previous eras—the post–Cold War period wasn't half bad.

There were numerous reasons for this, some of which had little to do with American strategy or policies. But international politics are prominently shaped by the policies of the system's leading power, and after the Cold War the United States had as much capacity to shape the system as any other great power in modern history. This being so, it is hard to escape the conclusion that U.S. grand strategy—which was specifically geared toward preventing renewed conflict and instability and driving forward the positive trends at work—played an essential role in making the post–Cold War order as benign as it has been.

Consider just a few ways in which American strategy influenced the post–Cold War world. The maintenance of U.S. military presence and alliances in Europe and East Asia helped tamp down potential instability and security competitions, and kept historical powers such as Japan and Germany anchored firmly in the West.[14] With the U.S. presence still in place, there was no need for these or other key countries to provide fully for their own security, which markedly reduced the incentives for them to engage in arms-racing and other kinds of destabilizing behavior that defined previous eras. Likewise, the extension of American alliance commitments to eastern Europe helped smother incipient conflicts and security dilemmas following the breakdown of Soviet hegemony, and reduced incentives for nuclear proliferation or major military buildups by historically insecure states such as Poland or Romania.[15] In the Balkans, U.S.-led military interventions between 1995 and 1999 were admittedly belated and hesitant, and incurred a great deal of domestic criticism. But nonetheless, they helped end ethnic cleansing of vulnerable populations and doused persistent conflicts before they could destabilize southeastern Europe more broadly.

Nor were these the only areas where U.S. policy had such effects. In the former Soviet space, a forward-leaning American diplomacy helped achieve the denuclearization of Ukraine, Belarus, and Kazakhstan (all of which had inherited sizable nuclear arsenals from the dying Soviet Union), and dramatically reduced the danger of "loose nukes" by helping Russian officials secure poorly guarded nuclear materials.[16] And in dealing with international outlaws such as Iraq or North Korea, U.S. policy prevented them from dominating or further destabilizing key regions. For all the problems that Saddam Hussein posed for regional and international security from the early 1990s onward, for instance, it was U.S. policy that reversed his aggression against Kuwait in 1990–91, and it was U.S. policy that kept his dangerous and megalomaniacal regime largely bottled up in the years thereafter. In sum, American engagement suppressed renascent geopolitical competition and upheaval in key areas and provided the reassurance that permitted global economic integration and other positive trends to continue.

U.S. policy affected the contours of the post–Cold War order in other ways, too. Direct U.S. engagement helped create and strengthen international economic institutions such as the World

Trade Organization, foster an array of regional and bilateral free trade pacts, and bring the single most important non-Western economy, China, into the international economic order to an unprecedented degree. In countries from Guatemala in the early 1990s to Georgia in the early 2000s, U.S. support helped strengthen democratic reformers, pressure authoritarian rulers, and promote political liberalization.[17] Finally, and not least, the fact that the United States maintained relatively robust military spending from the early 1990s on, and that it continued to provide global public goods such as security and freedom of the seas so that other countries did not have to, helped ensure that the international order did not swing back toward unstable multipolarity in the early twenty-first century.

American policy was not solely responsible for these developments, but it was the single common thread that tied them together. If the goal of America's post–Cold War strategy was to sustain and deepen a stable, liberal order in which the United States enjoyed global primacy, then that strategy would have to be considered, on balance, a success.

NOT OVER YET

But does America still enjoy that primacy, and can it sustain such an engaged and ambitious strategy in the future? The answer one increasingly hears is no. The world, many say, is rapidly entering a new era of multipolarity, and Washington has no choice but to retrench. "This time it's real," writes one scholar: American supremacy is vanishing fast.[18]

This argument is not baseless, for America's margin of superiority has slipped from its post–Cold War peak. In 1994, the United States accounted for nearly one-fourth of global GDP and 40 percent of world military spending, with those numbers rising even higher by the early 2000s. By 2015, however, these statistics had fallen—not dramatically, but not trivially—to 22.4 percent of global GDP and 33.8 percent of world military spending. The share of global wealth and power wielded by America's core treaty allies had also declined, from roughly 47 percent of global GDP and 35 percent of global military spending in 1994 to roughly 39 and 25 percent, respectively, in 2015. Meanwhile, the share wielded by the chief challenger to American primacy rose dramatically. In 1994, China accounted for just 3.3 percent of global GDP and 2.2 percent of world military spending; by 2015 two decades of booming economic growth and double-digit annual increases in military spending had taken those numbers to 11.8 and 12.2 percent, respectively.[19] By these common measures of global power, the world is not as unbalanced as it used to be.

As the global power gap has narrowed, Washington has also been faced with more—and arguably more severe—threats to its position and interests than at any time since the Cold War. Great-power competition has returned, as Russia and China test the contours of an order that they never fully accepted, and that they now have greater capacity—economic, military, or both—to challenge. Moscow and Beijing are seeking to assert primacy within their own regions, probing the distant peripheries of the U.S. alliance system, and developing military capabilities that severely threaten America's ability to project power and uphold its security commitments in eastern Europe and the western Pacific. China's antiship ballistic missiles and its coercion of its neighbors, like Russia's hybrid-warfare activities and its anti-access/area-denial (A2/AD) capabilities, represent growing challenges to U.S. military superiority in key areas of Eurasia, and to the benign regional orders Washington has sought to maintain.[20]

Meanwhile, the long-standing challenge of handling rogue actors has also become more difficult as those actors have become more empowered. North Korea boasts a sizable nuclear arsenal and is rapidly developing a reliable intercontinental strike capability with which to underwrite its serial provocations.[21] Iran is fanning sectarianism, fighting multiple proxy wars, and destabilizing an already-disordered Middle East as it also emerges from punishing international sanctions. The Islamic State is losing ground militarily, but it has shown the capacity of nonstate actors to sow chaos across a crucial region while also spreading and inspiring terrorism across the globe. The world is ablaze, it sometimes seems. In virtually every key region, the United States confronts rising challenges to the post–Cold War order.

The world ideological climate is now more contested as well. After being in retreat for decades, authoritarian regimes are increasingly pushing back against liberalizing currents, as the 2008 global financial crisis and its aftermath have raised questions about whether democracies can deliver the goods. Russia, China, and other authoritarian regimes have meanwhile reentered the global ideological competition in significant ways, touting the virtues of centralized control and "state capitalism," and pushing back against Western concepts of political liberalism and human rights. Even countries that are part of the U.S.-led alliance system have regressed politically. Hungarian prime minister Viktor Orbán has proclaimed the rise of the "illiberal state" as an antidote to the weaknesses of liberal democracy, and his example has gained admirers in Poland, Slovakia, and elsewhere. As a result of all this, although democracy remains very robust by historical standards, the advance of electoral democracy has stalled over the past decade, and some contend that a "democratic recession" is under way.[22] If history ever ended, it has restarted once more. In the realm of ideas, as in the realm of geopolitics, American primacy seems less daunting than before.

Finally, there are questions about the trajectory of America's own engagement with the world. The United States has experienced significant real declines in defense spending since 2011, forcing difficult trade-offs among force structure, readiness, and modernization. Indeed, Washington is increasingly facing a crisis of strategic solvency, as America's undiminished commitments outstrip its shrinking capabilities.[23] At the same time, the wars in Iraq and Afghanistan have encouraged pro-retrenchment sentiments at home; they have also raised doubts regarding America's judgment in starting wars and its ability to conclude those wars successfully. Overseas, U.S. partners in Europe, the Middle East, and East Asia now appear concerned that America might undertake a broad-based withdrawal from key regions; for their part, Americans seem less convinced as to why the United States should retain such an assertive strategy when there is no obvious existential threat to national security to justify it. According to one poll conducted in 2013, 52 percent of Americans—the highest proportion in decades—believed that the country should now "mind its own business internationally and let other countries get along the best they can on their own."[24] Not least, there is the simple fact that a candidate who derided U.S. alliances and overseas commitments, who angrily denounced the pursuit of free trade and globalization, and who promised—on the stump, at least—major changes in American foreign policy was elected president in 2016. These factors have collectively fed into a narrative of national ennui and decline that is more pronounced than at any time since the 1970s.

Yet if this narrative is not baseless, it is overstated. For the idea that the era of American primacy has passed—that we are now entering or have already entered a truly multipolar world—is far from the truth. By virtually all key measures, the United States still has substantial, even massive, leads over its closest competitors. In 2016 the United States claimed a nearly US$18.6 trillion GDP that was almost US$7.5 trillion larger than China's, and it possessed a per capita GDP (a crucial measure of how much money a government can extract from its citizens to pursue geopolitical ends) roughly four times that of China. In the military realm, U.S. annual defense spending was still nearly three times that of China as of 2015—a reminder that although China is closing the gap on Washington in certain respects, the overall gap remains significant indeed.[25]

In fact, America's global lead is probably far bigger than indicated by simple numerical measures such as GDP and percentage of global military spending. GDP is a commonly used but problematic way of comparing U.S. and Chinese economic strength. It is merely a snapshot, rather than a fully explanatory measure of how wealth accrues over time; it does not account for factors such as the damage that China is doing to its own long-term economic potential through the devastation of its natural environment; it understates important U.S. advantages such as the fact that American citizens own significant minority shares in foreign corporations. By a more holistic measure of national economic strength—"inclusive wealth," which takes account of manufactured capital, human capital, and natural capital—the United States was still roughly 4.5 times wealthier than China as recently as 2010. Add in the enormous long-term economic problems that China faces—from declining growth rates, to a massive asset bubble, to a rapidly aging population—and forecasts of coming Chinese economic supremacy become more tenuous still.[26]

The U.S. military lead is even more extensive. As a recent study by Stephen Brooks and William Wohlforth concludes, although China's ongoing military buildup presents significant, even severe, *regional* challenges for the United States, at the *global* level there is still simply no comparison. The United States possesses massive advantages in high-end power-projection capabilities such as aircraft carriers, fourth- and fifth-generation tactical aircraft, nuclear-powered submarines, AWACS, and heavy unmanned aerial vehicles. These advantages have been amassed over decades, through enormous and accumulating investments, and so it will take decades—if not longer—for China to come close to matching the United States. These metrics, moreover, do not reflect the other, more intangible advantages that the U.S. military possesses—the years of recent experience in complex operations, the extraordinarily high levels of human capital, the flexible command-and-control structures that permit initiative and adaptation. "Rather than expecting a power transition in international politics," Brooks and Wohlforth write, "everyone should start getting used to a world in which the United States remains the sole superpower for decades to come."[27]

Finally, any consideration of global power dynamics must evaluate the role of allies: the United States has dozens of them, whereas China and Russia have few, if any. (Those that they do have, countries such as Belarus and North Korea, make up a veritable international most-wanted list.) America's allies give it geopolitical leverage, diplomatic influence, and military access that other countries can only envy; they add enormously to the overall weight of the Western coalition of which Washington remains leader. As of 2015, the United States and its core treaty allies in Asia and Europe accounted for roughly three-fifths of global wealth and global military spending—a share that was moderately diminished from twenty years earlier, but still very impressive by nearly all other historical comparisons.

There may come a time when U.S. primacy has vanished or diminished to the point of strategic insignificance, but that day is still a long way off. And so, rather than abandoning a grand strategy that has worked well over the past twenty-five years, America should instead work to sustain and reinvigorate that grand strategy for a period in which its primacy remains impressive, even if more contested than before.

KEEPING A GOOD THING GOING

Doing so requires embracing five principles that are vital to positioning the United States for continued grand strategic success. First, and most broadly, American officials and public observers need to scope the grand strategy debate correctly. Every four years, a thunderstorm of proposals rain down for some "new grand strategy for America"—for a fundamentally revised approach to the world. With the rise of Donald Trump, that debate has suddenly become all the more urgent and real. Yet the United States does not need a fundamentally revised grand strategy; it already has one that has worked well over time and remains broadly consonant with global power realities today. The focus of the grand strategy debate, then, should be on adapting a generally successful approach at the margins, not coming up with something radically new from scratch.

Of course, change at the margins can still be consequential, and there is certainly room for fruitful debate on key policy questions. Advocates of an engaged and assertive globalism can profitably argue about when and how the United States should use force, how it should apportion resources among theaters, and how it should respond to specific issues, from Russian aggression in Ukraine to Chinese expansionism in the South China Sea. Heated debates on individual policy matters were part and parcel of a generally consistent grand strategy during the Cold War; there is no reason that America's post–Cold War grand strategy cannot similarly accommodate such debates today. Moreover, it is natural to expect oscillations in the overall energy and ambition of U.S. statecraft. Dating back to World War II, such oscillations have generally helped preserve long-term balance in American strategy and enabled U.S. statecraft to periodically revert to a broadly effective mean. Successful grand strategy always entails debate, learning, and adaptation within a larger framework of continuity. Understanding this point is central to orienting the grand strategy debate today.

Second, and more specifically, the United States will need to shore up the military foundation of its grand strategy by reinvesting in defense. Military power is hardly the only tool of U.S. policy, but military dominance has been a fundamental enabler of the global influence and stability that America has enjoyed over the past twenty-five years. And for all of America's globalist ambitions, maintaining that military dominance has been easily affordable during the post–Cold War era. At the peak of the superpower contest in the 1950s, U.S. military spending regularly consumed 10 to 12 percent of GDP; since the mid-1990s, the number has usually been between 3 and 4 percent. In a relatively benign environment, Washington has had its primacy on the cheap.[28]

Today, however (as discussed in greater detail in chapter 6), America is rapidly reaching the limits of this approach. At present, the demands on U.S. defense dollars are becoming greater than at any time in the post–Cold War era, and Washington faces major upcoming investments needed to modernize its nuclear deterrent and perpetuate its conventional edge. Yet American defense dollars are simultaneously becoming scarcer, as post-2011 budget cuts take the defense budget down toward 3 percent of GDP and even lower.[29] These trends are unsustainable—sooner or later (and probably sooner), growing demands and decreasing resources will erode the military foundation of American grand strategy, undercut the credibility of U.S. commitments, and thereby jeopardize the stability and influence that U.S. strategy has provided. "Strategy," Bernard Brodie famously wrote, "wears a dollar sign," and Washington will get only what it pays for in global affairs.[30]

This does not mean reverting to Cold War–era levels of defense spending or anything like them. What it does mean is removing the Budget Control Act spending caps that have driven defense expenditures downward over the past several years and replacing them with an agreement that controls spiraling entitlement costs and provides for steady, long-term growth in defense spending. Put another way, the United States can surely preserve an acceptable level of military primacy if it is willing to spend in the neighborhood of 4 percent of GDP on defense, and to focus that spending on investments such as the A2/AD-busting capabilities needed to preserve

U.S. deterrence and power projection in increasingly contested regions. It probably cannot do so at 3 percent of GDP or below.[31]

Third, and related, the United States needs to firm up the coalition aspect of its grand strategy by getting more out of—and diversifying—its relationships with allies and partners. America's post–Cold War primacy has always rested on its leadership of a community of capable, like-minded nations, and U.S. allies and partners have been crucial contributors on issues from upholding regional stability to encouraging democracy and markets overseas. In the coming years, moreover, shoring up U.S. alliances against the Russian and Chinese challenges will constitute a fundamental endeavor of American statecraft. Yet, as noted previously, the share of global wealth and power held by America's core treaty allies has fallen over the past two decades. U.S. primacy remains intact, but the overall relative strength of the U.S.-led coalition is slipping.

There are two principal pathways to addressing this core grand strategic challenge. One is by getting more out of existing U.S. allies, by pushing them to embrace policies that will stretch their resources further. Encouraging greater defense specialization and sharing of resources within NATO, pushing Asian and eastern European allies to adopt more cost-effective defense strategies based on A2/AD capabilities, and fostering greater multilateral ties among allies (particularly in Asia) all represent ways of getting more allied bang for the buck. Likewise, as Washington increases its own commitments to the European and Asia-Pacific theaters—as it is already starting to do—it should make clear that additional U.S. activity is also contingent on U.S. allies upping their security game.

Equally important, the United States should offset the relative decline of some traditional allies by deepening newer partnerships. Global power is not just shifting to America's rivals—it is also shifting to an array of states that are formally nonaligned but are nonetheless increasingly willing to work with Washington and its allies on a range of critical international issues. India, Brazil, Indonesia, Vietnam, and the United Arab Emirates, to take some key examples, have all forged deeper ties with the United States over the past decade or so on issues ranging from counterterrorism to maritime issues to regional security in the Middle East and the Asia-Pacific region. By improving flexible partnerships with such states, the United States can position itself to more effectively address emerging geopolitical challenges and opportunities, and to sustain a global *im*balance of power in support of key aspects of the international order.

Fourth, even as the United States focuses on shoring up the partnerships and power that make its grand strategy possible, it must also show discipline in employing that power. U.S. strategy has arguably been most successful when it has focused on the core tasks of preserving the basic stability and well-being of the international system and creating broad conditions in which political and economic liberalism can advance. These are the tasks for which American power is best suited, and in view of the return of great-power competition and other key threats, they are likely to pose the most crucial challenges in the years to come. Conversely, the United States has gotten into trouble when its immense power has encouraged strategic indiscipline—overestimating America's ability to rapidly transform foreign societies, or overreaching in the use of force. Such indiscipline is invariably punished through unforeseen and unwelcome geopolitical consequences abroad, and through the undermining of public support for robust American internationalism at home. This was the case with Vietnam during the Cold War; it has certainly been the case with Iraq more recently. And at a time when the U.S. margin of superiority has eroded from its post–Cold War peak, strategic profligacy is a luxury that Washington cannot afford.

To be clear, maintaining strategic discipline does not mean foreswearing all uses of force or assuming that all military interventions will lead inexorably to massive, multiyear commitments. Nor does it mean forsaking the active promotion of democracy and human rights. There will still be times when limited, coercive uses of force are appropriate to protect U.S. interests in key regions. There are cases today in which threats to the international order can be met only by force—think of the Islamic State, for example. U.S. alliance commitments must ultimately be backed by force when necessary. And finally, the nonmilitary aspects of democracy promotion—from economic assistance to emerging democracies to the activities of institutions such as the National Endowment for Democracy—will have a key role to play in the more competitive ideological environment that is now emerging.

But being disciplined does require a basic sense of limits and humility. It requires recognizing the limitations of military force as a tool of political transformation in historically illiberal societies. It requires accepting that there are problems and injustices that not even a superpower can solve, and that wisdom lies in discerning where American interests are most implicated and where American power can make a critical difference. Above all, it requires realizing that overextension can be just as dangerous as underinvestment when it comes to sustaining America's post–Cold War statecraft. Great power must be rationed as well as used if it is to be effective and enduring; acknowledging this point represents a fourth principle for U.S. strategy.

Fifth and finally, sustaining America's post–Cold War strategy entails persuading the American public to recommit to that strategy and the investments it requires. The state of American opinion on that subject is currently ambiguous. Polling data indicates that public support for most key aspects of American internationalism has recovered somewhat from where it was in 2012–13, and is again at or near postwar averages.[32] But the 2016 election cycle and its eventual outcome revealed strong support for candidates who advocated rolling back key elements of post–Cold War (and post–World War II) grand strategy, from free trade to U.S. alliances. This atmosphere reflects discontent with the failures and frustrations of U.S. grand strategy in the post–Cold War era, no doubt, yet it also reflects the fact that American strategy seems at risk of becoming a victim of its own success.[33] By helping to foster a comparatively stable and congenial environment, American policies have made it more difficult for Americans to remember why significant investments in the global order are needed in the first place.

Today, this ambivalence is becoming increasingly problematic, for the simple reason that properly resourcing American strategy requires making politically difficult trade-offs with respect to entitlements and other ballooning domestic costs. It is also becoming problematic, of course, because even if the American public seems to support particular aspects of American grand strategy, the public has shown itself willing to elect a president who appears to care little for the successful postwar and post–Cold War tradition, even if he has, so far, maintained more aspects of that tradition as president than his campaign rhetoric might have led one to expect. In the future—and indeed, looking beyond Trump's presidency—sustaining American grand strategy will thus require more intensive political efforts.

American leaders will need to more effectively make the case for controversial but broadly beneficial policies such as free trade, while also addressing the inevitable socioeconomic dislocations such policies cause.[34] They will need to more fully articulate the underlying logic and value of alliances and other commitments whose costs are often more visible—not to say greater—than their benefits. They will need to remind Americans that their country's leadership has not been a matter of charity; it has helped produce an international order that is exceptional in its stability, liberalism, and benefits for the United States. Not least, they will need to make the case that the costs that the country has borne in support of that order are designed to avoid the necessity of bearing vastly higher costs if the international scene returned to a more tumultuous state. After all, the success of American statecraft is often reflected in the bad things that don't happen as well as in the good things that do. Making this point is essential to reconsolidating domestic support now and in the future—and to preserving a grand strategy that has delivered pretty good results for a quarter century.

TWO

FOOLS RUSH OUT

There is, then, a strong case for substantial continuity in U.S. grand strategy. But what would happen if America instead adopted a fundamentally different grand strategy, one that was far more modest and restrained? In view of the undeniable difficulties it faces today, should the United States dramatically reduce, and perhaps eliminate, the network of security commitments and overseas force deployments that have been the linchpin of its global posture since World War II? In recent years, a growing chorus of scholars and strategic thinkers has answered this question in the affirmative. They have argued that Washington's long-standing global posture has become unnecessary and counterproductive—unnecessary because it is no longer required to maintain a favorable international environment, and counterproductive because it squanders limited resources while creating more problems than it solves. The solution, these scholars contend, is to embrace a minimalist strategy of "offshore balancing."

In its simplest form, offshore balancing envisions slashing U.S. force posture and alliance commitments overseas and undertaking a marked retrenchment in U.S. policy more broadly. Its guiding premise is that such retrenchment can lead to greater security at lesser cost—that less, in other words, can really be more.[1]

At present, this seems to be a beguiling proposition. Offshore balancing has long been the grand strategy of choice among leading international relations "realists" such as John Mearsheimer, Stephen Walt, Christopher Layne, and Barry Posen. In the post–Iraq War and post–financial crisis context, retrenchment's appeal has grown stronger still. Interest in offshore balancing has "jumped from the cloistered walls of academe to the real world of Washington policy making," wrote Layne in 2012. That strategy, another proponent of offshore balancing agrees, is "an idea whose time has come."[2] Whether that is true remains debatable, of course, but it is undeniable that the election and presidency of Donald Trump—who campaigned on a platform emphasizing skepticism if not outright hostility toward U.S. alliances, forward force deployments, and other manifestations of American globalism—have brought themes of retrenchment and restraint to the forefront of public debate.

So far, however, discussions of offshore balancing—particularly within academia—have remained one-sided and incomplete. Precisely because offshore balancing has such wide support within academia, analysts have rarely subjected the idea to the probing, sustained assessment that is necessary to fully appreciate both its strengths and its weaknesses.[3] This chapter seeks to rectify that imbalance via a critical analysis that outlines the ideas and logic underlying offshore balancing and more rigorously tests its key claims. The need for such assessment is acute. The United States will confront crucial decisions regarding its overseas posture and policies in coming years, making a thorough exploration of strategic options and alternatives imperative.

The results of this analysis are not kind to offshore balancing. The allure of the strategy is the promise, as Walt writes, that it can help the United States maximize its security and influence and also "minimize the resistance that its power sometimes provokes."[4] Yet, upon closer scrutiny, the allure of offshore balancing is largely an illusion. The purported economic and geopolitical dividends of that strategy are oversold, while the probable costs and risks are badly understated. In essence, the case for offshore balancing rests on a set of precarious judgments about what would happen following a dramatic U.S. retrenchment. When those judgments are interrogated, the argument for offshore balancing collapses. Were the United States to adopt this strategy, it would probably not enjoy greater security at lesser cost. Instead, it might very well jeopardize U.S. influence, tempt far greater insecurity and instability, and ultimately expose the country to a much higher long-term price.

PATTERNS OF POSTWAR GRAND STRATEGY

For roughly seventy years, the United States has pursued an engaged and assertive grand strategy to mold the global order. The day-to-day and even year-to-year manifestations of that strategy have shifted over time, but the core goals have remained the same. U.S. policymakers have sought an open and prosperous world economy based on free trade and nondiscrimination. They have pursued a peaceful international environment conducive to the flourishing of democracy, even as they have inevitably cooperated with nondemocratic powers. Perhaps most important, they have worked to prevent hostile actors from dominating any of the three overseas regions— Europe, East Asia, and the Persian Gulf—of vital geostrategic or geoeconomic value to the United States, and to forge stable, advantageous configurations of power in each of these areas.[5] Together, these objectives have guided U.S. grand strategy since World War II, providing broad continuity in American statecraft.

The pursuit of these goals, in turn, has been anchored by Washington's "most consequential strategic choice": its willingness to make numerous overseas security commitments, and to substantiate them via forward deployment of U.S. forces.[6] In Europe and East Asia, these commitments took shape formally and quite early in the postwar period, with the creation of NATO in Europe and a hub-and-spokes system of alliances in the Asia-Pacific region. In the Persian Gulf, U.S. presence and guarantees developed more gradually and with a lower public profile. Regional variations aside, however, commitments to the core geopolitical zones of Eurasia have long constituted a central pillar of postwar strategy.

From their origins, these commitments functioned primarily to deny any U.S. rival control over a region that was vital to the nation's security. Yet they also fulfilled other crucial purposes. U.S. presence dampened historical rivalries within the Western world, stifling counterproductive security competitions and facilitating unprecedented multilateral cooperation. It fostered—particularly in Europe and East Asia—the climate of reassurance in which liberal economies and polities could thrive. It retarded the spread of nuclear weapons by mitigating the insecurity that might otherwise drive allies such as Japan or Germany to seek the bomb. Not least, it thrust U.S. power deep into the most important areas of the world, giving Washington leverage on myriad issues. In essence, security guarantees and forward deployments were the backbone of U.S. strategy, providing the influence and stability necessary to achieve a broad array of objectives. It was a testament to the success of those arrangements during the Cold War that U.S. policymakers largely kept them in place—or expanded them—in the post–Cold War era.[7]

Nothing lasts forever, though, and after the Cold War, some critics did question whether this forward-leaning posture remained necessary in a world without a rival superpower.[8] The specter of retrenchment has loomed larger in recent years. Two unsatisfying post-9/11 wars, persistent budgetary pressures, and the increasingly contested state of U.S. primacy have fueled widespread skepticism about the future of American globalism. That skepticism has given strength to calls for a very different grand strategy.

THE LOGIC OF OFFSHORE BALANCING

Offshore balancing is a simple and fairly elegant concept. It rests on the belief that three overseas regions—Europe, East Asia, and the Persian Gulf—are vital to U.S. security for the resources, wealth, and geography that they possess. Like most mainstream observers of U.S. policy, then, offshore balancers agree that the overarching goal of U.S. strategy must remain to prevent an unfriendly power from dominating any of these regions. Where they depart from the existing approach is in arguing that permanent U.S. deployments and alliance commitments are not necessary or desirable to attain this end. Rather, offshore balancers believe that Washington should rely on local actors to contain threats and maintain a balance of power in those regions, bolstering them with economic, diplomatic, or indirect military support (such as arms sales) where necessary. Only when a crucial regional balance collapses or threatens to collapse altogether—only when a hostile power is poised to overrun the area—should the United States intervene and go "onshore" with its own military forces. Once U.S. forces defeat the aggressor and restore the balance, they should retreat offshore again.[9]

Offshore balancing is therefore not an *isolationist* strategy, because it recognizes the U.S. interest in maintaining favorable configurations of power overseas. It is a *minimalist* strategy, because it aims to do so with far fewer obligations and resources. Indeed, while offshore balancers sometimes differ regarding specific policy recommendations, they unanimously agree that the strategy envisions a marked retrenchment of U.S. presence and commitments. The United States should withdraw from NATO's military command and perhaps the alliance itself, for instance, or at least denude

Europe of permanently stationed U.S. troops. It should foreswear onshore peacetime deployments in the Persian Gulf and rely on "over-the-horizon" capabilities in case of a major crisis. Regarding East Asia, most offshore balancers favor retaining strong air and naval capabilities to hedge against a rising China. Yet they have also advocated, variously, withdrawing U.S. troops from South Korea, ending the ambiguous security commitment to Taiwan, modifying or terminating the alliance with Japan, and removing U.S. forces from that country. All of this retrenchment would be accompanied by significant cuts in U.S. force structure.[10] In short, offshore balancing entails a much more austere U.S. posture overseas.

It also entails a more austere, realpolitik approach to foreign policy writ large. Because offshore balancers are overwhelmingly international relations "realists"—analysts who believe that cold balance-of-power considerations trump all else—they argue that Washington should ruthlessly downgrade initiatives that are not crucial to this core issue. The United States should not pursue "ideological" objectives, such as human rights or democracy promotion, if that means alienating unsavory authoritarian regimes that can nonetheless contribute to stable regional balances.[11] Nor should it contest the efforts of countries such as Russia or China to carve out reasonably defined spheres of influence in their own neighborhoods—by bringing Ukraine or Taiwan to heel, for example—so long as those efforts do not fundamentally threaten the regional order.[12] Most important of all, Washington must assiduously avoid uses of force that are not absolutely necessary to maintain acceptable regional balances. Humanitarian intervention, wars of counterproliferation or regime change, prolonged counterinsurgency and nation-building—such "wars of choice" are costly and self-defeating diversions from the strategy's central mission.[13] The United States must therefore couple reductions in its alliances and overseas deployments with a broader move toward foreign policy restraint.

Offshore balancing, then, would constitute a major departure from the postwar pattern of U.S. grand strategy. It would not, however, be without precedent in the U.S. experience. The United States practiced something like offshore balancing in the early twentieth century, when it eschewed large peacetime commitments to Europe and East Asia, but intervened to prevent (or reverse) the conquest of those regions during the world wars.[14] U.S. strategy in the Persian Gulf before 1990 followed a similar pattern, with Washington relying primarily on local actors to maintain the balance, and then intervening militarily when Iraq's invasion of Kuwait threatened to destroy that balance.[15] Offshore balancing, its proponents thus claim, is not a new strategy. It is a time-honored formula to which the country should return.

Why should the United States so dramatically change its approach to the world? For offshore balancers, the answer is that the existing grand strategy has outlived its usefulness. U.S. security pledges and forward deployments made sense during the Cold War, when U.S. allies were weak and vulnerable and the Soviet Union was strong and threatening. Now, however, many U.S. allies are wealthy countries that could essentially look after themselves in the more benign environment that emerged after the Soviet collapse. There is no near-term danger of a hostile state overrunning Europe or the Persian Gulf, offshore balancers argue, and even in the Far East, China confronts numerous rivals that will oppose any bid for regional dominance. Such extensive U.S. commitments are thus no longer necessary; the United States' forward posture has become superfluous and profligate. It serves as "welfare for the rich," allowing allies to free ride while simultaneously overtaxing ever more strained U.S. resources. "The Pentagon has come to depend on continuous infusions of cash simply to retain its current force structure," Barry Posen writes, "levels of spending that ... the United States' ballooning debt have rendered unsustainable."[16]

If the current strategy has become unnecessary and unaffordable, offshore balancers believe, it has become deeply counterproductive as well. The perpetuation of such a muscular posture after the Cold War has not made the United States safer, but instead magnified the key threats that the country faces. The retention and even expansion of the United States' overseas presence since the Cold War has antagonized Russia and China, driving them to increase their own capabilities and causing downward spirals in their relations with Washington.[17] Likewise, offshore balancers argue that recent U.S. policy has actually inflamed problems such as terrorism and nuclear proliferation. Regarding proliferation, they claim that calls for "regime change" and the stationing of U.S. troops in close proximity to states such as Iran and North Korea have exacerbated the insecurity that drives countries to seek the bomb. Regarding terrorism, they contend that it is precisely U.S. military presence in Muslim countries that incites jihadist attacks. For offshore balancers, it is U.S. assertiveness and presence—not U.S. weakness or withdrawal—that foster so much insecurity and conflict.[18]

From this perspective, overhauling U.S. grand strategy would bring numerous benefits. First, it would strengthen America's long-term strategic position by setting its global posture on a more sustainable footing. Offshore balancers claim that present U.S. strategy is unstable and self-defeating, because it places disproportionate burdens on the United States and fights the ongoing global diffusion of power. Offshore balancing, conversely, would turn that diffusion to U.S. advantage. No longer would Washington allow capable allies to free ride to its own long-term detriment. Rather, retracting U.S. presence would force key regional powers, from Germany to Japan to Saudi Arabia, to take greater responsibility for their national and regional security. The strategy would thus use the natural balancing mechanism within international politics—the tendency of countries to do what they must to survive—to preserve a stable and congenial global order, while distributing the costs of maintaining that order more equitably. What offshore balancing would achieve, Christopher Layne writes, is not "burden-sharing" but "burden-shifting."[19]

This burden-shifting would enable a second and closely related benefit: it would greatly reduce U.S. costs. Offshore balancers claim that their strategy would, by definition, free the United States from the costs of military conflicts like the Iraq War and other "discretionary" interventions. They also anticipate broader financial dividends from shifting to a leaner force structure. One scholar estimates that an offshore balancing–type approach would let Washington reduce its ground forces by roughly half and cut the Navy and Air Force by one-quarter to one-third. Similarly, Christopher Preble of the Cato Institute argues that such a strategy could permit significant cuts in carrier strike groups, tactical fighter wings, and other high-cost capabilities, as well as major reductions in ground forces. The result would make U.S. strategy less economically onerous and better position the country for long-term prosperity and fiscal rectitude.[20]

Third, offshore balancers argue that retrenchment would actually enhance U.S. security by easing the blowback that Washington's own policies have created. In great-power relations, retracting the U.S. security footprint in Europe and East Asia would reduce tensions with Russia and China, thereby decreasing the possibility of conflict or even war.[21] The effects would prove equally beneficial elsewhere. Scholars such as Robert Pape contend that an end to U.S. forward presence and long-term troop deployments in the Gulf would assuage Muslim anger and significantly defuse the threat of jihadist terrorism.[22] Likewise, because offshore balancers claim that it is U.S. activism and presence that drive countries such as Iran and North Korea to seek security in nuclear weapons, they believe that pulling back would address the root cause of the proliferation problem.[23] Across an entire range of critical issues, retrenchment could thus markedly improve U.S. fortunes.

In fact, if one takes its core claims at face value, offshore balancing seems a nearly optimal grand strategy. It promises the best of all worlds, offering greater security and a better long-term position, all at substantially lower costs. The question, then, is whether the logic and claims of that strategy actually withstand real scrutiny. The answer, unfortunately, is that they do not. When one more closely examines the probable effects—both financial and geopolitical—of a shift to offshore balancing, it becomes clear that the purported advantages of the strategy are less impressive than they initially appear. The risks and liabilities, by contrast, are significant indeed.

HOW MUCH CHEAPER?

Begin with the issue of financial cost. One much-touted benefit of offshore balancing is that it will slash seemingly exorbitant U.S. defense outlays and thereby put the United States on far firmer fiscal ground. There would indeed be some savings. Washington would certainly save money by refusing to use force in any instance when a key regional balance was not in critical danger.[24] More broadly, a military sized for offshore balancing would be somewhat smaller and cheaper, and with far fewer overseas bases, than the current force. The savings would probably prove smaller than expected, however, because a variety of factors suggest that the financial dividends of offshore balancing are significantly oversold.

The first factor is that the existing grand strategy—even with defense budgets of roughly US$600 billion annually—is simply not as expensive as sometimes portrayed. During the 1950s, the United States consistently spent over 10 percent of GDP on defense, and in the 1980s the figure was often over 6 percent. During the post–Cold War era, by contrast, total defense spending (including money for wars in Iraq and Afghanistan) has generally hovered between 3 and 4 percent of GDP, rising to 4.7 percent in 2010, but dropping back under 4 percent in 2013 and sinking further since.[25] By historical standards, the United States has spent comparatively *little* of its wealth on defense in the post–Cold War era, and the costs of U.S. policy have been far less backbreaking than one might think. This would remain the case even if the United States undertook a significant military buildup to deal with a more dangerous global environment—even the most aggressive buildups being considered today would still keep Pentagon spending at or below 4 percent of GDP.[26]

The second and related reason for skepticism is that offshore balancing—if properly resourced—would permit only modest cutbacks. A military capable of executing offshore balancing must still be capable of intervening decisively in regional conflicts and fighting its way back onshore if the balance breaks. It must possess the air and naval power needed to dominate the global commons and push into contested areas in time of crisis; it must also retain—or very quickly mobilize—sufficient ground forces to intervene effectively if a regional balance begins to crumble. As Evan Montgomery of the Center for Strategic and Budgetary Assessments has noted, an offshore balancing military would therefore need to be capable of rapid, decisive global power projection, with all the costs involved.[27] "While day-to-day demands on the U.S. military would be less in offshore balancing than in [a strategy of forward presence]," another analyst concurs, "it is not clear whether total military requirements would be less burdensome."[28]

Moreover, shuttering overseas bases and stationing U.S. forces closer to home would not greatly mitigate such costs. As one RAND Corporation study points out, for instance, relocating two squadrons of F-16s from Italy to the United States would reduce operational costs by just 6 percent annually. Similarly, the Congressional Budget Office has estimated that returning nearly all overseas Army forces to the United States would yield annual savings of less than US$1.5 billion. "At the level of grand strategy," the RAND study concludes, "the cost differences between CONUS [domestic] and OCONUS [overseas] presence are insignificant."[29]

The savings would prove similarly negligible when it comes to nuclear forces. Some offshore balancers contend that their strategy can accommodate major cuts in the U.S. nuclear arsenal. Yet here too, the practical requirements of an adequately resourced offshore balancing strategy would actually be quite significant. The United States would need to possess very robust nuclear forces if it sought to preserve extended deterrence while simultaneously retracting its conventional force presence. For if, as the Obama administration noted in its 2010 Nuclear Posture Review, "strengthening the non-nuclear elements of regional security architectures is vital" to achieving further reductions in the U.S. nuclear arsenal, then *weakening* those nonnuclear elements via American retrenchment would logically place a higher premium on nuclear weapons.[30] Under an offshore balancing scenario, Washington would also need to retain the escalation dominance that would allow it to intervene in critical regional contingencies without fear of being coerced or blackmailed by a nuclear-armed aggressor. Accordingly, doing offshore balancing right would require major—and by all accounts very expensive— investments toward modernizing the U.S. nuclear arsenal in the years and decades ahead.[31]

Once these issues are considered, the financial advantages of offshore balancing appear less formidable. One scholar estimates that an offshore balancing–sized military would cost 2.5 percent of GDP.[32] Yet it is highly questionable whether such a force—featuring much-reduced air, naval, ground, and nuclear capabilities—could actually accomplish its stated objectives without incurring unacceptable risk.[33] And even leaving that issue aside, such spending is just 0.5 percent of GDP lower than actual defense spending in the late 1990s, and perhaps 1 percent of GDP lower than projected spending in the coming years.[34] Put differently, under extremely generous and probably unrealistic assumptions, offshore balancing *might* allow

America to cut defense spending by 16 to 29 percent compared to relevant post–Cold War figures. Such savings would, of course, have a positive budgetary impact, reducing national deficits that ranged from US$465 billion to US$1.55 trillion during the Obama years by perhaps US$100 billion to US$200 billion annually. But even under best-case conditions, these savings would still fall far short of balancing the federal budget. In fact, because defense's share of that budget is just 16 percent and falling, and because current and projected deficits are driven primarily by rising entitlement costs (49 percent of spending and growing as of 2016), it is simply misleading to suggest that the defense cuts that offshore balancers envision hold the key to a sustainable fiscal future for America.[35]

One might also ask whether offshore balancing merely trades relatively marginal short-term savings for higher long-term costs. The fact is that regional balances have often proved less robust than offshore balancers would expect. After all, in each case in which the United States pursued offshore balancing in the twentieth century—in Europe and East Asia during the era of the world wars, and in the Gulf before 1990—it eventually had to fight a major conflict to restore a regional balance that had collapsed or was in grave danger. In each case, fortunately, U.S. forces successfully defeated the aspiring hegemon. But one wonders whether, overall, the more economical course would have been to make the peacetime commitments that would have fortified the balance and perhaps prevented matters from reaching such a dangerous and costly climax. Indeed, in Europe and East Asia particularly, this belated realization that offshore balancing was penny-wise but pound-foolish led Washington to adopt a very different approach after World War II. Times have changed, but the fact remains: the financial case for offshore balancing is not as compelling as it might seem.

OVERSTATED SECURITY BENEFITS:
TERRORISM AND NUCLEAR PROLIFERATION

The promise of financial benefits is only part of the allure of offshore balancing. The strategy also purports to better position the United States to address critical security issues, namely terrorism and nuclear proliferation. If this optimism were warranted, it would offer a powerful argument for retrenchment. Here too, however, the merits of offshore balancing are exaggerated, while unacknowledged dangers and dilemmas lurk just below the surface.

Take the issue of terrorism. To be clear, offshore balancers are right that U.S. onshore presence in the Persian Gulf (and the broader Middle East) has sometimes acted as a stimulant to extremist violence. The stationing of U.S. troops in Saudi Arabia from 1990 onward was one important cause of al-Qaeda's deadly campaign against American targets, and the U.S. invasion and occupation of Iraq in 2003 and afterward helped reinvigorate a jihadist movement that had been pummeled following 9/11. More generally, scholarly research indicates that contesting foreign troop deployments and occupation is one driver of suicide terrorism.[36] There is thus something to the argument that U.S. policies have fueled the fires of jihad. What is more dubious is the claim that shifting to offshore balancing would significantly ameliorate the problem.

The primary cause for doubt is that while stationing U.S. troops in Muslim countries has historically been *one* cause of anti-American terrorism, it has never been *the only* one. That phenomenon also grew out of anger at U.S. support for authoritarian Middle Eastern regimes, Washington's relationship with Israel, the encroachment of Western cultural and economic influences on Muslim societies, and other grievances that were prominent in early al-Qaeda pronouncements and still resonate today. In 2010, for instance, an al-Qaeda spokesman announced that it would take more than withdrawing U.S. troops from Muslim lands to make jihadist attacks stop. The United States would also have to end its support to Israel, prohibit all trade and investment in that country, terminate all aid to "the hated regimes of the Muslim world," cease "all interference in the religion, society, politics, economy, and government" of the region, and so on. Similarly, as one expert notes, "Even U.S. intelligence liaison, which involves sharing information, training, and other forms of exchange, is . . . a sensitive issue" for al-Qaeda and other jihadists. Anti-American terrorism has always had a complex genesis, and avoiding U.S. military presence would address but one of the relevant complaints.[37]

Were the United States to embrace offshore balancing, it would actually aggravate some of those grievances further. A true offshore balancing strategy would make the United States *more* reliant on authoritarian Arab regimes—in Saudi Arabia, Egypt, Jordan, and other countries—as bulwarks of stability in the region. It would imply an increase in military sales, intelligence partnerships, and other support for these governments, and a tolerance for precisely the sort of friendly dictators approach that Muslim radicals deplore. In the same vein, while many offshore balancers call on Washington to distance itself from Israel, Colin Kahl and Marc Lynch have rightly noted that the logic of the strategy would certainly increase U.S. dependence on that country as the strongest, friendliest military power in a very volatile region.[38] In effect, then, offshore balancing would require doubling down on policies that have long stoked jihadist resentment.

Offshore balancing represents a problematic framework for counterterrorism in other ways, too. As the aftermath of the U.S. drawdown in Iraq in 2011 demonstrated, removing American forces from a still-unstable situation can compromise counterterrorism gains made to date and permit the insecurity in which extremist groups prosper. "Had a residual U.S. force stayed in Iraq after 2011," one senior adviser to the U.S. military in Iraq has written, "the United States would have had far greater insight into the growing threat posed by ISIS and could have helped the Iraqis stop the group from taking so much territory. Instead, ISIS's march across northern Iraq took Washington almost completely by surprise."[39]

Moreover, offshore balancing would weaken the infrastructure and partnerships that have been used to fight terrorist organizations. As Robert Art of Brandeis University has written, America's post-9/11 campaign in Afghanistan relied heavily on overseas bases and contingents that would presumably be subject to reductions or liquidation under an offshore balancing scenario. (The more recent anti–Islamic State campaign also relied on such assets.) Similarly, U.S. forward deployments and commitments have long provided leverage that Washington can use to secure greater assistance on the "quieter phase of fighting terrorism"—the intelligence sharing, diplomatic cooperation, and other behind-the-scenes measures that are essential to countering extremist groups.[40] Were the United States to reduce its security posture, one would expect that this leverage would also shrink. In sum, offshore balancing is no panacea regarding counterterrorism: it offers some advantages but brings major liabilities as well.

The balance sheet is even less favorable regarding nuclear proliferation. Offshore balancers say that U.S. presence and assertiveness actually motivate proliferation, and, as with the causes of terrorism, this argument holds some truth. "There is only one way that a country can reliably deter a dominant power," Kenneth Waltz observed, "and that is by developing its own nuclear force."[41] From the Cold War to the present, in fact, U.S. power and posture have sometimes been goads to proliferation. China began seeking nuclear weapons during the 1950s largely to counter the threat posed by U.S. presence in East Asia and to resist potential coercion by Washington. More recently, an unintended—but not unforeseen—consequence of the Iraq War was apparently to convince Iran and North Korea to accelerate their nuclear programs so as to avoid Saddam Hussein's fate.[42]

Yet if pushing enemies toward the bomb has been a periodic hazard of U.S. policy, it is highly doubtful that shifting to offshore balancing would rectify the situation. For starters, while U.S. strategy may provide one reason why "rogue states" seek nuclear weapons, there are plenty of others. Academic research shows that states go nuclear for numerous reasons, from concerns of international or domestic prestige to desires to wield the bomb as a tool of offensive or coercive leverage. Saddam Hussein, for instance, sought nuclear weapons in the late 1970s and 1980s not only for their defensive deterrent value, but also to enable aggressive, revisionist policies against Israel. Similar dynamics have been present in other cases.[43] The causes of proliferation, like the causes of terrorism, have long been quite complex, so changing U.S. strategy would affect only a single part of the problem.

If anything, offshore balancing would make that problem far worse by surrendering the leverage that Washington has used to keep proliferation comparatively limited. What offshore balancers too easily forget is that, whatever their liabilities, U.S. force presence and security commitments have, on aggregate, served as massive barriers to proliferation. U.S. security guarantees have provided the safety and reassurance that reduce the perceived need for U.S. allies to seek nuclear weapons. Those arrangements, the Obama administration's 2010 Nuclear Posture Review noted, limit proliferation "by reassuring non-nuclear U.S. allies and partners that their security interests can be protected without their own nuclear deterrent capabilities."[44] Meanwhile, the implicit threat that American protection might be withdrawn if such countries do go nuclear provides powerful influence that has often been used to dissuade prospective proliferators. In case after case over the past several decades—from Germany and Italy to Japan, South Korea, and Taiwan—this combination of factors has been central to keeping the nuclear club surprisingly small and exclusive.[45]

In this context, it is hard to see how adopting offshore balancing would put the nuclear genie back in the bottle in a case like North Korea. But it is easy to imagine how that shift would dramatically increase proliferation pressures elsewhere. In East Asia, retrenchment would cause consternation and insecurity among countries that live in the shadow of a rising China and have long refrained from nuclear acquisition largely because of the U.S. presence. In the Middle East, the proliferation pressures that Iran's nuclear program has already awakened—despite the Iran nuclear deal of 2015—in countries such as Saudi Arabia and Egypt would become even harder to contain. Even in eastern Europe, the combination of U.S. withdrawal and Russian assertiveness could tempt countries such as Poland—with its tragic past and significant technological potential—to reconsider their own nuclear forbearance.[46] The overall result of offshore balancing would likely be a more proliferated world, with intensified regional security competitions taking on a new and dangerous nuclear dimension. Should that scenario come to pass, offshore balancing would no longer look like such a bargain. For rather than reducing a major threat to U.S. interests, it would have amplified it instead.

U.S. INFLUENCE AND GLOBAL (IN)STABILITY

Offshore balancing is thus unlikely to significantly enhance the U.S. position on key security challenges such as proliferation and terrorism, and in important ways it may actually backfire. But what about the broadest and most important test of any prospective grand strategy—the question of how effective it will be in sustaining American influence and preserving the relatively stable, congenial environment that the United States has long enjoyed? Offshore balancing is premised on the idea that retrenchment need not jeopardize that environment, because it will reduce great-power pushback, force free riders to contribute more, and thereby preserve systemic stability at lower costs. Some offshore balancers even argue that their strategy will strengthen U.S. influence by allowing Washington to play hard to get.[47] Viewed critically, however, this best-of-all-worlds scenario seems much too rosy, and a more pernicious set of consequences appears all too likely.

The fundamental reason is that both U.S. influence and international stability are thoroughly interwoven with America's robust forward presence. Regarding influence, the protection that the United States has afforded its allies has equally afforded Washington great sway over those allies' policies. "The more U.S. troops are stationed in a country," one statistical analysis finds, "the more closely that country's foreign policy orientation aligns with that of the United States."[48] During the Cold War and after, for instance, the United States has used the influence provided by its security posture to veto allies' pursuit of nuclear weapons, to obtain more advantageous terms in financial and trade agreements, and even to affect the composition of allied nations' governments.[49] More broadly, America has used its alliances as vehicles for shaping political, security, and economic agendas in key regions and bilateral relationships, thus giving the United States an outsized voice on a range of important issues. To be clear, this influence has never been as pervasive as U.S. officials might like or as some observers might imagine. But by any reasonable standard of comparison, it has nonetheless been remarkable.

One can tell a similar story about the relative stability of the postwar order. As even some leading offshore balancers have acknowledged, the lack of conflict in regions such as Europe in recent decades is not something that has occurred naturally. It has occurred because the "American pacifier" has suppressed precisely the dynamics that previously fostered geopolitical turmoil. That pacifier has limited arms races and security competitions by providing the protection that allows other countries to underbuild their militaries. It has soothed historical rivalries by affording a climate of security in which powerful countries such as Germany and Japan could be revived economically and reintegrated into thriving and fairly cooperative regional orders. It has induced caution in the behavior of allies and adversaries alike, deterring aggression and dissuading other destabilizing behavior. As John Mearsheimer has noted, the United States "effectively acts as a night watchman," lending order to an otherwise disorderly and anarchical environment.[50]

What would happen if Washington backed away from this role? The most logical answer is that both U.S. influence and global stability would suffer. With respect to influence, the United States would effectively be surrendering the most powerful bargaining chip it has traditionally wielded in dealing with friends and allies, and jeopardizing the position of leadership it has used to shape bilateral and regional agendas for decades. The consequences would seem no less damaging where stability is concerned. As offshore balancers have argued, it may be that U.S. retrenchment would force local powers to spend more on defense, while perhaps assuaging certain points of friction with countries that feel threatened or encircled by U.S. presence. But it equally stands to reason that removing the American pacifier would liberate the more destabilizing influences that U.S. policy had previously stifled. Long-dormant security competitions might reawaken as countries armed themselves more vigorously; historical antagonisms between old rivals might reemerge in the absence of a robust U.S. presence and the reassurance it provides. Moreover, countries that seek to revise existing regional orders in their favor—think Russia in Europe, or China in Asia—might indeed applaud U.S. retrenchment, but they might just as plausibly feel empowered to more assertively press their interests. If the United States has been a kind of Leviathan in key regions, Mearsheimer acknowledges, then "take away that Leviathan and there is likely to be big trouble."[51]

Scanning the global horizon today, one can easily see where such trouble might arise. In Europe, a revisionist Russia is already destabilizing its neighbors and contesting the post–Cold War settlement in the region. In the Gulf and the broader Middle East, the threat of Iranian ascendancy has stoked regionwide tensions manifesting in proxy wars and an incipient arms race, even as that region also contends with a severe threat to its stability in the form of the Islamic State and other jihadist groups. In East Asia, a rising China is challenging the regional status quo in numerous ways, sounding alarms among its neighbors—many of whom also have historical grievances against each other. In these circumstances, removing the American pacifier would likely yield not low-cost stability, but increased conflict and upheaval.

That conflict and upheaval, in turn, would be quite damaging to U.S. interests even if it did not result in the nightmare scenario of a hostile power dominating a key region. It is hard to imagine, for instance, that increased instability and acrimony would conduce to the robust multilateral cooperation necessary to deal with transnational threats ranging from pandemics to piracy. More problematic still might be the economic consequences. As Michael Mandelbaum has argued, the enormous progress toward global prosperity and integration that has occurred since World War II (and now the Cold War) has come in the climate of relative stability and security provided largely by the United States.[52] One cannot confidently predict that this progress would endure and continue amid escalating geopolitical competition in regions of enormous importance to the world economy.

Perhaps the greatest risk that a strategy of offshore balancing would run, of course, is that a key region might not be able to maintain its own balance following U.S. retrenchment. That prospect might have seemed far-fetched in the early post–Cold War era. But in East Asia today, the rise and growing assertiveness of China have highlighted the medium- to long-term danger that a hostile power could in fact gain regional primacy. If China's economy continues to grow rapidly, and if Beijing continues to increase military spending significantly, then its neighbors will ultimately face grave challenges in containing Chinese power even if they join forces in that endeavor. This possibility, ironically, is one to which leading advocates of retrenchment have been attuned. "The United States will have to play a key role in countering China," Mearsheimer writes, "because its Asian neighbors are not strong enough to do it by themselves."[53]

If this is true, however, then offshore balancing becomes a dangerous and potentially self-defeating strategy. As mentioned above, it could lead Japan and South Korea to seek nuclear weapons, stoking arms races and elevating regional tensions. Alternatively, and perhaps more worryingly, it might encourage the scenario that offshore balancers seek to avoid, by easing China's ascent to regional hegemony. As Robert Gilpin has written, "Retrenchment by its very nature is an indication of relative weakness and declining power, and thus retrenchment can have a deteriorating effect on relations with allies and rivals. Sensing the decline of their protector, allies try to obtain the best deal they can from the rising master of the system. Rivals are stimulated to 'close in,' and frequently they precipitate a conflict in the process."[54]

In East Asia today, U.S. allies rely on U.S. reassurance to navigate increasingly fraught relationships with a more assertive China, precisely because they understand that they will have great trouble balancing Beijing on their own. A significant American retrenchment might therefore tempt these countries to acquiesce to, or bandwagon with, a rising China if they felt that prospects for successful resistance were diminishing as the United States retreated. If U.S. presence in Asia were weakened, one Thai commentator has predicted, Asian countries would have to conclude that "the region will no longer be a place where only one major power plays a dominant role," and hedge their bets accordingly.[55] In the same vein, retrenchment would compromise alliance relationships, basing agreements, and other assets that might help Washington check

Chinese power in the first place—and that would allow the United States to surge additional forces into theater in a crisis. In sum, if one expects that Asian countries will be unable to counter China themselves, then reducing U.S. influence and leverage in the region is a curious policy. Offshore balancing might promise to preserve a stable and advantageous environment while reducing U.S. burdens. But upon closer analysis, the probable outcomes of the strategy seem more perilous and destabilizing than its proponents acknowledge.

BALANCING OFFSHORE OPTIMISM

Is offshore balancing the right grand strategy for the United States? Its supporters firmly believe that the time to adopt that strategy has arrived. They claim that Washington's current global posture has become outdated and counterproductive, and that a more reserved approach can actually deliver better results at a better price. In the post-Iraq climate, such claims have understandable appeal. They have given offshore balancing growing salience in the U.S. grand strategy debate; they have even surfaced, via Trump's rhetoric and policies, in the broader U.S. political debate.

If something sounds too good to be true, though, it probably is—and upon closer examination offshore balancing falls squarely within this category. Offshore balancers are not wrong to point out certain ways in which the current U.S. posture is imperfect. The trouble, however, is that their preferred alternative is not compelling. On issues ranging from financial cost, to core security challenges such as terrorism and proliferation, to preservation of the favorable international environment that the United States has enjoyed, the likely upsides of offshore balancing are far more modest than advertised and the likely downsides are far more severe. Offshore balancers tout their strategy as the path to cut-rate security and stability for the United States. Yet on aggregate, the more likely upshot might well be to jeopardize the stability, security, and influence that U.S. policy has long afforded, and to trade moderate short-term economies for higher long-term risks and costs.

To be sure, none of this is to argue dogmatically against any flexibility or adaptation in American statecraft. Change within continuity is always a hallmark of effective grand strategy, and postwar U.S. grand strategy has been no exception. There has long been an ebb and flow to U.S. engagement overseas; administrations have responded to their predecessors' successes and failures by changing U.S. posture at the margins while still remaining within the overarching paradigm of proactive globalism. In the coming years and decades, this sort of "strategic recalibration" will remain essential to preserving the long-standing benefits of energetic engagement, while also enabling U.S. policy to roll with the punches and respond effectively to emerging opportunities and challenges.[56] What will prove equally essential, however, is to avoid the extreme of wholesale retrenchment—and to reject the false promise of offshore balancing.

THREE

BARACK OBAMA AND THE DILEMMAS OF AMERICAN GRAND STRATEGY

Did the Obama administration have a grand strategy? If so, was it effective? Before Obama's presidency even ended, these questions were unleashing fusillades of contradictory commentary. Sympathetic observers credited Obama with a wise, well-integrated grand strategy that enhanced American power for "the long game."[1] Detractors, by contrast, argued that Obama's strategy of "overarching American retrenchment and accommodation" had been pernicious—even devastating—to national security.[2] Still other prominent observers rejected the very idea of an Obama grand strategy, charging that his policies lacked any coherent design.[3] Finally, and further muddying the waters, Obama himself was sometimes dismissive of grand strategy, once remarking, "I don't really even need George Kennan right now."[4] Now that the president's tenure has ended, it is useful to revisit these issues and come to grips with grand strategy under Obama.

In fact, the Obama administration did have a fairly clear and consistent grand strategy—if one defines grand strategy realistically, as a set of basic principles that guide policy. And that grand strategy reflected a mixture of continuity and change vis-à-vis the foreign policy tradition Obama inherited. In many ways, Obama's grand strategy fit squarely within the broad contours of American statecraft during the postwar and post–Cold War eras, as its broadest objective was maintaining U.S. primacy and a liberal international order. Yet Obama simultaneously sought to define his grand strategy in opposition to the purported mistakes of George W. Bush, and therefore emphasized altering the more recent arc of U.S. policy. In particular, Obama stressed the need to inject greater restraint, economy, and precision into the use of U.S. military power; to double down on diplomatic engagement with friends and rivals alike; and to rebalance American policy geographically, in light of the emergence of the Asia-Pacific region as the cockpit of twenty-first-century geopolitics and geoeconomics. To be sure, the *degree* of change in Obama's grand strategy was sometimes less than advertised (or alleged), but across these three dimensions meaningful shifts did occur.

Obama's grand strategy might thus be summarized—at least in the president's own view—as preserving U.S. leadership of an eminently favorable international order, but doing so at reduced costs, via more supple and energetic diplomacy, and in ways that better reflected the shifting landscape of global power. These were the most consistent "big ideas" in Obama's statecraft; they anchored key initiatives across issues and regions.[5]

The mere existence of a grand strategy does not ensure its success, however, and here the administration's record was more ambiguous than either defenders or detractors claimed. In some ways, Obama's grand strategy was what the United States needed after the George W. Bush years. It promoted some necessary adjustment and recalibration of U.S. leadership; it better oriented America to address enormous long-term challenges such as the rise of China and global climate change; it provided the country with a strategic breather after a period of overexertion. Moreover, in a number of key areas—from diplomacy with Iran to U.S. posture in the Asia-Pacific region—it drove policies that were broadly constructive in their effects.

In other ways, however, Obama's grand strategy was more problematic. Its implementation entailed some notable and costly failures, particularly in the greater Middle East, while also exposing key tensions and limitations at the very core of his statecraft. Additionally, on issues from Iraq and Syria to the United States' broader global posture, Obama's statecraft periodically raised the question of whether the president had overlearned from his predecessor's mistakes—and thus committed the opposite errors himself. Finally, with the surprise election of Donald Trump as president in November 2016, there was significant uncertainty as to how much of Obama's grand strategic legacy—and how much of American grand strategy more broadly—would ultimately endure. Grand strategy is never easy, of course, and not all the difficulties the administration encountered were entirely or even primarily of its own making. But these difficulties nonetheless revealed some fundamental dilemmas of U.S. grand strategy during the Obama years.

MAKING SENSE OF GRAND STRATEGY

Grand strategy is frequently maligned by its detractors, in part because it is oversold by its advocates. Contrary to the common mystique, a grand strategy is neither a road map nor a cure-all for the complexity of global affairs. It is simply an integrated set of concepts that offers broad direction to statecraft. A grand strategy consists of considered assessments of the global environment, a country's core interests and objectives, the most important threats and opportunities, and the ways finite resources can be deployed across key issues. These assessments constitute a conceptual framework that steers policy—the concrete initiatives through which states engage the world.

Grand strategy is therefore vital to effective statecraft. Yet doing grand strategy can be devilishly hard. It requires making sense of a messy world and reconciling competing priorities. It demands a strong overall sense of direction as well as the flexibility to adapt as the unexpected intervenes. It requires synchronizing the sources of national power to achieve important ends, while also preserving that power so that it endures. Throw in the perpetual vicissitudes of global and domestic politics, and it becomes clear how demanding the task can be. Grand strategy, then, is no panacea; it can never impart perfect vision and efficacy to statecraft. At best, it can impart a bare, essential minimum of those qualities to a country's dealings with an unruly world.[6]

In terms of its content, U.S. grand strategy has featured strong elements of both continuity and change over time. The continuity reflects the fact that many drivers of the country's statecraft—its geography, its liberal values, its power position within an interdependent global environment—change slowly, if at all. And so, since World War II, that continuity has been manifested in an enduring, bipartisan commitment to shaping the global order through assertive economic, diplomatic, and military engagement. Yet the precise *manner* of that engagement has evolved from year to year and from administration to administration. Different leaders have made different choices about how assertively to press U.S. interests, what issues or regions to emphasize, and how best to employ the tools of American power to address given challenges. Likewise, changing circumstances at home and abroad have regularly compelled adjustments in American policy. Appreciating the interplay of continuity and change is thus crucial to understanding U.S. grand strategy historically and to grasping American grand strategy under Obama.

CONTINUITY AND CHANGE IN OBAMA'S
GRAND STRATEGY

Obama's critics often portrayed his policies as dramatic departures from the tried-and-true patterns of U.S. statecraft. In reality, there was much continuity with the past. As discussed in previous chapters, since World War II, U.S. officials have consistently sought a stable and prosperous international order, one that would be congenial to America's liberal values, and one in which the United States and its allies would enjoy preponderant power. After the Cold War, Washington essentially doubled down on this project in the highly favorable climate of unipolarity, which featured the United States as the sole superpower in the new global order.

After 1989, every U.S. administration aimed to maintain America's remarkable post–Cold War primacy, to further spread liberal institutions overseas, and to contain or roll back the major threats to this advantageous environment. Every administration, moreover, pursued these goals through policies that were deeply ingrained in U.S. strategic culture—promoting free trade and democracy; maintaining and expanding U.S. alliances overseas; preserving a globe-straddling military with unrivaled capabilities; and confronting "rogue states," nuclear proliferation, terrorism, and other dangers. These initiatives all reflected a long-standing, bipartisan commitment to *sustaining U.S. leadership and primacy, and preserving the liberal international order that American power has traditionally underpinned.*[7]

They also constituted the first and broadest pillar of U.S. grand strategy under Obama. From 2009 onward, every major U.S. strategy document restated the goal of perpetuating U.S. primacy and shaping an international order that reflected American interests and values.[8] And in practice, Obama undertook nearly all the same endeavors that have traditionally marked American globalism.

The administration affirmed that unrivaled military primacy represented the "backbone" of American leadership, and despite significant post-2010 budget cuts, the United States in 2015 still spent nearly three times as much on defense as any other country.[9] Likewise, Obama maintained and even marginally expanded the vast system of U.S. alliances and security commitments; overseas force deployments remained robust, even as their regional distribution continued to shift. The administration also consistently opposed nuclear proliferation, terrorism, and other key threats. Not least, it used all aspects of national power to address the most significant dangers, as shown by its punishing counterterrorism campaign against al-Qaeda from 2009 to 2011 and the counter–Islamic State campaign beginning in 2014.

The administration stayed within the historical mainstream in other ways, too. Obama promoted the United States' long-standing globalization / free trade agenda, principally by pursuing international agreements—the Trans-Pacific Partnership (TPP) and the Transatlantic Trade and Investment Partnership (TTIP)—meant to further liberalize and integrate the Asia-Pacific and North Atlantic economies. The president also selectively promoted human rights and democracy, even intervening militarily in Libya in 2011 to protect civilians and encourage the emergence of more pluralistic governance. One can dispute the efficacy of these various policies, but continuity with the broad contours of U.S. globalism clearly represented the foundation of Obama's strategy.

That strategy also entailed real change, however, because Obama emphasized correcting the perceived mistakes of more recent U.S. statecraft. Obama's view, as he repeatedly argued in 2008 and after, was that he had inherited a mess. America was suffering from the punishing effects of the Great Recession and from military overstretch due to the Iraq and Afghanistan wars. It was confronting a shifting global power structure, in which key regional and global players were contending for greater influence, and in which U.S. supremacy—while still vast—was starting to slip from its post–Cold War peak. Finally, the country was facing the legacy of an administration that, from Obama's perspective, had fundamentally mismanaged American power—by overinvesting in the Middle East at the expense of other priorities, by launching a costly war in Iraq that had empowered U.S. rivals and undercut the struggle against terrorism, and by employing a unilateralist ethos that had generated more resistance than cooperation.[10]

To be fair, this critique of Bush was somewhat overwrought, for it downplayed the progress Bush had made in areas such as U.S.-India and U.S.-China relations, as well as his second-term efforts to correct first-term errors such as alienating key allies and bungling the occupation of Iraq.[11] But Obama's team still believed—not without justification—that the overall pattern of Bush's statecraft had been more damaging than constructive. The administration's task, then, was to maintain U.S. leadership while adapting it in light of changing global circumstances and the painful lessons of the previous administration.

This imperative informed the second pillar of Obama's grand strategy, which entailed *taking a more restrained, economical, and precise approach to using U.S. military power.* From 2009 onward, the administration stressed the need to begin winding down the manpower-intensive, open-ended stabilization operations that characterized the war on terror under Bush, and to take a "more targeted approach" that "dismantles terrorist networks without deploying large American armies."[12] It called for allies and local partners to bear greater responsibility when force was required. And of course, the administration repeatedly urged caution in contemplating any large-scale military operations, to minimize the risk of another draining misadventure. His guiding principle, Obama famously remarked, was "Don't do stupid shit."[13] Or, as the administration's 2012 Defense Strategic Guidance made clear, preserving U.S. military dominance entailed husbanding that dominance to a greater degree.[14]

That document also noted another impetus to, and dimension of, military restraint under Obama—reduced defense spending.

U.S. military spending always contracts after major wars. Under Obama, the pressure was increased by the president's domestic policy priorities, the effects of the Great Recession, and the legacy of Bush-era deficit spending. These factors, combined with partisan gridlock that triggered the sequester mechanism created by the Budget Control Act of 2011, caused constant-dollar U.S. defense spending to fall from US$759 billion in 2010 to US$596 billion in 2015.[15] These reductions compelled significant cuts in force structure and a shift to a more modest defense strategy; they also accentuated the need for cheaper, more discriminating approaches to the use of force.[16]

The policy implications of this approach would soon become apparent. The Obama administration relied heavily on drones, Special Operations Forces (SOF), and other "light-footprint" approaches as primary tools of counterterrorism, even as it aggressively targeted al-Qaeda.[17] In Libya, it emphasized "leading from behind"— letting U.S. allies and partners take greater initiative—while keeping American boots largely off the ground.[18] In Iraq, the administration gradually wound down U.S. involvement between 2009 and 2011, and ultimately withdrew completely in December 2011. In Afghanistan, by contrast, Obama escalated U.S. involvement in 2009–2010 by deploying roughly 60,000 additional troops as part of an effort to win a "necessary war" against the Taliban and al-Qaeda. Yet in line with his broader approach to military intervention, he also hedged against an open-ended commitment by imposing a time limit on the surge of U.S. forces. "We have been at war now for eight years, at enormous cost in lives and resources," Obama said in December 2009; it was necessary to begin bringing these conflicts to an end.[19] And from 2011 to 2014, Obama showed deep reluctance to be drawn into Syria's civil war, even after the flagrant transgression of his own "red line" on chemical weapons, for fear of another Middle Eastern morass.[20]

Finally, this same approach guided the military campaign that increasingly came to define Obama's second term. Even after the Islamic State conquered vast swaths of Iraq and Syria in 2013–14, thereby unleashing an avalanche of criticism of Obama's earlier restraint, the administration declined to "Americanize" the conflict by sending any significant number of ground troops into combat. Instead, it carefully circumscribed the American commitment, utilizing unique U.S. enablers—SOF, airpower, logistics—to empower Iraqi and Syrian ground forces to roll back Islamic State gains.[21] Across these initiatives, Obama sought to correct his predecessor's mistakes—and sustain American power—by establishing a more disciplined, limited-liability approach to military action.

The imperative of adapting U.S. leadership also informed the third pillar of Obama's grand strategy, which involved *doubling down on diplomacy with friends and rivals alike.* Contrary to Obama's critique, the Bush administration had never ignored diplomacy—it had scored a major diplomatic breakthrough with India, for instance, and launched new multilateral endeavors such as the Proliferation Security Initiative (PSI), which fostered international cooperation to counter the spread of weapons of mass destruction. Yet from Obama's perspective, the combination of the Iraq War, the harsher aspects of the war on terror, and the sometimes Manichean ethos of Bush's post-9/11 statecraft had alienated too many international observers and foreclosed too many diplomatic opportunities. Redoubled, "comprehensive engagement" was therefore essential—essential to repairing America's international reputation, to enabling greater multilateral cooperation on complex global issues, to improving relations with challengers as well as adversaries, and to regenerating U.S. leadership on a more consensual, lower-cost basis.[22]

This approach motivated the series of immensely (critics would say naively) aspirational speeches Obama gave during 2009, on issues ranging from relations with the Islamic world to the need for eventual nuclear abolition. The specifics of each speech were important, but the broader grand strategic purpose was to begin rebuilding U.S. soft power by demonstrating that the country was ready to "turn the page" on the Bush years.[23] Similarly, this approach motivated an array of diplomatic initiatives over the course of Obama's presidency, from repeated (and repeatedly unsuccessful) efforts to broker Israeli-Palestinian peace, to recurring international and bilateral talks aimed at combating climate change.

Perhaps most important, the emphasis on intensified diplomacy undergirded Obama's persistent willingness to engage adversaries and other problematic actors—and often, to take the first step in doing so. There were high-profile diplomatic openings to Myanmar in the first term and to Cuba in the second, which were geared toward ending outdated hostilities and using engagement rather than isolation to change an interlocutor's behavior. There was also the much-touted "Russia reset." That initiative was meant to foster greater cooperation on issues ranging from arms control and Afghanistan to Iran and North Korea, while also reinforcing perceived positive political tendencies in Moscow during the presidency of Dmitri Medvedev (May 2008–May 2012); it entailed early U.S. concessions on issues such as revising plans for a ballistic missile defense system in eastern Europe.[24]

Most notably, there was American policy toward Iran. From 2009 onward, Obama averred that a nuclear Iran was unacceptable. Over time, and partially under pressure from Congress, he would employ powerful coercive levers—including economic sanctions and, reportedly, cyberattacks—to compel Tehran to halt its nuclear program. Yet Obama also sought to engage Tehran diplomatically, first by offering to conduct direct and unconditional talks with the regime in 2009, and later by complementing increased pressure with persistent diplomatic outreach, both bilateral and multilateral. Tactically, Obama did so to enlist broader international support for economic sanctions and other pressures. More fundamentally, he did so to locate a peaceful, positive-sum solution to the nuclear issue, and to demonstrate that diplomacy could provide imperfect but acceptable ways of protecting U.S. interests at much lower cost than military force. "Part of our goal here has been to show that diplomacy can work," Obama explained.[25]

The fourth and final pillar of Obama's strategy also emphasized reorienting U.S. leadership, in this case to reflect the changing geography of international power. When Obama took office, it was becoming clear that the world's center of economic and military gravity was shifting from West to East—that the Asia-Pacific region was emerging as the future cockpit of global economic and military dynamism, and that the rise of China as a full-fledged rival for regional primacy presented arguably the greatest long-term challenge for U.S. statecraft. It was also clear that although the Bush administration's immense military investment in the greater Middle East had not prevented it from undertaking a number of constructive initiatives in the Asia-Pacific region and making initial moves to bolster the U.S. strategic position there, it had nonetheless distorted the balance of resources and top-level attention between those two regions.[26]

The corresponding strategic imperative was to *rebalance American engagement geographically*. Washington must de-leverage its strategic investments in the Middle East and simultaneously redouble its efforts to shape the future of a dynamic Asia-Pacific region. Or as Secretary of State Hillary Clinton wrote in 2011, "We will need to accelerate efforts to pivot to new global realities."[27]

In practice, this idea powerfully reinforced the inclination toward restraint, retrenchment, and light-footprint military strategies in the Middle East. More affirmatively, it was the logic behind the administration's much-touted Asia pivot. The United States had never been absent from the Asia-Pacific region, of course, and so the rhetoric surrounding the pivot was sometimes grander than the reality. Yet that initiative still featured myriad efforts to sustain the sine qua non of U.S. influence in the Asia-Pacific region—U.S. regional military primacy—in the face of China's rise, from the decision to eventually station 60 percent of U.S. naval and air assets in that region, to a "Third Offset strategy" focused on developing advanced capabilities and concepts needed to preserve U.S. conventional deterrence. The pivot also featured enhanced efforts to modernize America's alliances, disperse and harden U.S. force posture, and build deeper defense relationships with nonallied countries from India to Indonesia.[28]

Importantly, the pivot included nonmilitary components, which were meant to be just as prominent as the defense-related initiatives. There was intensified engagement to ensure a liberal, U.S.-facing regional economic order, mainly via negotiation of the TPP, which was finalized in late 2015 (although, as discussed subsequently, it was later thwarted by political opposition within the United States). On the diplomatic front, Washington worked to forge and strengthen relationships with key players across the Asia-Pacific region, and to increasingly empower regional institutions such as the Association of Southeast Asian Nations, or ASEAN. Finally, although all this activity was geared toward fortifying a favorable regional order against disruptions that a more bellicose China might cause, the administration also intensified engagement with Beijing—through creation of the U.S.-China Strategic and Economic Dialogue (an evolution of earlier senior bilateral dialogues), attempts to negotiate a bilateral investment treaty, and other steps—as part of a continuing, multidecade effort to bring China into that regional order as a constructive participant. "Most of the history of the 21st century is going to be written in the Asian–Pacific region," Assistant Secretary of State Kurt Campbell commented, and U.S. policy increasingly reflected that fact.[29]

The Obama administration did not lack a grand strategy, then, nor did it engage in a flight from American primacy. Rather, it pursued a multipronged grand strategy aimed at sustaining U.S. leadership by adjusting it to new challenges and realities. The key question thus becomes how effective that grand strategy really was. And here the answer is more ambiguous. Across several key issues, the record of Obama's grand strategy consisted of a mixture of geopolitical insights and generally constructive policies, on one hand, with failures, limitations, and unresolved strategic dilemmas, on the other.

DOUBLE-EDGED DIPLOMACY

Consider one calling card of Obama's strategy—his emphasis on intensifying U.S. diplomacy, particularly vis-à-vis adversaries and rivals. As noted, this approach was based on an overdone critique of Bush-era policies. Yet it was nonetheless true that a superpower whose energies had been taxed by Iraq as well as a punishing financial crisis, and whose soft power had been badly depleted, was going to have to rely more on diplomatic outreach to advance its interests. And so Obama's diplomacy did yield some meaningful gains.

If nothing else, the opening to Cuba was an exercise in enlightened loss-cutting, for it distanced the United States from a policy that had long served to isolate Washington as much as Havana. Likewise, climate change diplomacy with China was arduous and often frustrating, but it ultimately produced a bilateral deal to begin limiting greenhouse gas emissions in 2014, which facilitated a broader international agreement in 2015. The near-term gains delivered by those accords were modest (and the long-term gains were subsequently thrown into doubt by the election of Donald Trump as president), but they did increasingly orient international diplomacy toward addressing an enormous long-term threat that, as Obama commented, "could define the contours of this century more dramatically than any other."[30]

For its part, the Russia reset hardly delivered warmer long-term relations with Moscow, but it did enable successful transactional diplomacy. Some of the dividends were the New Start Treaty of 2011 (which further reduced U.S. and Russian deployed nuclear weapons), enhanced cooperation on logistics for the U.S. mission in Afghanistan, Russian acquiescence to humanitarian intervention in Libya in 2011, and support for greater multilateral pressure on North Korea and Iran.[31] Additionally, although the process was beyond ugly, coercive diplomacy—pursued in cooperation with Moscow—allowed Washington to partially disarm the Assad regime of chemical weapons following the red line saga in 2013.[32]

Most notably, the administration's blend of coercion, international coalition-building, and engagement did eventually deliver a nuclear deal with Iran in 2015. That deal was imperfect in many ways, and it left open the question of what would happen after its key provisions expired. But provided that Tehran adhered to the deal, it nonetheless froze and/or rolled back key aspects of Iran's nuclear program for at least a decade—far longer than any military intervention might have accomplished, and at far less cost. In doing so, it averted, or at least significantly delayed, the twin nightmare scenarios U.S. planners had long feared: another major military conflict in the Middle East, or an Iran that was largely unconstrained in pursuit of the bomb.[33] The nuclear deal thus illustrated that coercive diplomacy, when pursued with focus and persistence, could yield constructive results in the post-Iraq context.

Unfortunately, the Iran deal also illustrated prominent dangers that accompanied that endeavor. One critique of Obama's diplomacy has been that the administration often became so invested in its search for agreement with adversaries that it lost leverage either in the negotiations themselves or in the broader bilateral relationship. It appears that Obama encountered this problem vis-à-vis Iran. During the negotiations, the administration retreated fairly significantly on important side issues such as limits on Iran's ballistic missile program. Moreover, although Obama could be quite tough in applying nuclear-related pressures, based on published reports he seems not to have embedded those pressures within a broader program for pushing back against increasingly assertive Iranian behavior throughout the region, such as its growing influence with the sectarian, Shia-led government in Baghdad, its support for Houthi rebels in Yemen, and its intervention in Syria on behalf of Assad. The widespread perception among U.S. partners, at least, was that the quest for a nuclear deal was helping Iran become ascendant in the Middle East, while the United States was retreating after Iraq.[34]

This perception related to a second problem, which was that the Iran negotiations caused significant fallout between Washington and its regional partners. An inherent dilemma of engaging enemies is that it can discomfit insecure friends. Although the administration sought to counter this dynamic via arms sales and other security assistance to Israel and key Gulf states, it was never particularly successful. In fact, Obama's undisguised ambivalence toward partners such as Saudi Arabia, as well as the perception of retrenchment fostered by U.S. withdrawal from Iraq and the failure to strike Syria after Assad's chemical weapons attacks in 2013, made it even harder to reassure those partners that the nuclear deal did not presage a larger regional realignment that would empower Iran at their expense. That belief, in turn, apparently contributed to panicked behavior by an exposed Saudi Arabia, whose effort to push back unilaterally against Tehran in early 2015 led it into a war in Yemen that further destabilized the region.[35]

Engagement with Tehran thus provided an acceptable solution to the nuclear issue, but it complicated containment of Iran's regional influence and tested America's own regional relationships. Diplomacy with adversaries can be a double-edged sword; Obama's strategy demonstrated the possibilities and perils of that endeavor.

LIMITATIONS OF THE LIGHT FOOTPRINT

The same was true of Obama's approach to using force, particularly his preference for light-footprint interventions. That preference reflected a sensible desire to set the war on terror on a more sustainable footing, and to get away from manpower-intensive strategies that often inflamed local sensitivities and allowed enemies to bleed U.S. troops and the U.S. Treasury alike. In practice, this approach indeed enabled intervention at reduced risk of quagmire; in some cases, it delivered operational success.

A focused, light-footprint approach proved devastatingly effective against core al-Qaeda, for example. Obama's first term saw an estimated 400 U.S. drone strikes, compared to roughly 50 during Bush's entire presidency. Those strikes, along with SOF raids and other tools, killed dozens of al-Qaeda leaders and hundreds of midlevel operatives, and severely disrupted al-Qaeda's operations. "Drones have turned al-Qaeda's command and training structures into a liability," wrote terrorism and Middle East expert Daniel Byman, "forcing the group to choose between having no leaders and risking dead leaders."[36]

There were other successes, too. Al-Qaeda in the Arabian Peninsula (AQAP) took a beating from drone strikes, assistance to local security forces, and other light-footprint methods prior to 2015. Similarly—although the rise of the Islamic State was a tremendous setback for U.S. policy—a light-footprint strategy centered on airpower, SOF, and other enablers allowed Syrian and Iraqi partner-forces to roll back that group's territorial gains from 2014 onward. By the end of Obama's presidency, U.S. operations had helped those partners liberate key points from Manbij to Fallujah, and to begin operations against remaining Islamic State strongholds in Mosul and Raqqa, while also killing perhaps 45,000 enemy fighters in exchange for a handful of American combat deaths.[37] In these cases, Obama's approach leveraged unique U.S. capabilities to wage a cost-effective war on terror.

Yet the light footprint was no panacea. It disrupted extremist organizations, but did little to address the underlying failures of governance that allowed terrorist groups to thrive. In 2013–14, Obama was touting progress against AQAP as the very model of a newer, smarter counterterrorism strategy. By early 2015, however, Yemen was disintegrating amid chaos so severe that the U.S. military mission had to withdraw from the country. As AQAP exploited this chaos to seize a greater territorial foothold, it seemed fair to ask whether the light footprint had achieved anything more than simply "mowing the grass."[38]

The weaknesses of the light footprint were equally apparent in other contexts. The Libyan intervention was an early archetype of this approach, featuring an emphasis on allied contributions and a reliance on precision airpower and U.S. enablers. This campaign succeeded in halting Qaddafi's onslaught and eventually pushing him from power. Yet even as American officials were hailing the war as "the right way to run an intervention," the same light-footprint approach was depriving the United States and its coalition partners of the ability to influence events or provide security following Qaddafi's demise.[39] The strategic upshot of the intervention, then, was not the emergence of stable democracy, but a rapid erosion of internal order, the unleashing of instability that created a haven for extremists and spilled over into neighboring countries, and the need for two subsequent military interventions—one by France in Mali, one by the United States in Libya—to address the mess left by the original conflict. The light footprint may have limited the short-term military costs of intervention in Libya, but it contributed to the higher, longer-term geopolitical costs that conflict produced.[40]

Obama's presidency thus showed that the light footprint offered a way of utilizing U.S. military power while containing the country's near-term exposure—no small benefit after Iraq. It also showed, however, that limited investments could produce limited—and sometimes strategically counterproductive—results.

DILEMMAS OF DE-LEVERAGING

The weaknesses of the light footprint highlighted another tension in Obama's grand strategy, pertaining to the broader concept of de-leveraging U.S. investment in the greater Middle East. By virtually any measure, the Bush administration's investments of time and resources in the region were out of proportion with the strategic gains achieved there. And so de-leveraging—lessening Washington's strategic investment of resources to be more commensurate with American interests in the region—was indeed critical to restoring a healthier equilibrium in U.S. global engagement, and to positioning the country for success not just in Asia but globally.

The problem, however, is that the "how" of de-leveraging can be just as important as the "whether." And so a key test for the Obama administration was whether it would adjust its regional posture in ways that allowed it to lock in existing gains, particularly in Iraq, and rebalance from a position of strength, or whether it would jeopardize existing gains and the prospects for long-term stability by de-leveraging too significantly or too hastily. This is a perpetual dilemma for great powers experiencing overstretch—how does one retrench without undercutting important interests? And it was here that Obama ran into trouble.

In Afghanistan, for instance, the need to de-leverage conflicted with Obama's oft-stated belief that this "necessary war" had to be won, and with his postelection realization that winning would be a longer and costlier proposition than originally expected. Caught between competing imperatives, Obama split the difference. He significantly escalated U.S. involvement in hopes of reversing the downward trajectory of the war and enabling a later withdrawal on favorable terms, while also announcing that this surge would last only until mid-2011.[41] From a de-leveraging perspective, that decision reflected an understandable desire to hedge against indefinite diversion of resources. Yet it also limited the military impact of the surge, reduced U.S. leverage in pushing for a potential negotiated settlement, and encouraged damaging hedging behavior by local partners in Afghanistan and Pakistan. In effect, the administration pursued a worst-of-both-worlds policy, one that incurred significant additional resource commitments but simultaneously undercut the probability that these commitments would make it possible to de-leverage from a position of greater stability and success.

In fairness, Afghanistan was a hard enough problem that it may have been beyond Washington's ability to solve at acceptable cost. In Iraq, however, where the trajectory of events was far more favorable when Obama took office, the problem was that he was insufficiently attentive to the more manageable imperative of sustaining that trajectory. The administration did modify Obama's campaign pledge to withdraw one brigade per month, in favor of a more gradual and realistic downslope. But particularly during the critical 2010–11 period, the White House appears to have increasingly focused simply on winding down a conflict that Obama had long pledged to end, rather than on making the residual—and far from prohibitive—investments necessary to lock in U.S. influence and ensure some lasting stability following the Bush administration's surge. This tendency, now well documented by administration insiders and independent observers alike, was evident in the decreasing personal attention that Obama paid to Iraq; it was equally evident in the White House's ambivalent stance on potentially leaving behind a residual force after 2011.[42]

Reasonable people can debate whether such a force, or other continuing investments, might have prevented the disastrous sequence that culminated in the Islamic State overrunning a third of the country.[43] What is clear is that Obama's approach helped deprive

Washington of tools and presence it might have used to influence Iraq's trajectory—to moderate Nouri al-Maliki's sectarian governance, to mitigate the hollowing out of the Iraqi military, or simply to better understand the threat that the Islamic State posed to an increasingly fragile Iraqi state. By late 2014, then, whatever stability had existed in 2011 had unraveled completely, and an administration that had earlier boasted of ending the Iraq War had to start yet another intervention in that country, under far worse circumstances than when it had departed. That war, moreover, threatened to complicate the same longer-term global rebalancing that the U.S. drawdown had been meant to facilitate. Obama had been determined to learn from Bush's mistake of getting into Iraq too carelessly; he ended up committing the opposite error of getting out too completely and precipitately.

De-leveraging can thus be a prudent strategic move for a country that is overinvested in a given area. But de-leveraging responsibly sometimes requires making, or sustaining, marginal investments to protect gains made along the way. Obama understood the first imperative; the second, he learned the hard way.

NATO, RUSSIA, AND THE RESOURCE BALANCE

The challenges of Obama's grand strategy were also evident with respect to NATO and Russia. Obama initially enhanced diplomatic engagement with Moscow, to elicit cooperation on key issues and perhaps mellow Russian policy over time. The reset was fairly effective on the first count; it manifestly failed on the second. Russia's overall strategic behavior became more truculent with time (particularly after Vladimir Putin returned to the presidency in 2012), culminating in the invasion and annexation of Crimea, destabilization of Ukraine, military intervention in Syria, persistent efforts to undermine the European Union (EU) and NATO, and even intervention in electoral processes in Europe as well as the

United States itself. In retrospect, the administration failed to recognize that a revisionist Russia was again emerging as a major threat, and its attachment to the reset—for all the transactional diplomacy it enabled—may have discouraged stronger steps to protect NATO's exposed eastern flank or otherwise address this challenge.[44]

To its credit, the administration steadied the ship thereafter, mounting a firm but measured response to Putin's aggression in Ukraine. U.S. officials declined to risk a major confrontation over Ukraine itself, an area in which Moscow possessed escalation dominance and a profound asymmetry of motivation. But they did work to impose multilateral economic sanctions that—combined with falling oil prices—took a significant toll on Russia's economy, while also beginning to prepare NATO to confront a renewed threat from the east. By late 2016, the long post–Cold War slide in European defense budgets had apparently bottomed out, the alliance was implementing a quasi-permanent troop presence in eastern Europe, and Washington and its allies were working to improve interoperability, prepositioning, rapid response, anti-access/area denial defeat, and other critical capabilities.[45] In view of budgetary constraints and competing priorities on both sides of the Atlantic, these measures were probably close to what the traffic could bear.

As Obama's presidency ended, however, there remained two strategic questions the administration had yet to answer. First, were the actions taken actually sufficient to deter an increasingly risk-acceptant Putin and to mitigate NATO's significant local inferiority in the east? As RAND Corporation analysts noted in 2016, NATO was still far from being able to mount a credible defense of the Baltic states, and its forces there would be quickly destroyed by a determined Russian assault.[46] More broadly, Washington and NATO were only beginning to grapple with the more likely dangers posed by coercion short of war—the use of cyberattacks, paramilitary fighters, and other subversive tactics to undermine Russia's neighbors without triggering a NATO military response.[47] Not least, Putin's efforts to undercut U.S. interests and project Russian power continued unabated. The Kremlin mounted an operationally successful intervention to shore up the Assad regime in Syria beginning in September 2015, and it undertook—despite warnings from Obama himself—an audacious campaign to influence the U.S. presidential elections in 2016 through hacking, the dissemination of "fake news," and other methods.[48] Obama had started late in addressing the Russian challenge; there remained much ground to cover as his administration wound down.

Second, and more broadly, how would the renewed Russian threat complicate the United States' global defense calculus? From the start, a key premise of the Asia pivot—and of Obama's overall defense strategy—was that Europe would remain quiescent, and that Washington could thus continue its post–Cold War drawdown on the Continent.[49] Yet with that premise now invalidated, it remained unclear how Washington would reconcile the rising demands of European deterrence with the requirements of the Asia pivot and renewed military operations in the Middle East—all at a time when its overall military resources were undergoing a fairly significant decline. By 2016–17, in fact, the question was no longer how much the United States could safely cut defense after a decade of manpower-intensive counterinsurgency operations; it was whether the country was now approaching a state of strategic insolvency as its capabilities declined and its commitments became steadily more taxing. The Obama administration had wagered that the demands on U.S. military power would become fewer in the post-Iraq context. With that gamble having failed, the country's military posture was being stressed anew.

PROSPECTS AND PROBLEMS OF THE PIVOT

The prospects of the pivot, then, would ineluctably be influenced by events and policies elsewhere. But what about Asia-Pacific strategy itself? Here, the administration deserved credit for reweighting U.S. global engagement to reflect shifting long-term power dynamics, and for better positioning the country for what was likely to be the defining geopolitical rivalry of the twenty-first century—the struggle for regional and perhaps eventually global influence between the United States and China.

The Pentagon, for instance, increasingly oriented itself for long-term competition in the region. It deployed more advanced capabilities, such as F-22 and F-35 fighters, to the Asia-Pacific region; began investing in high-end future capabilities such as undersea drones and a new long-range bomber; and started developing advanced operational concepts relevant to regional contingencies. It also strengthened and diversified U.S. force posture by deploying additional assets to the Asia-Pacific region and stationing them across a larger number of facilities. Alliance relationships across the region were strengthened or modernized; the U.S.-Philippines alliance was fundamentally revived via an agreement that gave U.S. forces access to Filipino bases for the first time in a quarter century. (By the end of Obama's presidency, however, the election of Rodrigo Duterte as president of the Philippines—and Duterte's subsequent erratic and frequently anti-American conduct once in office—had cast somewhat greater uncertainty on the future of the relationship.) Defense relationships with nonallied countries also improved, as demonstrated by normalization of U.S.-Vietnam defense relations and continued progress in U.S.-India relations. Finally, through its Maritime Security Initiative, Washington began linking friendly South China Sea littoral states into a more cohesive security network.[50]

The United States' Pacific posture improved in other ways, too. Intensive diplomatic engagement enhanced U.S. involvement in ASEAN and the East Asia Summit, and opened or further developed important bilateral relationships with countries from Myanmar to Indonesia. Additionally, the signing of the TPP in 2015 demonstrated that there was strong regional demand for closer economic and strategic ties to Washington, and brought an agreement representing 40 percent of global GDP tantalizingly—if, in the end, frustratingly—close to fruition. In sum, the pivot was not just rhetoric.[51] It fortified America's regional position and fostered a web of opportunities, relationships, and initiatives that Obama's successors could, if they chose to do so, exploit. As Obama's presidency wound down, however, there nonetheless remained great uncertainty—in Washington and the Asia-Pacific region—as to the future of the region. That uncertainty, in turn, reflected three factors that U.S. policy had *not* effectively addressed.

First, there were growing questions as Obama's presidency progressed as to whether the U.S. political system would in fact support the intensified Asia-Pacific engagement that the administration had pursued. In late 2013, for instance, a government shutdown caused by partisan gridlock forced Obama to cancel a trip to the region, raising doubts about U.S. steadiness and competence. Far more seriously still, amid growing domestic hostility to trade, the prospects for congressional approval of the TPP were problematic at best even before the 2016 presidential election—and they became downright dismal following Donald Trump's victory. When Trump withdrew the United States from that agreement in January 2017, he effectively collapsed the economic pillar of the pivot—and with it a major component of Obama's regional strategy.

Second, pivot notwithstanding, China's behavior became significantly more bellicose during the Obama years. From China's assertion of expansive maritime claims, to its illegal land reclamation and militarization of disputed features in the South China Sea, to its increasing propensity to coerce and intimidate its neighbors, Beijing consistently tested the regional order more sharply than at any time since the Cold War.[52] And for all the diplomatic and military fruits of the rebalance, the Obama administration frequently failed to generate the leverage necessary to halt or significantly alter this conduct over any sustained period. In other words, U.S. policy might have given Washington an enhanced regional posture, but it did not dissuade China from seeking to improve its own position—often in aggressive and destabilizing ways.[53]

Third, and as a result of these first two factors, there was increasing concern as Obama's presidency ended that the pivot might not suffice to preserve a favorable regional climate against this rising and increasingly disruptive China. Despite the Pentagon's myriad Asia-Pacific initiatives, the regional military balance continued shifting adversely—in part because post-2010 defense cuts somewhat muted the military impact of the pivot, and more fundamentally because of a continuing, decades-long Chinese modernization program. The United States would face a "progressively receding frontier" of its regional primacy, RAND Corporation analysts predicted, as Chinese modernization created intensifying challenges to U.S. power-projection capabilities and ability to uphold key security commitments.[54] Meanwhile, China's "gray-zone" coercive activities in the South China Sea and elsewhere were changing military and geopolitical facts on the ground, as its economic diplomacy sought to exploit the collapse of the TPP and draw the region more tightly into Beijing's economic orbit.[55] As of early 2017, it was thus clear that the pivot had been necessary and generally positive. Whether it would ultimately be sustainable and successful remained far murkier.

THE OVERREACH/UNDERREACH DILEMMA

Many of these issues tied into a final matter, which might be termed the overreach/underreach dilemma. Grand strategy requires calibrating the use of power—acting assertively enough to achieve important goals, but not so hyperactively as to risk blowback and exhaustion. From day one, the Obama administration chose to err—insofar as it had to err—on the side of underreach. It argued that the greatest danger to American primacy and the liberal order was excessive activism rather than excessive restraint, and that, as the 2015 *National Security Strategy* put it, the United States must therefore exhibit great discretion and "strategic patience" in addressing a world full of complex and sometimes insoluble challenges.[56]

This was probably a prudent judgment to make when Obama became president—a moment when even former Bush administration officials acknowledged that the country was "out of steam."[57] It protected against another enervating military misadventure; it gave the country a strategic breather after a period of intense and often disillusioning involvement abroad. Much as Henry Kissinger and Richard Nixon recognized in the late 1960s that a degree of retrenchment was necessary to sustain U.S. globalism, Obama—with his assiduous avoidance of overreach—may eventually receive credit for a similar insight.

The trouble, however, is that underreach can ultimately be quite dangerous as well. Excessive restraint can undermine an international system that has long rested on assertive U.S. leadership. The consequences of nonintervention can be just as messy and pernicious as the consequences of intervention. It is impossible to pinpoint where the critical crossover is—where the perils of underreach surpass the perils of overreach. But this point does exist, and it was arguably closer on key issues than the administration acknowledged.

Consider Syria. Obama was certainly right to emphasize the myriad dangers of intervention, from the lack of attractive military options to the potentially high costs involved. Yet even so, many of the president's advisers reportedly advocated more assertive steps in Syria between 2011 and 2013, in no small part because they believed that the costs of nonintervention could eventually exceed those of intervention.[58] And indeed, given the truly baleful consequences of letting that conflict rage—a humanitarian catastrophe rivaling Rwanda, the rise of the Islamic State and the destabilization of the Middle East, the return of Russian military intervention in that region, the decreased confidence of U.S. regional partners in Washington's leadership, the unprecedented pressure on the European project, the insecurity and toxic spillover that contaminated that continent and points far beyond—it is hardly irresponsible hawkery to suggest that a more forceful approach, earlier in the conflict, may have been warranted.[59]

Or consider the state of the world as Obama's presidency ended. Simply put, 2016 was not 2009 anymore—the global scene had become considerably more disordered since Obama arrived. The Middle East was in chaos; Europe and East Asia were experiencing growing geopolitical instability; great-power competition was sharper than at any time since the Cold War. A perpetually provocative North Korea had reportedly attained a survivable nuclear arsenal and was rapidly progressing toward a nascent intercontinental strike capability; terrorist activity had reached an all-time high in 2015.[60] The world was burning, it often seemed; the liberal order was under growing pressure. And meanwhile, what had seemed in 2009–10 like a needed strategic breather had turned into a period of prolonged military retrenchment that was leaving U.S. primacy increasingly frayed around the edges.

To be clear, the United States was neither fully responsible for these problems, nor could it fully resolve them. But in these circumstances, and given how many countries around the world still looked to Washington for stability in periods of crisis, perhaps it was time for "strategic patience" to give way to strategic reassertion. Perhaps it was time to move beyond retrenchment, and to undertake the sort of renewed geopolitical offensive and military buildup that had allowed the United States to reassert itself after previous periods of respite. All told, Obama's grand strategy certainly protected the United States from the dangers of overreach. Whether it protected the country from the perils of underreach was far more debatable.

MIXED LEGACY, POTENT DILEMMAS

No grand strategy is perfect, or even close to it. The world is too messy, the choices are too hard, the constraints are too real, the trade-offs are too inescapable. All grand strategies have shortcomings; even the good ones leave problems in their wake.

This is worth remembering in evaluating Obama's grand strategy. His administration sought to sustain U.S. leadership of a liberal international order, while also adapting that leadership in important ways. And in retrospect, there was real merit in that approach. Obama's grand strategy showed recognition that greater discipline and restraint were probably needed after Iraq, and it was sensitive—in a way that the approach of Obama's predecessor too frequently was not—to issues of cost and other constraints. It grasped the need to recalibrate the use of U.S. military power after two manpower-intensive interventions; it helped reweight and refocus American engagement following a period of overinvestment in the Middle East. It allowed Washington to reap some benefits of energetic diplomacy on issues from climate change to Iran, while also enhancing U.S. ability to compete in a dynamic Asia-Pacific region. This was hardly a spectacular performance, but by comparative standards it wasn't half bad. To paraphrase Robert Kaplan, prudence and restraint are rarely admired—until their absence reminds one that the alternatives can be far worse.[61]

Criticism is also warranted, however, for Obama's grand strategic ledger had a debit side. There were some costly setbacks, most notably the failure to de-leverage in Iraq and the Middle East in a way that promoted stability rather than catastrophic instability. There were significant tensions and trade-offs associated with all the core elements of Obama's grand strategy, from the limitations of the light footprint to the dangers of diplomacy with Iran and Russia. There were areas—such as the Asia-Pacific region, or Europe after 2014—in which U.S. policies were generally well conceived and necessary, but there nonetheless remained great uncertainty about whether those policies would ultimately succeed. Finally, there was the question of whether Obama had perhaps overlearned the painful lessons of the Bush years—whether in averting the undeniable danger of overreach he had exposed the country to the opposing danger of underreach, just as the world was again demanding more, not less, of the United States' stabilizing influence. Obama's grand strategy had its virtues, then, but it entailed potent drawbacks and strategic dilemmas as well. The overall result was an ambiguous record in steering the ship of state.

This was perhaps not surprising, given the inherent difficulty of grand strategy and the real challenges that Obama confronted. The trade-offs associated with a light-footprint approach to military intervention; the rewards and risks of engagement with adversaries; the difficulties associated with right-sizing U.S. involvement in the Middle East; the challenge of balancing commitments across regions; the question of how to preserve a favorable climate in the Asia-Pacific region in the face of China's rapid rise; and the balancing act required to avoid the twin perils of overreach and underreach: these dilemmas probably would have tested the abilities of any president. The fact that they tested Obama thus spoke to the constraints and trade-offs imposed by geopolitical circumstances, as well as to the limitations and ambiguities of his own statecraft.

It was perhaps fitting, then, that the election of Donald Trump to the presidency in late 2016 brought both the limitations and the value of Obama's strategy into sharper relief. The immediate effect was to make Obama's grand strategic legacy seem increasingly precarious. For the nation had now elected a president who had pledged to roll back Obama-era policies such as the Iran deal, climate change diplomacy, and the TPP—and who did, in several cases, actually begin to unwind those policies once in office. Moreover, the country now had a leader who had promised—rhetorically, at least—an unprecedented presidential departure from the postwar patterns of American globalism, and whose conduct threatened to upend so many aspects of U.S. diplomacy.

How Trump would actually govern remained an open question, of course, not just in the immediate aftermath of his election but throughout the tumultuous opening months of his presidency. If, over time, he ended up following through on even a significant fraction of his campaign rhetoric, he might erase a large part of Obama's grand strategic record and upend U.S. foreign relations in the process. But in doing so, he might also pay the Obama administration an unintended and sadly ironic compliment. For he might underscore that although future presidents could well do better than Obama had in addressing the challenges and dilemmas of American grand strategy in the early twenty-first century, they could also do far, far worse.

FOUR

IS AMERICAN
INTERNATIONALISM DEAD?

"A world is collapsing before our eyes," wrote Gérard Araud, the French ambassador to the United States, upon learning of Donald Trump's election as president in November 2016.[1] Many American internationalists probably felt just the same way. For roughly four generations prior to Trump's victory, the United States had pursued a robust and engaged internationalism supported by a bipartisan political consensus. In November 2016, however, American voters elected a candidate who condemned many aspects of that internationalist tradition in harsh and unapologetic tones. The country that had spent decades erecting an international order based on free trade, multilateral cooperation, a global alliance network, and the promotion of democratic values had now chosen as its leader a man who voiced skepticism—if not outright scorn—toward nearly all the key components of this ambitious American project. In the wake of the election, there was thus a pervasive sense of despair among many foreign leaders—and no less, among members of the American foreign policy establishment. "The U.S. is, for now, out of the world order business," Robert Kagan wrote. After more than seventy years, American internationalism was pronounced politically dead.[2]

True understanding often comes only with time, of course, and it will be years before we know what Trump's rise ultimately means for the arc of American engagement with the world. Indeed, Trump's statecraft itself remains a work in progress. Yet it is not too soon to begin placing Trump's ascent in historical perspective, and to start grappling, on the basis of the evidence at hand, with what his victory tells us about the state of American internationalism today. This question is, after all, of profound geopolitical importance. Given the central role the United States has played in building and sustaining the postwar international order, the political collapse of American internationalism would be an epochal, globe-shaking event.

As it turns out, though, the answer to that question is more complicated than it may initially seem. On the one hand, there is evidence to suggest that—Trump's rise notwithstanding—the political fundamentals of American internationalism actually remain fairly strong. On the other hand, there are also good reasons to believe that American internationalism may indeed be in deep political trouble—that the 2016 campaign simply revealed previously undiagnosed cancers that have now begun to metastasize. In other words, American internationalism is not yet politically flatlining, and many of its individual elements still appear quite popular with the domestic audience. But it nonetheless faces deeper structural challenges that facilitated Trump's ascendancy—and that could ultimately, if left unaddressed, pose a serious threat to that tradition's survival.

THE INTERNATIONALIST TRADITION

For more than seventy years, American internationalism has been rooted in an enduring twofold logic of interdependence and indispensability. After World War II, American policymakers concluded that the global arena had become fundamentally interdependent: the United States could not be secure in a world dominated by aggressive dictators or stalked by instability and war, just as it could not be prosperous in a world plagued by protectionism and depression. They also concluded that the United States, by dint of its unequaled power, was uniquely and indispensably suited to creating a broader global order that would protect American interests and values in an interdependent world. As General George Marshall, the chief of staff of the U.S. Army, commented in 1945, Washington could no longer pursue a narrow conception of national interest or limit its strategic horizons to the Western Hemisphere: "We are now concerned with the peace of the entire world."[3]

During the postwar decades, American officials thus sought to fashion an open international economy that would foster positive-sum relationships and prevent another slide into depression and war. They worked to preserve geopolitical stability in key regions from western Europe to East Asia, and to prevent aggressive authoritarian states such as the Soviet Union from dominating those regions or disrupting international peace. They sought to sustain a global balance of power that favored the United States and its democratic allies, and—on the whole if not in every specific case—to advance liberal concepts such as democracy and human rights. They created a global institutional architecture that emphasized international cooperation and multilateralism. And to attain these ends, U.S. policymakers embraced a historically unprecedented degree of activism and engagement in the form of military alliances and overseas troop deployments, leadership of international institutions and the global economy, and myriad other initiatives. America's postwar internationalism, as Henry Kissinger once remarked, was based on "the notion of a predominant United States, as the only stable country, the richest country, the country without whose leadership and physical contribution nothing was possible, and which had to make all the difference for defense and progress everywhere in the world."[4]

American activism abroad, in turn, was supported by a bipartisan political consensus at home. To be sure, the old bromide that politics stops at the water's edge was always more aspiration than reality. The internationalist consensus emerged only after significant congressional and public debate in the 1940s, and postwar America saw fierce political disputes over issues ranging from the "loss" of China to the Iraq War. The *degree* of support for an ambitious global agenda also waxed and waned over the years, and from time to time—from Vietnam to Iran-Contra and beyond—there were recurring crises in public resolve and confidence regarding America's global mission. But broadly speaking, America's two major political parties and majorities of their supporters consistently accepted the basic logic of American internationalism—and so the U.S. political system consistently provided the wherewithal to pursue that strategy.

Over a period of decades, the American people and their elected representatives funded defense expenditures far greater than what would have been necessary simply to protect the continental United States. They faced up to the idea that American troops might fight and die to defend faraway frontiers. And they accepted—often reluctantly—the notion that Washington should take primary responsibility for leading the global economy, U.S. alliances, and international institutions, despite the myriad costs and frustrations involved.[5]

Americans accepted these costs not out of any special altruism, of course, but because they believed that the benefits of living in—

and leading—a stable, prosperous, and liberal world order were ultimately greater. But if the postwar era was thus characterized, as Daniel Deudney and G. John Ikenberry write, by a "bipartisan consensus . . . on the paramount importance of American leadership," then the 2016 presidential election and its results surely called into question whether that consensus still exists.[6]

THE TRUMP DISRUPTION

In foreign policy, as in so many things, Donald Trump's presidential campaign represented a frontal assault on the established order. If a commitment to internationalism has represented the soul of American statecraft since World War II, Trump often seemed determined to violate every shibboleth of the faith en route to the White House.

Trump repeatedly derided U.S. alliances as "obsolete," and he suggested that Washington might not honor its defense commitments to vulnerable NATO allies.[7] He questioned decades of U.S. nonproliferation policy, saying that Japan and South Korea should perhaps get nuclear weapons to enable American retrenchment.[8] He lambasted free trade agreements ranging from NAFTA ("the single worst trade deal ever approved in this country") to the Trans-Pacific Partnership (TPP) ("a rape of our country") and advocated a return to high tariffs and economic protectionism.[9] He sharply condemned international institutions from the United Nations to the World Trade Organization, and proposed measures—such as a ban on Muslim immigrants and refugees, and the construction of a great wall on the Mexican border—to fortify America against the insecurities of the outside world.[10] He scorned the idea that the United States had either a moral or a practical calling to promote democracy and human rights abroad, and he advocated a partnership with the international leader—Vladimir Putin—whose country often seemed to pose the greatest near-term danger to the global order.[11] Across an array of issues, Trump thus rejected key initiatives and accomplishments of postwar U.S. statecraft.

Trump also rejected the postwar consensus in more fundamental ways, by attacking its underlying geopolitical logic. Both during the campaign and after, Trump ridiculed the core intellectual pillar of American internationalism: the idea that U.S. foreign policy should be a positive-sum endeavor in which the American people thrive by helping others thrive. Instead, Trump cast international relations as an inherently zero-sum endeavor, one in which gains for other nations represent losses for the United States—and in which a gullible Washington is all too frequently taken to the cleaners. "We're taken advantage of by virtually every nation in the world," he claimed.[12]

Similarly, Trump cast doubt on the value of the multilateralism that had generally guided postwar U.S. leadership, arguing—on issues from trade to counterterrorism—that the world's sole superpower would do better with a unilateral approach that freed it from the strictures of international law and global opinion.[13] He questioned whether events in faraway parts of the world—eastern Europe or East Asia, for instance—really mattered to American well-being, thereby contradicting the interdependence logic at the heart of postwar foreign policy. He contended that the pursuit of global openness left the United States weaker and more vulnerable rather than stronger and more prosperous.[14] And he harkened back to the more coercive, mercantilist ethos of an earlier era, arguing that the United States should use its military dominance not for nation-building but for plundering the resource wealth of weaker countries.[15]

Indeed, although Trump's critics sometimes claimed that his policy proposals were unmoored from any discernible philosophy, the reality was rather different.[16] Consciously or not, Trump was often advocating a return to the foreign policy doctrines—protectionism, unilateralism, continentalism, mercantilism—that had predated the rise of American internationalism. In doing so, he willingly courted and reciprocated the enmity of the bipartisan foreign policy establishment that had shaped America's approach to the world for generations, arguing that this group was not a select priesthood to be heeded but a corrupt cabal that had led the nation from disaster to disaster. In the 1930s, Franklin Roosevelt famously welcomed the hatred of his political enemies. Trump took a similar tack in dismissing the establishment as "nothing more than the failed Washington elite looking to hold onto their power."[17]

To be clear, Trump did not campaign on a platform of classical isolationism, his critiques of alliances, globalization, and international institutions notwithstanding. He argued, for instance, that the United States must build unrivaled military strength to get its way in global affairs. He called for a more ruthless and aggressive campaign against terrorist organizations such as the Islamic State. He promised to take a more confrontational posture toward adversaries such as Iran.[18] In all this, Trump had much in common with the Jacksonian school of American foreign policy—a tradition that does not advocate wholesale withdrawal from the world, but rather emphasizes narrowing U.S. interests while also pursuing those interests more unilaterally and assertively.[19] Yet whatever the label, Trump unmistakably argued for a significant departure from the ambitious, globally oriented internationalism that had long characterized U.S. policy, calling for a return to the more parochial nationalism abandoned by Washington after World War II.

And whereas every other presidential candidate who had challenged the postwar tradition failed at the ballot box, Trump triumphed. Dwight Eisenhower stepped in to defeat the quasi-isolationist Robert Taft for the Republican nomination in 1952. Richard Nixon trounced George McGovern and his "Come home, America" platform in 1972. Neither Pat Buchanan nor Ross Perot broke through in 1992 or 1996. Yet Trump—despite espousing views that most foreign policy experts, including hundreds of GOP wonks, considered to be dangerous and disqualifying—rolled through sixteen challengers for the Republican nomination and bested a card-carrying member of the foreign policy establishment for the presidency.[20] Add in Senator Bernie Sanders's success in attracting strong support in the Democratic primaries by harshly critiquing globalization and other tenets of U.S. policy, and it seems all the more evident that the foreign policy mainstream took a beating.

So, was the 2016 election merely an aberration within the long history of American internationalism? Or does Trump's victory indicate deeper and perhaps more irrevocable changes in American attitudes on foreign affairs? As it turns out, there are two plausible interpretations of this issue, and they point in very different directions.

NOT DEAD YET

Start with the optimistic interpretation. It is always dangerous to read too much into the outcome of any single election, and it may be particularly dangerous to read too much into what happened in 2016. For one thing, the 2016 campaign was not fought primarily over philosophical first principles. It did not feature particularly probing debates about America's place in the world. Rather, it was defined largely by the historic unpopularity of both candidates and featured comparatively little substantive discussion of most foreign policy issues.[21] Moreover, Trump might have been decisively defeated—some polls showed him trailing by double digits in mid-October—were it not for a series of remarkably lucky breaks late in the campaign, particularly then–FBI Director James Comey's announcement that he had reopened the investigation of Hillary Clinton's use of a private e-mail server during her tenure as secretary of state.[22] Finally, although Trump won the election, he *did* decisively lose the popular vote to a candidate who distanced herself from the TPP in the heat of the Democratic primaries but whose views were nonetheless just as reliably internationalist as those of any of her recent Democratic predecessors.[23] In light of these issues, it is tempting to see 2016 as a political fluke—a sui generis event that tells us little about public support for U.S. foreign policy.

This is not simply wishful thinking, for there is a good deal of evidence to bolster this interpretation. If political support for American internationalism were plummeting, one would expect to see unambiguous downturns in public opinion toward U.S. alliances, international trade, and other key initiatives. Yet, while there certainly are signs of public alienation from American internationalism—as discussed subsequently—most polling data collected during the period around Trump's election tells a different story.

According to public opinion surveys taken in the heat of the 2016 campaign, for instance, 65 percent of Americans saw globalization as "mostly good" for the United States, and 64 percent saw international trade as "good for their own standard of living."[24] Even the TPP—which Clinton disowned under pressure from Sanders, and which Trump used as a political punching bag—enjoyed 60 percent support.[25] Reaching back slightly further to 2013, an overwhelming majority—77 percent—of Americans believed that trade and business ties to other countries were either "somewhat good" or "very good" for the United States.[26] In other words, if Americans are in wholesale revolt against globalization, most public opinion polls are not capturing that discontent.

Nor are they registering a broad popular backlash against other aspects of American internationalism. Although Trump delighted in disparaging U.S. alliances during the campaign, some 77 percent of Americans still saw being a member of NATO as a good thing. A remarkable 89 percent believed that maintaining U.S. alliances was "very or somewhat effective at achieving U.S. foreign policy goals."[27]

Similarly, opinion polls have revealed little evidence that the American public is demanding significant military retrenchment. In 2016, three-quarters of respondents believed that defense spending should rise or stay the same. The proposition favoring more defense spending had actually increased significantly (from 23 percent to 35 percent) since 2013.[28] Support for maintaining overseas bases and forward deployments of U.S. troops was also strong.[29] Regarding military intervention, polls taken in recent years have indeed shown a widespread belief that the U.S. wars in Iraq and Afghanistan were not worth the cost, but these sentiments do not seem to have translated into a broader skepticism regarding the utility of military force. In 2016, for instance, 62 percent of Americans approved of the military campaign against the Islamic State, demonstrating broad agreement that the United States should be willing to use the sword—even in faraway places—when threats emerge.[30]

Polling on other issues reveals still more of the same. For all of Trump's critiques of international institutions, international law, and multilateralism, nearly two-thirds of Americans (64 percent) viewed the United Nations favorably in 2016, and 71 percent supported U.S. participation in the Paris Agreement on combating climate change.[31] And, although polls indicating that over 50 percent of Americans preferred to let other countries "get along as best they can" on their own are far more troubling, here too the overall picture painted by recent survey data is somewhat brighter.[32] As of 2016, more than half—55 percent—of Americans believed that the United States either did too little or the right amount in confronting global problems.[33] When asked if the United States should continue playing an active role in world affairs, nearly two-thirds answered affirmatively.[34]

As one comprehensive analysis of the survey data thus concluded, at present there is just not overwhelming evidence—in the polls, at least—to suggest a broad-gauged public rejection of internationalism: "The American public as a whole still thinks that the United States is the greatest and most influential country in the world, and bipartisan support remains strong for the country to take an active part in world affairs."[35]

On some issues, in fact, Trump's behavior since becoming president has actually affirmed the continued resilience of American internationalism. Early indications that the administration was considering imposing a high border tax on imports from Mexico, or perhaps even withdrawing from NAFTA, were met with a sharply negative political response—including from many Republican senators and representatives otherwise supportive of Trump. As Senator Lindsay Graham of South Carolina eloquently tweeted, "Any policy proposal which drives up costs of Corona, tequila, or margaritas is a big-time bad idea. Mucho Sad."[36] Likewise, when Trump harangued Australian prime minister Malcolm Turnbull in an early phone conversation, internationalist senators, led by John McCain, leaped to the defense of the alliance.[37] When Trump demanded that South Korea pay a greater share of the costs for a missile defense system, in contravention of an earlier agreement, other Republican legislators urged the president to focus on pressuring Pyongyang rather than Seoul.[38]

What all of this quickly made clear was that although Trump's rhetoric might have appealed to some portion of his electoral base, there was simply no winning political coalition in early 2017 for tearing up NAFTA, undermining American alliances, or fundamentally deconstructing American internationalism. Indeed, as Trump subsequently moderated his conduct on these issues—by proclaiming, albeit grudgingly and belatedly, his support for NATO and other U.S. alliances, and by pledging to seek revision rather than immediately terminating NAFTA—it increasingly appeared as though the president was simply adjusting to this reality.[39]

Finally, even if American internationalism is under pressure today, it is worth bearing in mind that we have been here before. Trade has *always* been a contested issue because it creates losers as well as winners. Grumbling about freeloading allies dates back to the birth of NATO. Indeed, the idea that American internationalism was ever an *easy* sell would come as news to the spirits of Dean

Acheson and Dwight Eisenhower.[40] And although predictions of the political demise of American internationalism have been made many times before, they have just as often been proved wrong.

In the final throes and aftermath of the Vietnam War, for instance, the United States was gripped by desires for geopolitical retrenchment, which carried George McGovern to the Democratic presidential nomination, led to major cuts in defense spending, and even spurred efforts within Congress to withdraw large numbers of U.S. forces from Europe. There was a strong sense of dissatisfaction with the burdens imposed by U.S. leadership of the international economic order—not just in the body politic, but within the Nixon administration itself. "Foreigners are out to screw us," Treasury Secretary John Connally remarked. "Our job is to screw them first."[41] It often seemed that political support for American international leadership was evaporating: following the withdrawal from Vietnam, only 36 percent of Americans felt "it was important for the United States to make and keep commitments to other nations."[42] And yet within just a few years' time, the United States was undertaking a renewed Cold War offensive against the Soviet Union, pursuing democracy and human rights promotion with unprecedented fervor, and serving as the foremost evangelist of the intensified economic and financial globalization unleashed in the 1970s. The logic of American internationalism has been tested before, and it has repeatedly proved resilient.

One can thus make a good case for optimism in assessing the prospects of internationalism. At the very least, it is far too early to pronounce that tradition politically dead. But if there nonetheless seems to be a whistling-past-the-graveyard quality to this interpretation in light of the simple fact that Donald Trump was elected president in 2016, that's because there is also a far more pessimistic—and equally plausible—way of reading the national mood. From this perspective, Trump's rise was not an aberration or a glitch. It was, rather, the culmination of a quiet crisis that has gradually but unmistakably been weakening the political foundations of American internationalism. That crisis may not yet be manifesting itself in dramatic, across-the-board changes in how Americans view particular foreign policy issues. But as Trump's election indicates, its political effects are nonetheless becoming profound.

GOING, GOING . . .

This glass-half-empty interpretation starts from the premise that America's postwar internationalist project was not just extraordinary in scope. It was also the product of extraordinary circumstances. For most of its history, the United States pursued what might be thought of as a pre-internationalist foreign policy. Only the triple whammy of the Great Depression, World War II, and then the Cold War led to the rise of the internationalist tradition.[43] These events provided a vivid reminder, for those Americans who experienced them, of what the costs and dangers of *not* sustaining an open, secure international order could be, and thus impelled Americans to make the sacrifices necessary to forge the postwar system. These events also provided another crucial inducement to heroic exertions: the looming presence of dangerous, morally abhorrent enemies whose very existence helped foster a degree of national unity and rally Americans to the cause.

As these circumstances—and even memories thereof—gradually faded, however, the benefits of Washington's global role became less tangible for many Americans because it was harder to identify precisely what catastrophe U.S. engagement was meant to avert. As America lost its most powerful enemies, the cohesion and purpose they provided also dissipated. "Without the Cold War," John Updike's title character famously asked in the novel *Rabbit at Rest*, "what's the point of being an American?"[44] In the early 2000s, the patriotic fervor that followed 9/11 temporarily masked these dynamics. But as some of the highest-profile policy initiatives of the post-9/11 era—namely, the Iraq and Afghanistan wars—produced deeply disappointing results, and as the 2007–08 financial crisis and its aftermath reminded Americans that their resources were finite indeed, it was only natural that the political stars would eventually align for someone willing to challenge the established orthodoxy. Donald Trump, then, was not some political black swan. He was Pat Buchanan—who ran on a remarkably similar platform of geopolitical retrenchment and economic nationalism in the 1990s— with better timing.[45]

Meanwhile, the political defenses of American internationalism were also being softened up in other ways. By almost any standard, American internationalism has been broadly successful in creating a remarkably advantageous world order.[46] But aspects of that tradition have undoubtedly been misfiring of late.

Burden-sharing within America's alliances has, in fact, become increasingly unbalanced since the Cold War. Whatever the polls may say, ally-bashing has become a bipartisan sport in Washington. "The blunt reality," warned Robert Gates—no America Firster—in 2011, "is that there will be dwindling appetite and patience in the U.S. Congress—and in the American body politic writ large—to expend increasingly precious funds on behalf of nations that are apparently unwilling . . . to be serious and capable partners in their own defense."[47] Similarly, it is undeniable that U.S. nation-building missions since 2001 have often been costly and unrewarding. After all, it was not Trump but Obama who first called for the country to shift from nation-building abroad to nation-building at home.[48] Whatever their views on other parts of American internationalism, many Americans apparently agreed. Whereas 29 percent of Americans believed that promoting democracy abroad should be a key diplomatic priority in 2001, by 2013 the number was only 18 percent.[49] When Trump slammed these aspects of American internationalism, he was pushing on an open door.

He was also pushing on an open door in attacking a foreign policy establishment that almost unanimously opposed his candidacy.[50] That bipartisan establishment had served as the stewards of American internationalism for decades, and in different circumstances its opposition might have been fatal to a candidate with no foreign policy experience or expertise. What Trump intuitively understood, however, was that the credibility of the experts had been badly tarnished in recent years.

As Tom Nichols has observed, the deference that experts command from the U.S. public has been declining for some time, and this is certainly the case in foreign policy.[51] After all, under George W. Bush one group of experts led the country into a war in Iraq that a majority of Americans have long since come to see as a mistake. Under Barack Obama, a second group of experts then oversaw a precipitate withdrawal from that country, resulting in the security vacuum that enabled the rise of the Islamic State, a terrorist organization even more terrifying than al-Qaeda. When Trump—who had, of course, supported the invasion of Iraq before he opposed it—dismissed establishment criticism by repeatedly pointing out that this was the very establishment that had brought the United States such costly fiascos, his rejoinder probably resonated with many voters who had grown skeptical of just how smart the experts really were.[52]

These issues related to another, more fundamental contributor to the crisis of American internationalism: the rupturing of the basic political-economic bargain that had long undergirded that tradition. From its inception, internationalism entailed significant and tangible costs, both financial and otherwise, and the pursuit of free trade in particular inevitably disadvantaged workers and industries that suffered from greater global competition. As a result, the rise of American internationalism during and after World War II went hand in hand with measures designed to offset these costs by ensuring upward social mobility and rising economic fortunes for the voters—particularly working- and middle-class voters—being asked to bear them. Domestic policies such as progressive taxation, Keynesian full employment initiatives, support for unionization, and social safety net programs were thus just as critical to American internationalism as were overseas endeavors such as alliances, trade deals, and forward military deployments.[53] Political elites also assured voters that, over time, the rising economic tide that came with open markets would lift all boats, even if freer trade created dislocations in the short term. This bargain has gradually been fraying since as far back as the late 1970s, however, and in recent years it increasingly seems to have broken.

For the fact is that many Americans—particularly less-educated Americans—are not seeing their economic fortunes and mobility improve over time. Rather, their prospects have worsened in recent decades. As an article by Jeff Colgan and Robert Keohane notes, the real median household income for Americans without high school diplomas dropped by nearly 20 percent from 1974 to 2015, while real median household income for Americans with high school diplomas but no college education fell by 24 percent.[54] Likewise, as Nicholas Eberstadt has written, members of these groups often face crippling economic insecurity, from sharply declining work rates among American men to sharply rising levels of household debt. "Even though the American economy still remains the world's unrivaled engine of wealth creation," Eberstadt writes, "those outside the bubble may have less of a shot at the American Dream than has been the case for decades, maybe generations."[55] This economic insecurity reflects a variety of deep structural causes, from automation to the shift to a postindustrial economy that has left many industrial workers behind. Yet it has been exacerbated by the weakening of the social safety net, the regressive tax reforms, and the generally anti-union ethos that have characterized government policy since the late 1970s—and also, to some degree, by core aspects of U.S. statecraft.[56]

The pursuit of globalization and free trade, for example, has been broadly beneficial to U.S. economic and financial power, and it has tremendously improved the economic fortunes of the American population writ large. But as Harvard scholar Dani Rodrik warned twenty years ago, globalization has also exposed "a deep fault line between groups who have the skills and mobility to flourish in global markets and those who . . . don't."[57] Sure enough, the economic gains from globalization have been pocketed largely by well-educated Americans in the upper deciles of the income distribution.[58] Meanwhile, globalization has resulted in declining economic prospects for working-class Americans whose jobs can be outsourced or whose industries have been rocked by intensifying foreign competition from lower-wage economies.

To give just the most prominent example, expanding trade with China has been a bipartisan goal of U.S. policy for decades, meant to enhance American prosperity and draw China deeper into the existing international system. And in aggregate terms, it has undoubtedly succeeded in both of these aims. But that policy—which culminated in the granting of permanent normal trade status and World Trade Organization membership to China—also led to the loss of over 2 million U.S. jobs in manufacturing and related industries between 1999 and 2011.[59] It bears restating, when discussing such issues, that most U.S. manufacturing job losses over the past several decades are the result of automation rather than trade, and that globalization gets blamed for far more evils than it deserves. But China-related job losses have constituted an economic bloodbath by any measure, one that has surely led many of the affected to question whether U.S. policy truly reflects their interests. The result was a brewing political backlash that Trump, with his strident condemnations of trade in general and China in particular, was able to channel and exploit.

Indeed, although there is plenty of public opinion polling that paints a reassuring picture of American views on trade and globalization, there are also clear indications that such a backlash is occurring. In 2016, a plurality of Americans (49 percent) agreed with the statement that "U.S. involvement in the global economy is a bad thing because it lowers wages and costs jobs," a sentiment perfectly tailored to Trump's protectionist message.[60] During the GOP primaries, an even larger proportion (65 percent) of Trump's voters agreed that U.S. involvement in the international economy was a bad thing. During the general election, Trump performed particularly well in areas where competition from trade was most intense.[61] And while this shift in GOP views on free trade is striking, given that party's traditional support for free trade, Bernie Sanders clearly tapped into similar sentiments in the Democratic primaries.[62] More broadly, it is hard not to see concerns about economic insecurity looming large in the growing proportion of Americans who believe that the United States is overinvested internationally—and who therefore prefer for the "U.S. to deal with its own problems, while letting other countries get along as best they can." In 2013, 52 percent of Americans—the highest number in decades—agreed with a version of this statement. In 2016, the proportion was even higher, at 57 percent.[63]

In sum, American voters may still express fairly strong support for free trade and other long-standing policies in public opinion surveys. But it is simply impossible to ignore the fact that, among significant swaths of the population, there is nonetheless an unmistakable and politically potent sense that American foreign policy has become decoupled from the interests of those it is meant to serve.

This point, in turn, illuminates a final strain that Trump's rise so clearly highlighted: the growing sense that American internationalism has become unmoored from American nationalism. American internationalism was always conceived as an enlightened expression of American nationalism, an approach premised on the idea that the well-being of the United States was inextricably interwoven with that of the outside world. But the inequities of globalization have promoted a tangible feeling among many voters that American leaders have been privileging an internationalist agenda (one that may suit cosmopolitan elites just fine) at the expense of the well-being of "ordinary Americans."[64] In the same vein, to the extent that immigration from Mexico and Central America has depressed wages for low-skilled workers and fueled concerns that the white working class is being displaced by other demographic groups, it has fostered beliefs that the openness at the heart of the internationalist project is benefiting the wrong people.[65] "Many Jacksonians," writes Walter Russell Mead of the coalition that brought Trump to power, "came to believe that the American establishment was no longer reliably patriotic."[66]

This belief, of course, is hard to measure with any certainty. But it can presumably be seen in the 92 percent of Trump's supporters who favored building a wall on the Mexican border, in the 57 percent of Americans who believed that the United States had focused too much on other people's problems and not enough on its own, and in the continuing erosion of Americans' confidence in government.[67] It can be seen in the nearly half (48 percent) of white working-class Americans who in early 2017 agreed with the statement "I often feel like a stranger in my own country," and in the 68 percent who believed that "the American way of life needs to be protected from foreign influence."[68] Viewed from this perspective, Trump's rise was no fluke at all. An anti-internationalist candidate was primed to burst through the growing cracks in that foreign policy tradition.

THE FATE OF AMERICAN INTERNATIONALISM

What does all this tell us about the future of American internationalism? The answer involves elements of both interpretations offered here. It is premature to say that a "new isolationism" is taking hold, or that Americans are systematically turning away from internationalism, in light of the idiosyncrasies of Trump's victory and the fact that so many key aspects of internationalism still poll fairly well.[69] Yet no serious observer can contend that American internationalism is truly healthy given Trump's triumph, and the 2016 election clearly revealed the assorted maladies that had been quietly eroding its political vitality. American internationalism may not be slipping into history just yet, but its long-term political trajectory seems problematic indeed.

So, is it just a matter of time before American internationalism does collapse politically—before its political fortunes catch up to the drearier assessments that accompanied Trump's rise? Not necessarily. After all, the fact that internationalism has survived for over seven decades, and that it has weathered setbacks as severe as Vietnam and Watergate, reminds us that it is fundamentally a robust and resilient paradigm. And the fact that it retains some political currency today, underlying difficulties notwithstanding, reminds us not to discount the possibility that predictions of its demise may again prove exaggerated.

For the future of American internationalism ultimately hinges on powerful factors that have yet to fully take shape, some of which U.S. officials cannot really control and some of which they can. In the former category, the cold truth is that political support for a robust internationalism has historically waxed when the level of external threat is high—as in the early Cold War, the early 1980s, or after 9/11—and waned when it seems lower. Clear and present dangers provide a persuasive argument for why the costs of global engagement are worth bearing; they remind Americans how bad things can get in the absence of a steadying U.S. hand. This is the central irony of American internationalism: it is designed to keep the world safe and congenial, but works best politically when that world seems full of peril.

Bad news may thus be good news insofar as internationalism is concerned. It was no coincidence that American support for increased defense spending rose significantly after the Islamic State exploded onto the scene in 2014.[70] If, as seems likely, the world grows more threatening in the coming years, and especially if the United States faces sharpening challenges from rival great powers such as Russia and China, then the logic of American internationalism may once again reassert itself. Nations need enemies, as Charles Krauthammer once wrote, and American internationalism could surely use some enemies right now.[71]

Yet the fate of American internationalism will also hinge on things that U.S. leaders can more readily control—namely, how Washington responds to the various strains that Trump's rise has revealed. It would be a historic mistake to adopt the drastic departures that Trump often proposed during his campaign. A pure version of "America First" would be the epitome of a cure far worse than the disease. But it would equally be a mistake to think that no adjustment is necessary. From time to time, U.S. political leaders have confronted the challenge of updating American internationalism in light of pressing political and geopolitical problems. A similar task presents itself today.[72]

American leaders will need to aggressively defend U.S. interests and the global order while avoiding the costly quagmires that have left so many Americans disillusioned. They will need to drive harder bargains on burden-sharing and trade. They will need to ensure that the pursuit of an open and profitable trading system does not come at the expense of vulnerable populations at home. They will need to devise ways of better protecting the country's borders and ensuring homeland security without losing the dynamism and societal rejuvenation that immigration provides. They will need to strengthen the social safety net for those who need it most while also pursuing the reforms necessary to keep those programs—and the U.S. government—solvent over time. They will need to get back to first principles in explaining why America's global engagement really matters—and what would happen if Washington ceased to play such a role—while also giving more Americans a sense that their foreign policy truly does put them first.

What is needed, in other words, is an internationalism that puts American nationalism front and center—a calibrated and reasonable version of an "America First" agenda, not the cartoonish, pre-1941 version that Trump often touted on the road to the White House. Whether Trump—or, perhaps more realistically, the country's future leaders—can summon the wisdom, creativity, and purpose necessary to chart such a course will go far in determining whether American internationalism ultimately endures.

FIVE

FORTRESS AMERICA AND ITS ALTERNATIVES

America is an exceptional nation, but not when it comes to the wave of nationalism sweeping the globe. Across multiple continents, leaders and polities are pushing back against globalization and integration; they are reasserting national sovereignty as a bulwark against international tumult. In the United States, this nationalist resurgence has manifested in a sharp challenge to the internationalist project that has animated U.S. grand strategy since World War II.

For nearly seventy-five years, U.S. foreign policy has emphasized securing American interests through the leadership of an open, stable, and integrated global community, one in which Washington bears the heaviest burdens in exchange for enormous benefits. But today, American internationalism is under fire. As described in the previous chapter, the 2016 presidential election saw strident critiques of globalization, alliances, multilateralism, and other components of America's postwar project; the triumph of Donald Trump brought to power a candidate who proudly espoused a stark, pugilistic nationalism. Whether America is decisively turning away from its postwar grand strategic tradition remains uncertain; what seems clear is that American grand strategy will have a more nationalistic flavor in years to come.

But what might a more nationalistic grand strategy entail, whether during Trump's presidency or after? One model is "Fortress America"—a hard-line, nearly zero-sum approach that would actively roll back the postwar international order and feature heavy doses of unilateralism and latter-day isolationism. This model is dark but no longer inconceivable: the Trump campaign often espoused a Fortress America approach in its rhetoric, and the Trump administration has flirted with such an approach in some of its early policies. Yet there is also another model, a more benign version of American nationalism that might be thought of as internationalism with a nationalist accent. This approach would not fundamentally dismantle the postwar international order; the emphasis would be on securing better deals, more evenly distributing burdens, and enhancing America's relative position within that order. The first model represents the path to superpower suicide and a far uglier, more disordered world; the second would involve some real drawbacks and disruption, but could perhaps help sustain an internationalist project—and global order—that are presently under strain.

AMERICAN INTERNATIONALISM, PROPERLY UNDERSTOOD

America's postwar project has never represented a rejection of nationalism—nationalism, in this instance, being the pursuit of a foreign policy that aggressively prioritizes America's own national interests. Rather, America's postwar project has simply pursued U.S. national interests via internationalist means.

For U.S. policymakers, World War II showed that isolationism had failed because it was outdated—because in the twentieth century, the world had become smaller and more interconnected in security and economic terms alike. That conflict thereby moved U.S. policymakers to take a more expansive approach to global politics—to protect America's interests by constructing an overarching international system in which the country could be prosperous and secure. As we have seen, during the postwar decades, the United States undertook to lead an open and prosperous global economy, to underwrite stability and security in key regions, to advance liberal ideals such as democracy and human rights, and to embed U.S. primacy in a variety of multilateral institutions. This internationalist order-building project, G. John Ikenberry has written, was "the most ambitious and far-reaching . . . the world had yet seen."[1]

This project was never cost-free, of course, and it required setting aside some considerations of near-term unilateral advantage. The United States made military expenditures far in excess of what would have been required simply to defend American territory; it tolerated some free riding by allies from western Europe to the Western Pacific; it bore some of the heaviest burdens in responding to transgressions of the international order from the Korean War to the Persian Gulf War and beyond. Likewise, Washington's leadership of the international economy meant accepting a degree of economic discrimination by countries that exploited open U.S. markets without fully opening their own; it also required accepting responsibility for stabilizing and lubricating the international economy, with all the exertions those tasks entailed. Participating in international institutions—from the North Atlantic Treaty Organization (NATO) to the United Nations (UN)—meant accepting some multilateral constraints on how the United States could wield its unmatched power. The burdens and frustrations of American internationalism have often been exaggerated, but they have never been illusory.

What made the bargain worthwhile was that the United States also reaped great benefits. There have been broad if somewhat amorphous benefits, such as the security and well-being that have come from living in a world that has avoided both great-power war and global depression for generations. There have also been narrower benefits—the immense influence that the United States wields in all the world's key regions; the checks it has been able to impose on nuclear proliferation and other threats; the extraordinary international cooperation it has secured in pursuing its own foreign policy priorities, from combating communism during the Cold War to fighting terrorism today. On the economic front, too, economists generally agree that the pursuit of free trade and globalization has made the United States (and the world) far richer than it otherwise would have been—in fact, Washington has frequently translated its position of international leadership into an advantage in trade and other economic negotiations.[2]

American internationalism, then, has never been a matter of charity. It has simply represented an enlightened, positive-sum form of nationalism based on the idea that the United States can best achieve its own security and prosperity by helping others become secure and prosperous. Now, however, that conviction appears to be weakening, as a rawer, more atavistic form of American nationalism reappears.

NATIONALISM RESURGENT

The 2016 presidential election will likely loom large for future historians studying the patterns of American foreign policy. A word of caution here—one should not overinterpret the result of that election as proof that the U.S. public has decisively reverted to the narrower nationalism and isolationism of the pre–World War II years. After all, issues of trade and terrorism aside, foreign policy played a relatively small role in the election, and the candidate who won the popular vote—Hillary Clinton—espoused a foreign policy vision that was largely aligned with U.S. globalism.[3] Moreover, as discussed in the previous chapter, opinion polls from 2015 and 2016 showed that public support for key aspects of American internationalism—including alliances and free trade—remained close to postwar and post–Cold War averages. Seventy-seven percent of Americans thought that being a member of NATO was good for the United States in mid-2016; polls taken in late 2016 showed majority support for globalization and even the much-maligned Trans-Pacific Partnership (TPP) trade pact.[4] And although Donald Trump did win the election, he hardly carried a great mass of GOP isolationists into Congress on his coattails. One could plausibly conclude from all this that Trump's election was a black-swan event, largely disconnected from U.S. public opinion on foreign policy.

Yet there is also reason to see 2016 as an inflection point, at least in the near and medium term, in America's foreign relations. Concerns about the downsides of free trade and globalization—particularly the loss of U.S. manufacturing jobs and the increased vulnerability, economic and otherwise, that accompanies global integration—have been mounting for decades.[5] Opinion polling aside, disillusion with other aspects of American internationalism has also been rising. It was not Donald Trump but then–Secretary of Defense Robert Gates who admonished the NATO allies in 2011 that the alliance faced a "dim if not dismal future" absent progress toward more equitable burden-sharing.[6] And in the run-up to 2016, other signs of American world-weariness appeared. According to one survey conducted in 2013, 52 percent of Americans, the largest share in decades, believed that the country should "mind its own business internationally and let other countries get along the best they can on their own."[7] By 2016, the proportion of Americans agreeing with a similar statement was even higher.[8]

The 2016 election itself, moreover, was characterized by a striking degree of hostility toward America's internationalist project.

On the left, Bernie Sanders railed against the TPP and won fervent favor among working-class voters, environmentalists, and other opponents of globalization. Hillary Clinton—who had energetically backed the TPP while secretary of state—found Democratic opposition to the pact so severe that she repudiated that agreement during the primaries.[9] And, of course, Donald Trump won the election after campaigning on the most stridently, confrontationally nationalist platform of any major party candidate in generations. He called the TPP "a rape of our country," condemned existing free trade agreements, and promised to institute high tariffs and economic protectionism.[10] He derided NATO and suggested that key U.S. allies might be left to defend themselves.[11] He proposed extreme measures to strengthen U.S. sovereignty and border control, and voiced a harsh skepticism of many of the international institutions and arrangements that Washington had itself helped create. He even revived the 1930s-era slogan "America First," evoking a full-on rejection of the postwar international order and a return to prewar isolationism.[12]

Trump thus evinced a remarkable hostility to core aspects of American internationalism—and was, at the very least, not punished for it by U.S. voters. America had now elected a president who—in his campaign rhetoric, at least—embraced a fiery, populist nationalism, and who fundamentally challenged core aspects of American internationalism. The question in the wake of the election was thus not whether U.S. foreign policy would change during his administration—and potentially after—but how much.

FORTRESS AMERICA

Under one model, the change would be severe. "Fortress America" represents a hard-line version of American nationalism, infused with strong elements of unilateralism and isolationism. It rests on a nearly zero-sum logic of global affairs—specifically, the idea that other countries have systematically exploited American largesse and openness for years, and that providing public goods or participating in multilateral regimes is a losing bet for a self-interested superpower. It contends that the shift toward greater global integration has actually left America weaker and more vulnerable by undermining its sovereignty and its ability to defend itself from global upheaval, and that the active promotion of liberal values is a fruitless and quixotic quest. It holds that the United States should have—and be prepared aggressively to use—its enormous military strengths, but that it should wield those strengths only to protect narrowly conceived national interests, as opposed to protecting allies or some broader conception of international security. Accordingly, this approach entails an explicit rejection of America's positive-sum, internationalist project, and a reversion to more narrowly nationalistic policies that carry distinct echoes of the 1930s and even before.[13]

The first and central pillar of Fortress America is economic nationalism, and the idea, as President Trump remarked in his inaugural address, that "protection will lead to great prosperity and strength."[14] Under this approach, the United States would roll back its support for an open global economy by withdrawing from existing free trade agreements such as the TPP and the North American Free Trade Agreement (NAFTA) and imposing high tariffs to protect industries weakened by globalization. Washington would also operate outside of the World Trade Organization (WTO) process far more frequently, perhaps withdrawing from that organization altogether, and it would emphasize economic sovereignty and obtaining unilateral advantage over trade competitors such as China rather than upholding the global economic "rules of the road." U.S. policy would severely penalize American corporations engaged in offshoring or outsourcing, perhaps through high border taxes, and feature inducements to "buy American" and "hire American."[15] Not least, Fortress America would seek to insulate the United States from global economic shocks—perhaps by pursuing a latter-day "Manhattan Project" for achieving "energy independence" through all-in bets on fracking and development of domestically sourced alternative energies.[16]

Second, the United States would pull back from its military alliances and the provision of global security and other global public goods, on grounds that providing these goods simply encourages free riding on American exertions. At a minimum, Washington would therefore demand far higher rents for the global services it currently provides. Saudi Arabia might be asked to supply, free of charge, a certain quantity of oil in exchange for the U.S. Navy protecting the Straits of Tiran; Japan might be pressured to make far higher economic payments to retain U.S. security guarantees. More significantly, America might simply quit providing "welfare for the rich."[17] It might terminate its military alliances, cease providing security of the commons, and revert to a narrower—and, advocates would say, more self-interested—conception of national security and defense.

Third, and related, America would pursue a "muscular but aloof militarism"—an emphasis on building great military strength, but strength focused narrowly on the defense of the United States.[18] The Pentagon would invest heavily in capabilities needed to deter, defeat, or punish attacks on the homeland or U.S. citizens—everything from enhanced missile defenses, to recapitalization of the nuclear triad, to special operations forces and other tools of counterterrorism. Yet it would no longer emphasize a force posture or overseas presence associated with acting as a global constabulary and the primary provider of international security—unless it received far higher rents for its efforts. Postwar internationalists have wanted a military formidable enough to sustain global order; Fortress America would seek a military strong enough for America to be left alone.

Fourth, to facilitate this retraction of overseas commitments, U.S. officials would encourage devolution of responsibility to other powers. Washington would support authoritarian great powers such as Russia and China carving out greater spheres of influence, on grounds that preservation of order in eastern Europe and East Asia should be their responsibility, not America's. Similarly, the United States might encourage nuclear proliferation by countries such as Japan, Germany, and South Korea so that they could better meet their own security needs.[19]

Fifth, Fortress America would entail a "win and go home" approach to counterterrorism. Fortress America does not imply passivity against pressing threats—quite the opposite. The United States would take stronger measures against jihadist groups, from deployment of large numbers of ground troops, to intensified bombing campaigns and acceptance of greatly increased civilian casualties, to embracing controversial measures such as extraordinary rendition, "black sites," and torture. But after defeating such organizations, Washington would not pursue nation-building or stabilization missions, which are likely to prove costly and frustrating; it would declaim any responsibility for improving governance in the greater Middle East. The emphasis, rather, would be on hardening homeland defenses and husbanding American capabilities—until the next attack occurred, at which point the cycle would start anew.

Sixth, and related to the previous point, the United States would essentially abandon human rights and democracy promotion, by either military or nonmilitary means. America cannot successfully export its values to foreign societies, the thinking goes, and such efforts simply waste resources better used at home. Washington should thus focus on securing tangible geopolitical and economic interests, including through amoral deal-cutting with authoritarian regimes, rather than pursuing amorphous "ideals" such as liberal democracy.[20]

Seventh, Fortress America would entail stringent measures to strengthen American sovereignty and shield the country from unsettling by-products of globalization. Building a wall along the

Mexican border (and perhaps forcing Mexico to pay for it), deporting illegal immigrants en masse, and restricting and perhaps banning entry of refugees and citizens of Muslim-majority countries would all figure prominently in this approach. So might extreme homeland security measures, such as creation of a Muslim registry, designed to better keep tabs on "un-American" groups thought to pose a particular threat to internal security.

Eighth, and to enable much of the foregoing, Fortress America would seek to free America from the shackles of international law, international institutions, and multilateralism, on grounds that these arrangements too frequently inhibit the United States from fully exerting its unmatched power. Withdrawing from the UN (or simply kneecapping it through major funding cuts), as well as quitting multilateral treaties and legal regimes that infringe upon U.S. sovereignty or constrain the aggressive pursuit of U.S. interests, would be central to this model.[21] Multilateral diplomacy to address the threat of climate change would surely go by the wayside, in the belief that the Paris accords and other agreements infringe unacceptably on American sovereignty and economic interests. And whereas postwar internationalism has placed a high premium on multilateral consultation and action, Fortress America would emphasize preserving Washington's freedom of action by making unilateralism—whether in counterterrorism or any other arena—the approach of choice.

This description of Fortress America may initially seem like a caricature—a reincarnation of 1930s-era isolationism, updated for the modern age. But it is not entirely implausible. After all, Donald Trump at the very least flirted with virtually all of the ideas underlying Fortress America during his campaign and his first year in office, and with many of its specific policies, too. We do not have to imagine having a president who has argued that America is being played for a sucker "by every nation in the world, virtually," and who has derided America's internationalist postwar project as needless generosity to a rapacious and ungrateful world—we have one right now.[22] We don't have to imagine having a president who has advocated forsaking U.S. security commitments, pursuing economic protectionism, banning refugees and immigrants from Muslim-majority countries, tearing up multilateral agreements to combat climate change, and building an impenetrable wall along America's southern frontier—we have one right now. How far Trump will ultimately go on these and other issues remains uncertain, and so far it seems that—on some issues, at least—his policies may prove more moderate than his rhetoric.[23] But Trump's rise has nonetheless put many of the core concepts and initiatives of Fortress America front and center in the national debate—and made it worth considering what the consequences of such an approach might be.

ASSESSING FORTRESS AMERICA

So what effects would a Fortress America grand strategy have if it were actually implemented? This approach aims to reduce America's supposedly thankless global burdens, enhance American security and sovereignty, and revitalize allegedly eroded U.S. strengths. And in fact, there would be some near-term benefits. By some estimates, granting permanent normal trade status to China in 2000 caused the loss of over 2 million U.S. jobs; certain U.S. industries—particularly segments of U.S. manufacturing—might therefore gain from protectionism.[24] Shedding alliance commitments would reduce America's global military burdens; shedding the constraints imposed by international institutions and multilateralism would provide greater ability to act unilaterally and decisively. Stricter immigration and border controls might marginally reduce the danger of lone-wolf terrorist attacks, and deporting illegal immigrants could marginally stimulate the wages of poorly educated native-born workers.[25] Acceding to spheres of influence arrangements in East Asia or eastern Europe could conduce to better relations with Moscow or Beijing, at least temporarily.[26] Finally, a more aggressive counterterrorism strategy might defeat—at least in a narrow operational sense—groups like the Islamic State more rapidly, while an America that abandoned nation-building would presumably avoid draining quagmires. In sum, Fortress America would indeed reduce certain costs of U.S. grand strategy and provide some advantages, at least for a time.

Yet Fortress America would also have deeply pernicious effects that would outweigh any narrow, short-term benefits. Most broadly, it would shred the international order that Washington has long promoted. The relatively high levels of international stability and security that the world has enjoyed since World War II, the maintenance of an open global economy, the unprecedented spread of liberal concepts such as democracy and human rights, the multilateral cooperation to address common threats: all of these fundamental characteristics of the international system have rested on the geopolitical, economic, and ideological leadership of the United States, and all would, presumably, be endangered by a reversion to Fortress America. Indeed, if one accepts the relatively commonsensical premise that the actions of the world's preeminent power set the tone for the international system, then such dramatic changes in U.S. foreign policy would inevitably upend the global order as well.[27]

Of course, killing the liberal order would be a feature, not a glitch, of Fortress America. So the question is whether disrupting the international system could still pay dividends by enabling narrower national gains. The trouble here, however, is that Fortress America hinges on a fundamentally skewed assessment of the benefits and costs of American internationalism. As noted, there is strong evidence that an open trading system makes America far wealthier than it would be otherwise—even if the gains are unevenly distributed and some trade partners pursue predatory approaches. There is strong evidence that U.S. alliance commitments have suppressed regional instability which might otherwise erupt and force Washington to intervene—as happened during World War I and World War II—at enormous cost in lives and treasure. There is strong evidence that institutions such as the IMF, the World Bank, and the UN actually serve as force multipliers for U.S. power, by allowing America to project its voice through forums for which it pays only a fraction of the cost. And there is strong evidence that an international system in which democracy is dominant is likely to be more peaceful and advantageous for the United States over the long run, and that American policies have contributed enormously to the spread of democracy to date.[28] Fortress America misses just how beneficial the postwar order has been for America—and thus dramatically understates the costs of destroying that order.

Indeed, Fortress America would simply exchange modest short-term gains for far higher long-term costs—namely, the emergence of a less prosperous and less stable world, one in which liberal political institutions such as democracy are less prevalent, one in which collective action to confront common dangers is more difficult to achieve, and one in which the United States would ultimately suffer a great deal as well. And when one examines Fortress America more closely, even some of the shorter-term gains prove illusory. Fortress America emphasizes a more aggressive approach to counterterrorism—but by disrupting U.S. alliances and alienating Muslim communities at home and abroad, it would surely undercut both the international and domestic cooperation essential to any counterterrorism strategy. Fortress America emphasizes strengthening American sovereignty and aggressively curbing illegal immigration—but killing NAFTA and immiserating Mexico would only exacerbate the economic underdevelopment that drives migrants to the United States. "Energy independence" seems like a worthwhile goal, but realizing it would require the nearly impossible task of completely sealing the United States off from the global energy market.[29] Fortress America may seem alluring, but its key components are frequently unachievable, contradictory, or counterproductive.

In fact, Fortress America could prove profoundly self-destructive to American power. The United States has historically been able to wield preeminent global power with remarkably little global push-back, primarily because it has generally wielded that power in an inclusive, multilateral, and broadly beneficial way.[30] Yet if Washington were to adopt a more zero-sum policy based on promoting its interests at the expense of others, if it were to become more aggressively unilateral and standoffish, other countries might come to view U.S. power as more threatening than reassuring—and they might work more determinedly to counter American influence through diplomatic, economic, or other means. Fortress America would thus represent the self-inflicted death of the relatively benign American superpower that the world has known for the past seventy years, and the advent of a scarier superpower that would engender vastly increased international resistance.

A BETTER NATIONALISM

Fortunately, a nationalistic grand strategy need not be nearly so disastrous. It could represent a more benign and constructive nationalism—essentially, internationalism with a nationalist accent. This "better nationalism" would not dismantle the postwar order or undo America's postwar project, yet it would take a harder-edged and more disciplined approach to asserting U.S. interests within those contexts. In particular, this approach would emphasize striking better deals, more evenly distributing burdens, and better protecting American sovereignty and finite resources, while still preserving—even strengthening—America's global role and proactively sustaining the international system. This strategy truly would put "America first" by enhancing its relative position within a positive-sum order that has served the nation so well.[31]

The intellectual starting point for this approach is a recognition that American internationalism has been, on balance, enormously successful—but that aspects thereof are not working as well as they should be right now. For all its benefits, globalization has indeed injured certain sectors of American manufacturing and displaced U.S. workers; trade competitors such as China have pursued mercantilist and predatory policies while accessing open U.S. markets. U.S. alliances have kept the peace, but burden-sharing has become unbalanced. International institutions generally enhance U.S. influence, but have sometimes become dysfunctional or been turned to anti-American purposes. Democracy promotion makes sense, but armed nation-building has proved frustrating and costly. These issues, in turn, have fueled popular dissatisfaction with American internationalism and shown that a modified approach is necessary.

A resulting turn toward a more nationalist internationalism would hardly be unprecedented. During the 1980s, Ronald Reagan pursued a hard-nosed trade policy designed to punish discriminatory practices and ensure that the costs of globalization were not borne disproportionately by U.S. firms and workers, even as he also laid the foundations for the Uruguay Round of global trade negotiations. Before that, Richard Nixon worked assiduously to offload excessive burdens and enhance U.S. advantage within the confines of the postwar system. Nixon killed the Bretton Woods system of international finance by suspending dollar-gold convertibility at US$35 per ounce, thereby permitting dollar depreciation and advantageously restructuring U.S. trade relations.[32] He also enacted the Nixon Doctrine, which maintained U.S. alliances in Asia but forced those allies to take primary responsibility for defending themselves from insurgencies and other nontraditional threats.[33] Nixon thus put America first in a variety of foreign relationships, not to destroy American internationalism but to sustain it amid more difficult conditions. Today, a better nationalism would emulate this basic approach.

First, this strategy would involve what Reagan's treasury secretary, James Baker, called "free trade with a bite."[34] The United States would still lead an open global trading system, while acting more aggressively to punish unfair practices and ensure that global rules are actually respected. This could entail, as during the 1980s, selective use of targeted "301" sanctions to combat discriminatory measures and ensure fair access and equal opportunity for U.S. companies and goods.[35] It would likely involve a harder-edged approach to China—which has maintained numerous discriminatory practices despite joining the WTO—using just these methods.[36] Washington might also renegotiate existing agreements, such as NAFTA, to address problems and asymmetries that have emerged since their creation. And in the future, Washington might even distance itself from multilateral pacts—in which, it has been argued, U.S. leverage is diluted—in favor of bilateral deals. In this scenario, America might still ditch the TPP, as Trump did, but replace it with a U.S.-Japan trade deal. Crucially, all of these actions, particularly targeted sanctions, would be accompanied by ongoing negotiations to further open markets, and by assurances that the goal is making free trade genuinely fair and rules-based, rather than retreating into protectionism.

Second, a better nationalism would require sharper-elbowed alliance management. The United States would reaffirm alliance commitments, but make crystal clear that those commitments will eventually become unsustainable absent meaningful reforms and better burden-sharing. Along these lines, U.S. officials might make additional U.S. deployments in Europe or East Asia contingent on greater allied defense efforts, and continually seek ways of showing that the highest-performing allies will receive priority consideration in Washington. They might forthrightly explain to consistent underperformers (such as Taiwan) that keeping U.S. security guarantees over time requires developing and adequately funding a realistic defense strategy. Washington could also push NATO to devote greater institutional emphasis to counterterrorism challenges such as the counter–Islamic State fight—where NATO's institutional contribution, and that of some key members, has been anemic—and promote a better division of labor by providing more directive input into allies' defense strategy reviews. (The Pentagon did just this during the United Kingdom's 2015 Strategic Defence and Security Review.) These efforts would go hand in hand with continued reassurance, but greater candor with—and, frankly, pressure on—allies and partners would be essential.[37]

Third, and related, would be a significant military buildup focused on both self-defense and collective defense. The United States would reverse recent disinvestment in defense and address the ongoing erosion of its relative military strength—critical components of any strong, nationalist approach. Yet it would invest not only in self-defense capabilities emphasized by Fortress America, but also in enhanced forward presence in key regions and the capabilities— from additional attack submarines to fifth-generation strike fighters to heavy armored brigades—necessary to help properly motivated allies defend themselves. This buildup would not substitute for greater allied investments; it would be the carrot accompanying the aforementioned sticks. In the past, U.S. allies have been most inclined to do more in their own defense as part of a broader strengthening of collective defense; putting more U.S. skin in the game could therefore induce others to do likewise.[38]

This concept leads to a fourth element: an intensified campaign against radical jihadist groups that present the most immediate danger to U.S. lives and security. Like Fortress America, a better nationalism would cast off some self-imposed constraints of recent years—perhaps by using modest numbers of ground troops to clear out jihadist safe havens more quickly, or by accepting a marginally higher tolerance for civilian casualties.[39] But this approach would reject proposals—such as reviving torture or creating a Muslim registry—that would dramatically alienate global opinion and compromise international counterterrorism cooperation. Moreover, this approach would feature an insistence that intensified U.S. efforts be matched by America's Muslim partners, to include providing ground troops (perhaps supported by U.S. advisers and airpower), more aggressively attacking terrorist finances and ideology, and funding postconflict reconstruction. Admittedly, such contributions have traditionally been—and remain—far easier to demand than to achieve, but Washington might "start small" by increasing efforts to train small-unit leaders and senior officers, thereby creating pockets of greater competence within Arab militaries.[40]

Cooperation with Muslim partners relates to a fifth pillar of this approach. Here, U.S. officials would frankly acknowledge the limited returns and high costs of prolonged stabilization and nation-building missions, and the way in which such interventions can undermine domestic support for American internationalism. Washington would therefore cast a skeptical eye toward humanitarian military intervention, and insist that local forces and Muslim partners—supported by unique U.S. enabling capabilities—bear the brunt of any stabilization missions needed to prevent defeated terrorist groups from resurging. Yet this reticence would not be pursued as part of a broader geopolitical abdication or an outright abandonment of democracy and human rights promotion. Rather, in the best tradition of the Nixon Doctrine, this approach would represent an effort to minimize the most costly and frustrating aspects of American internationalism in order to sustain the broader tradition. Moreover, Washington would continue nonmilitary efforts to promote democracy and human rights overseas, for they represent cost-effective ways of advancing American interests and values alike.[41]

Regarding great-power relations, a sixth key area, a better nationalism would differ only marginally from current U.S. policy—but it would differ dramatically from Fortress America. Here, the emphasis would *not* be on establishing spheres of influence so that America could retrench. Although Washington would continue pursuing pragmatic cooperation where interests align, the emphasis instead would be on upholding U.S. commitments that restrain these great-power rivals (and that represent America's word of honor as a nation), and on pushing back more sharply when U.S. interests and sovereignty are transgressed. Chinese coercion of U.S. allies, harassment of U.S. vessels and aircraft operating in international waters, and violations of international law in the South China Sea; Russian intimidation of NATO members and intervention in the U.S. electoral process—these are actions a robust but sensible nationalism would more strongly oppose. And such opposition works better when supported by robust alliances and significant military power—two other aspects of this strategy. A true American nationalist, Theodore Roosevelt, highlighted the importance of maintaining geopolitical order and carrying a big stick; a better nationalism reflects both imperatives.[42]

The final aspects of this strategy can be briefly summarized. America would not quit or cripple international institutions, but would more aggressively use U.S. leverage to shape or reform them—by using the threat of selective funding cuts to overhaul the deservedly maligned UN Human Rights Council or UN peace-keeping operations, for instance. Likewise, a better nationalism might well emphasize strengthening U.S. sovereignty through better control of the southern border. But this would come as part of what then–Secretary of Homeland Security John Kelly called a "layered defense," one that treats Mexico and the Central American countries as partners rather than adversaries, and continues to assist them—via robust trade, public security assistance, and other means—in addressing the economic deprivation and citizen insecurity that drive illegal immigration.[43] Across these and other initiatives, the goal of a better nationalism is to improve, rather than abandon, America's internationalist tradition.

ASSESSING A BETTER NATIONALISM

So, what are the strengths and liabilities of this approach? For starters, all of the individual initiatives sketched previously entail their own drawbacks and dilemmas. Using targeted sanctions too aggressively could undermine rather than strengthen the global trading system; emphasizing bilateral rather than multilateral trade deals could have the same effect, while also making weaker trade partners less inclined to pursue such deals with the United States in the first place.[44] Getting tougher with allies risks upsetting what have been remarkably organic and constructive international relationships of long standing; it also raises the question of what Washington should do when one or more of its allies inevitably fails to improve performance sufficiently.[45] Taking even a modestly more aggressive approach to counterterrorism might improve operational effectiveness, but it also increases the probable military risks and costs. Pushing back harder on great-power coercion carries dangers of escalation and increased conflict. All these initiatives come with significant advantages, too, but they are by no means panaceas.

These points touch on a second and broader challenge. Although a better nationalism would be far milder than Fortress America, it would still involve significant international disruption. Getting better deals requires bargaining harder; bargaining harder means exerting real pressure on interlocutors. A better nationalism would thus require deliberately engendering greater friction with actors from China and Saudi Arabia to NATO and the UN; those actors would likely push back and find ways of making their displeasure known.[46] The result is likely to be a period of considerable turbulence in U.S. diplomacy, as existing arrangements shift and key relationships—with allies and rivals alike—are renegotiated. There is also, of course, the danger that the initiatives outlined here might prove insufficient to secure more advantageous arrangements and better burden-sharing. U.S. officials would then confront the unpalatable options of either escalating pressure and risking more severe ruptures and crises, or simply backing down and leaving the original problem unresolved.

This point underscores a third difficulty, which is that executing this approach effectively would require real skill and sophistication. As noted, all of the initiatives discussed here have their difficulties. Yet the overarching challenge is how to shock the system enough to achieve meaningful change—as Nixon did in the 1970s by ending Bretton Woods—without breaking it in the process. Pressure and reassurance are both essential, in other words, and careful calibration is at once vital and hard to achieve. Too much pressure can damage valuable relationships, cause confrontation with allies and competitors, and make Washington look like a dangerous bully. But too much reassurance can undercut the pressure that is essential to getting results. In the past, even presidents now recognized for their diplomatic achievements—such as Nixon and Reagan—often found this a tricky balance to strike. Asking a President Trump—who has frequently acted as a geopolitical blunderbuss—to do as well or better might be a tall order.

Pursuing a better nationalism, then, is no silver bullet. But it does carry distinct strategic advantages, especially when compared to Fortress America. First, it reflects the fact that America possesses great inherent ability to push for better terms in its myriad foreign relationships, because it is the only actor capable of providing public goods such as leadership of the international economy or security in key regions.[47] Today, ironically enough, this approach may be even better primed to succeed, because Trump's election and early presidency have already delivered a massive shock to the system. These events have shown actors around the world that they cannot take U.S. leadership for granted, at a time when resurgent global turmoil and insecurity are simultaneously reminding Washington's partners how vital that leadership is. If Trump or future presidents can act wisely and avoid overdoing it, perhaps they can leverage that shock to reset and rebalance key relationships in a constructive way.

Second, this strategy is broadly consistent with the national mood. As noted, the American people may be world-weary, but they are not fleeing headlong into 1930s-style isolationism. There is frustration with globalization and unequal burden-sharing—which Trump skillfully and demagogically channeled in 2016—but little evidence to suggest that the electorate desires simply to discard trade or alliances. Public views of American internationalism thus reflect ambivalence and dissatisfaction, not total rejection.[48] A better nationalism addresses and provides avenues for ameliorating that dissatisfaction, without going too far and dismantling an internationalism that has benefited the U.S. public quite well.

Third, if this strategy might thereby put American internationalism on sounder political footing, it could actually put the postwar international system itself on firmer footing as well. As scholars have noted, and as discussed here, that system has occasionally required tweaking, in the form of reallocating burdens, resetting key relationships, and marginally revising the leading power's role.[49] This was precisely what Nixon and other U.S. policymakers attempted during the 1970s, and their efforts helped sustain American leadership and the international system for another forty years. If American policymakers can emulate that approach today, perhaps they can once again shore up U.S. internationalism and extend a remarkably favorable order.

WHICH WAY WILL AMERICA GO?

The crucial question, then, is not which of these grand strategies is preferable from the perspective of U.S. interests, but which one will prevail today. And as Donald Trump's presidency unfolds, the clash between Fortress America and a better nationalism has shaped up to be a defining theme of the administration.

President Trump himself is clearly attracted to something like Fortress America. After all, Trump used the occasion of his inaugural address to paint a bleak picture of a zero-sum world in which postwar U.S. internationalism has served mainly to strengthen others at America's expense. "For many decades," he declared, "we've enriched foreign industry at the expense of American industry; subsidized the armies of other countries while allowing for the very sad depletion of our military; we've defended other nations' borders while refusing to defend our own; and spent trillions of dollars overseas while America's infrastructure has fallen into disrepair and decay."[50] After taking office, Trump quickly did several things that arguably reflected a Fortress America mind-set: withdrawing from the TPP (without proposing an alternative) and continuing to tout the merits of protectionism; berating longtime U.S. allies and reportedly telling them that Washington "wants our money back"; reemphasizing (at least rhetorically) the idea of fortifying the southern border and using trade sanctions to make Mexico pay for it; attempting to implement an executive order that would have banned immigration and refugees from several Muslim-majority countries; announcing that he was beginning the process of withdrawing the United States from the Paris climate change accords; and others.[51] Perhaps these were all just opening bids in a shrewd negotiating strategy, or political bones tossed to the president's electoral base. But since Trump has lambasted key tenets of U.S. internationalism for decades, perhaps Fortress America is what he truly prefers.[52]

Given the formidable power of the presidency in foreign affairs, this is disconcerting news for those who understand the likely consequences of Fortress America. Fortunately, however, there are also constraints and countervailing forces, many of which have become increasingly apparent since Trump took power. Some core features of postwar internationalism—such as U.S. alliances—are deeply institutionalized and difficult to unwind, and they benefit from strong, bipartisan support in the Congress. Moreover, most of Trump's own foreign policy advisers prefer a better nationalism to Fortress America. Michael Flynn, Trump's short-lived first national security adviser, called for "re-baselining"—not rupturing—U.S. alliances and other key relationships in remarks made during the transition. In February 2017, Secretary of Defense James Mattis made his first foreign trip to Asia to reassure U.S. allies.[53] On his first trip to Europe, Mattis blended reaffirmations of U.S. commitment to NATO with a blunt warning that the alliance might suffer over time without greater European efforts.[54] And in subsequent months, Trump's key national security aides repeatedly averred, to audiences both domestic and international, that the United States would not be withdrawing into a Fortress America–style shell, regardless of what the president may have said on the campaign trail. Meanwhile, some leading advocates of a more sharply nationalist approach—such as Steve Bannon, who served as Trump's chief political strategist during the early months of his presidency—left the administration or were otherwise marginalized.

The opening innings of Trump's presidency also showed that there is little sympathy within the GOP-controlled Congress for Fortress America. Key senators such as John McCain and Lindsey Graham have long blended hawkish nationalism with a deep commitment to U.S. global engagement; they have pushed back hard against administration efforts to undercut American alliances or undermine key trade agreements such as NAFTA.[55] Likewise, although some U.S. manufacturing concerns might favor protectionism, the most powerful elements of today's business community—such as large financial firms and the high-tech sector—are deeply dependent on global markets, capital, and talent, and appear willing to use their political clout to protect that access.[56] Finally, the foreign policy bureaucracy is internationalist to its core, and can be expected to use the dark arts of foot-dragging and bureaucratic warfare to resist isolationist or radical impulses. Indeed, insofar as Trump's policies have so far been less extreme than his promises, these factors largely deserve the credit.[57] Over time, and as the liabilities of Fortress America become increasingly clear, these same issues may, perhaps, pull the administration away from that model and toward a milder, better form of nationalist internationalism—if, that is, the administration can summon the discipline and consistency required to implement any sort of coherent geopolitical program.

Which of these two tendencies will prevail, and in what proportion and with what consistency, thus remain to be determined. One fears that President Trump may be inclined to pursue Fortress America—or at least aspects thereof—with all its destructive effects. One hopes, for the sake of the international order and America itself, that this administration—or its successors—will ultimately find its way toward a better nationalism that could actually be fairly constructive.

SIX

DOES AMERICA HAVE ENOUGH
HARD POWER?

If the United States does seek to continue playing something like its traditional role in sustaining the existing international system, how much military power will it need to do so effectively?[1] The question must be asked with increasing urgency today. For two decades after the Cold War, Washington enjoyed essentially uncontested military dominance and a historically favorable global environment—all at a comparatively bargain-basement price. Now, however, America confronts military and geopolitical challenges more numerous and severe than at any time in at least a quarter century, precisely as disinvestment in defense has left U.S. military resources far scarcer than before. The result is a creeping crisis of American military primacy, as Washington's margin of superiority is diminished and a gap emerges between U.S. commitments and capabilities. As Secretary of Defense Chuck Hagel noted in 2014, "We are entering an era where American dominance on the seas, in the skies, and in space—not to mention cyberspace—can no longer be taken for granted."[2] "Superpowers don't bluff," went a common Obama-era refrain—but today, America risks being left with a strategy of bluff as its preeminence erodes.

Foreign policy, Walter Lippmann wrote, entails "bringing into balance, with a comfortable surplus of power in reserve, the nation's commitments and the nation's power." If a statesman fails to preserve strategic solvency, if he fails to "bring his ends and means into balance," Lippmann added, "he will follow a course that leads to disaster."[3] America's approaching strategic insolvency is indeed fraught with peril. If left unaddressed, it will undermine U.S. alliances by raising doubts about the credibility of American guarantees. It will weaken deterrence by tempting adversaries to think aggression may be successful. Should conflict actually erupt in key areas, the United States may be unable to uphold existing commitments, or be able to do so only at prohibitive cost. Finally, as the shadows cast by U.S. military power grow shorter, American diplomacy is likely to become less availing, and the global system less responsive to U.S. influence. To be sure, the U.S. military remains far superior to any single competitor, and so far it has generally been sufficient to sustain a pretty good grand strategy. But today, American military power is gradually but unmistakably becoming insufficient relative to the grand strategy and international order it is meant to support.

Great powers facing strategic insolvency have three basic options. First, they can decrease commitments, thereby restoring equilibrium with diminished resources. Second, they can live with greater risk, either by gambling that their enemies will not test vulnerable commitments, or by employing riskier approaches—such as nuclear escalation—to sustain commitments on the cheap. Third, they can expand capabilities and thereby restore strategic solvency. Today, this third approach would probably require a concerted, long-term defense buildup comparable to the efforts of

Presidents Jimmy Carter and Ronald Reagan near the end of the Cold War.[4]

Much contemporary commentary favors the first option—reducing commitments—and denounces the third as financially ruinous and perhaps impossible.[5] Yet significantly expanding American capabilities would not be nearly as economically onerous as it may seem. Compared to the alternatives, in fact, this approach represents the best option for sustaining American primacy and preventing a slide into strategic bankruptcy that will eventually be punished.

PRIMACY AND POST–COLD WAR GRAND STRATEGY

Since World War II, the United States has had a military second to none. Since the Cold War, America has committed to having overwhelming military primacy. The idea, as George W. Bush declared in 2002, that America must possess "strengths beyond challenge" has featured in every major U.S. strategy document for a quarter century; it has also been reflected in concrete terms.[6]

From the early 1990s, for example, the United States consistently accounted for around 35 to 45 percent of world defense spending and maintained peerless global power-projection capabilities.[7] Perhaps more important, U.S. primacy was also unrivaled in key overseas strategic regions—Europe, East Asia, the Middle East. From thrashing Saddam Hussein's million-man Iraqi military during Operation Desert Storm, to deploying—with impunity—two carrier strike groups off Taiwan during the China-Taiwan crisis of 1995–96, Washington has been able to project military power superior to anything a regional rival could employ even on its own geopolitical doorstep.

This military dominance has constituted the hard-power backbone of an ambitious global strategy. After the Cold War, U.S. policymakers committed to averting a return to the unstable multipolarity of earlier eras, and to perpetuating the more favorable unipolar order. They committed to building on the successes of the postwar era by further advancing liberal political values and an open international economy, and to suppressing international scourges such as rogue states, nuclear proliferation, and catastrophic terrorism. And because they recognized that military force remained the *ultima ratio regum*, they understood the centrality of military preponderance.

Washington would need the military power necessary to underwrite worldwide alliance commitments. It would have to preserve substantial overmatch versus any potential great-power rival. It must be able to answer the sharpest challenges to the international system, such as Saddam's invasion of Kuwait in 1990 or jihadist extremism after 9/11. Finally, because prevailing global norms generally reflect hard-power realities, America would need the superiority to assure that its own values remained ascendant. It was impolitic to say that U.S. strategy and the international order required "strengths beyond challenge," but it was not at all inaccurate.

American primacy, moreover, was eminently affordable. At the height of the Cold War, the United States spent over 12 percent of GDP on defense. Since the mid-1990s, the number has usually been between 3 and 4 percent.[8] In a historically favorable international environment, Washington could enjoy primacy—and its geopolitical fruits—on the cheap.

Yet U.S. strategy also heeded, at least until recently, the fact that there was a limit to how cheaply that primacy could be had. The American military did shrink significantly during the 1990s, but U.S. officials understood that if Washington cut back too far, its primacy would erode to a point where it ceased to deliver its geopolitical benefits. Alliances would lose credibility; the stability of key regions would be eroded; rivals would be emboldened; international crises would go unaddressed. American primacy was thus like a reasonably priced insurance policy. It required nontrivial expenditures, but protected against far costlier outcomes.[9] Washington paid its insurance premiums for two decades after the Cold War. But more recently American primacy and strategic solvency have been imperiled.

THE DARKENING HORIZON

For most of the post–Cold War era, the international system was—by historical standards—remarkably benign. Dangers existed, and as the terrorist attacks of September 11, 2001, demonstrated, they could manifest with horrific effect. But for two decades after the Soviet collapse, the world was characterized by remarkably low levels of great-power competition, high levels of security in key theaters such as Europe and East Asia, and the comparative weakness of those "rogue" actors—Iran, Iraq, North Korea, al-Qaeda—who most aggressively challenged American power. During the 1990s, some observers even spoke of a "strategic pause," the idea being that the end of the Cold War had afforded the United States a respite from normal levels of geopolitical danger and competition. Now, however, the strategic horizon is darkening, due to four factors.

First, great-power military competition is back. The world's two leading authoritarian powers—China and Russia—are seeking regional hegemony, contesting global norms such as nonaggression and freedom of navigation, and developing the military punch to underwrite these ambitions. Notwithstanding severe economic and demographic problems, Russia has conducted a major military modernization emphasizing nuclear weapons, high-end conventional capabilities, and rapid-deployment and special operations forces—and utilized many of these capabilities in conflicts in Ukraine and Syria.[10] China, meanwhile, has carried out a buildup of historic proportions, with constant-dollar defense outlays rising from US$26 billion in 1995 to US$226 billion in 2016.[11] Ominously, these expenditures have funded development of power-projection and anti-access/area denial (A2/AD) tools necessary to threaten China's neighbors and complicate U.S. intervention on their behalf. Washington has grown accustomed to having a generational military lead; Russian and Chinese modernization efforts are now creating a far more competitive environment.

Second, the international outlaws are no longer so weak. North Korea's conventional forces have atrophied, but it has amassed a growing nuclear arsenal and is developing an intercontinental delivery capability that will soon allow it to threaten not just America's regional allies but also the continental United States.[12] Iran remains a nuclear threshold state, one that continues to develop ballistic missiles and A2/AD capabilities while employing sectarian and proxy forces across the Middle East. The Islamic State, for its part, is headed for defeat, but has displayed military capabilities unprecedented for any terrorist group, and shown that counterterrorism will continue to place significant operational demands on U.S. forces whether in this context or in others. Rogue actors have long preoccupied American planners, but the rogues are now more capable than at any time in decades.

Third, the democratization of technology has allowed more actors to contest American superiority in dangerous ways. The spread of antisatellite and cyberwarfare capabilities; the proliferation of man-portable air defense systems and ballistic missiles; the increasing availability of key elements of the precision-strike complex—these phenomena have had a military leveling effect by giving weaker actors capabilities which were formerly unique to technologically advanced states. As such technologies "proliferate worldwide," Air Force Chief of Staff General David Goldfein commented in 2016, "the technology and capability gaps between America and our adversaries are closing dangerously fast."[13] Indeed, as these capabilities spread, fourth-generation systems (such as F-15s and F-16s) may provide decreasing utility against even non-great-power competitors, and far more fifth-generation capabilities may be needed to perpetuate American overmatch.

Finally, the number of challenges has multiplied. During the 1990s and early 2000s, Washington faced rogue states and jihadist extremism—but not intense great-power rivalry. America faced conflicts in the Middle East—but East Asia and Europe were comparatively secure. Now, the old threats still exist—but the more permissive conditions have vanished. The United States confronts rogue states, lethal jihadist organizations, and great-power competition; there are severe challenges in all three Eurasian theaters. "I don't recall a time when we have been confronted with a more diverse array of threats, whether it's the nation state threats posed by Russia and China and particularly their substantial nuclear capabilities, or non-nation states of the likes of ISIL, Al Qaida, etc.," Director of National Intelligence James Clapper commented in 2016. Trends in the strategic landscape constituted a veritable "litany of doom."[14] The United States thus faces not just more significant, but also more numerous, challenges to its military dominance than it has for at least a quarter century.

DISINVESTING IN DEFENSE

One might expect the leader of a historically favorable international system to respond to such developments by increasing its own, relatively modest investments in maintaining the system. In recent years, however, Washington has markedly *dis*invested in defense. Constant-dollar defense spending fell by nearly one-fourth, from US$759 billion in 2010 to US$596 billion in 2015.[15] Defense spending as a share of GDP fell from 4.7 percent to 3.3 percent, with Congressional Budget Office projections showing military outlays falling to 2.6 percent by 2024—the lowest level since before World War II.[16] And although the Trump administration subsequently came to power pledging to undertake a historic military buildup, as of this writing it seemed that the U.S. defense budget was likely to increase only marginally—if at all—in 2018, leaving that budget at a level that Trump's own defense secretary privately acknowledged was insufficient to offset the effects of prolonged decline.[17]

Defense spending *always* declines after major wars, of course. Yet from 2010 onward, this pressure was compounded by the legacy of Bush-era budget deficits, the impact of the Great Recession, and President Obama's decision to transfer resources from national security to domestic priorities. These forces, in turn, were exacerbated by the terms of the Budget Control Act (BCA) of 2011 and the sequester mechanism. Defense spending absorbed roughly 50 percent of BCA- and sequester-related spending cuts, despite accounting for less than 20 percent of federal spending. By walling off most personnel costs and severely limiting flexibility in how cuts could be made, moreover, the sequester forced the Department of Defense to make reductions in blunt, nonstrategic fashion.[18]

Some military retrenchment was arguably sensible following the Iraq War. But prolonged exposure to this budgetary buzz saw has taken a toll. Readiness has suffered, with all services struggling to conduct current counterterrorism operations while also preparing for the ever-growing danger of great-power war. "The services are very good at counterinsurgency," the House Armed Services Committee noted in 2016, "but they are not prepared to endure a long fight against higher order threats from near-peer competitors."[19] The Army chief of staff, General Mark Milley, put it more bluntly in September 2016, stating that only one-third of the regular Army's brigade combat teams were ready for high-end combat, and warning that unready forces could result in a "butcher's bill paid in blood."[20] Modernization has also been compromised. Purchases of currently planned capabilities have been reduced or deferred; the ability to develop and field promising future capabilities is sharply constrained by budget caps and uncertainty. "We have . . . curtailed our modernization in a number of areas critical to staying ahead of our potential adversaries," Chief of Naval Operations John Richardson remarked.[21] This problem will only get worse—

in the 2020s, a "bow wave" of deferred investments in the nuclear triad and high-end conventional capabilities will come due.[22]

Finally, force structure has been sacrificed. The Army has fared worst—under Obama's final budget, it was slated to decline to 450,000 personnel by 2018, or 30,000 personnel fewer than prior to 9/11.[23] But all the services are at or near post–World War II lows in terms of end strength, and the U.S. military is now significantly smaller than the 1990s-era "Base Force," which was designed as "a minimum force that constituted a floor below which the nation should not go if it was to remain a globally engaged superpower."[24] Strategy is ultimately a function of resources, and Washington is paying for less capability relative to the threats it faces than at any time in decades.

THE CREEPING CRISIS OF U.S. MILITARY PRIMACY

The cumulative result of these developments has been a creeping crisis of U.S. military primacy. Washington still possesses vastly more military power than any challenger, particularly in global power-projection capabilities. Yet even this global primacy is starting to be contested. The United States now faces a Russia with significant extraregional power-projection capabilities as well as near-peer capabilities in areas such as strategic nuclear forces and cyberwarfare; China's military budget is now more than one-third of the U.S. budget, and Beijing is developing its own advanced power-projection capabilities.[25] Perhaps more important, U.S. global primacy is also becoming less relevant, because today's crucial geopolitical competitions are regional contests, and here the trends have been more adverse.

In East Asia, China's two-decade military buildup has allowed Beijing seriously to contest U.S. power projection within the first island chain. "The balance of power between the United States and China may be approaching a series of tipping points," RAND

Corporation analysts have written.[26] The situation in eastern Europe is worse. Here, unfavorable geography and aggressive Russian modernization have created Russian overmatch in the Baltic; U.S. and NATO forces are "outnumbered and outgunned" along NATO's eastern flank.[27] In the Middle East, the balance remains more favorable, but Iranian A2/AD and ballistic missile capabilities can significantly complicate U.S. operations, while the reemergence of Russian military power has narrowed U.S. freedom of action. In key areas across Eurasia, the U.S. military edge has eroded, even as the overall U.S. military lead remains significant.

This erosion, in turn, is having serious implications for American strategy. For one thing, U.S. forces will face far harder fights should conflict occur. War against Iran or North Korea would be daunting enough, given their asymmetrical capabilities (and, in North Korea's case, a growing nuclear arsenal). Even Iran, for instance, could use its ballistic missile capabilities to attack U.S. bases and allies, employ swarming tactics and precision-guided munitions against U.S. naval forces in the Persian Gulf, and activate Shiite militias and proxy forces, all as a way of inflicting higher costs on Washington.[28] Conflict against Russia or China would be something else entirely. Fighting a near-peer competitor armed with high-end conventional weapons and precision-strike capabilities would subject the U.S. military to an environment of enormous lethality, "the likes of which," Milley commented in 2016, it "has not experienced . . . since World War II."[29] U.S. forces might still win—albeit on a longer time line, and at a painfully high cost in lives—but then again, they might not.

According to open-source analysis, U.S. and NATO forces would have little chance of halting a determined Russian assault on the Baltic states. Facing severe disadvantages in tanks, ground-based fires, and airpower and air defenses, those forces would likely be destroyed in place. NATO would then face an agonizing dilemma— whether to mobilize its resources for a protracted war that would risk nuclear escalation or acquiesce to an alliance-destroying fait accompli.[30]

Similarly, whereas the United States would have dominated any plausible conflict with China in the 1990s, according to recent assessments the most likely conflicts would be nearer-run things today. Consider a conflict over Taiwan. Beijing might not be able to defeat Washington in a long war, but it could establish air and maritime superiority early in a conflict and thereby impose unacceptable losses on U.S. air and naval forces. The crucial "tipping point" in a Taiwan contingency could come in 2020 or even earlier; in the Spratly Islands, it could come within another decade.[31] "Looking forward," John Richardson warned in 2016, "I remain deeply concerned about the gap between what the American people expect of their Navy now and for the foreseeable future, and the available resources to deliver on those expectations."[32] As U.S. superiority erodes, America runs a higher risk of being unable to meet its obligations.

In fact, Washington's ability to execute its standing global defense strategy is growing increasingly doubtful. After the Cold War, the United States adopted a two "major regional contingency" (MRC) standard, geared toward preventing an adversary in one region from undertaking opportunistic aggression to exploit U.S. preoccupation in another. As the 1997 Quadrennial Defense Review put it, "Such a capability is the sine qua non of a superpower and is essential to the credibility of our overall national security strategy."[33] By 2012, however, budget cuts had already forced the Obama administration to shift to what might be thought of as a 1.5 or 1.7 war standard premised on decisively defeating one opponent while "imposing unacceptable costs" on another.[34] Yet now the U.S. capacity to execute even this less ambitious strategy is under strain, just as the international environment is raising questions about whether the strategy is ambitious enough.

This is because the Obama administration's 2012 defense strategy was announced prior to sequestration, and prior to Russian aggression in Ukraine in 2014—which raised the disturbing possibility that one of America's wars might be against a nuclear-armed, great-power competitor. And beyond these issues, events in Europe and the Middle East since 2011–12 have raised doubts about whether a 1.7 war standard is sufficient, given the possibility the Pentagon might confront conflicts in three strategic theaters. As the bipartisan National Defense Panel noted in 2014, "In the current threat environment the United States could plausibly be called upon to deter or fight in several regions in overlapping timeframes: on the Korean peninsula, in the East or South China Sea, in the Middle East, South Asia and quite possibly in Europe. . . . Additionally, the spread of al Qaeda and its spin offs to new areas in Africa and the Middle East means that the U.S. military must be able to sustain global counterterrorism operations and defend the American homeland even when engaged in regional conflict overseas."[35] In sum, the United States is nearing, if it has not already reached, the point of strategic insolvency. And even beyond the aforementioned risks, this situation poses great strategic challenges.

The cohesion of U.S. alliances will likely suffer, as American allies lose confidence in Washington's ability to protect them. We have gotten a taste of this already; Rodrigo Duterte's recent geopolitical reorientation of the Philippines has apparently been rooted, at least partially, in his skepticism regarding U.S. guarantees.[36] Adversaries, in turn, will become more likely to test U.S. commitments, as a way of gauging Washington's willingness to make good on increasingly tenuous promises and exploiting its declining ability to respond decisively. "The ability to contest dominance might lead Chinese leaders to believe they could deter U.S. intervention in a conflict between it and one or more of its neighbors," several military analysts have written, undermining deterrence and making the use of force seem more attractive.[37] Indeed, Russian intimidation of the Baltic states, Iranian expansionism in the Middle East, and increasingly aggressive Chinese coercion of the Philippines and Japan in recent years illustrate these dynamics in action.

Finally, as U.S. military power becomes less imposing, the United States will find its global influence less impressive. Norms, ideas, and international arrangements supported by Washington will lose strength, and will increasingly be challenged by actors who feel empowered to imprint their own influence on global affairs. More and more, the United States will confront what one pundit has called a "broken-windows world," as long-standing rules become more difficult to enforce.[38] U.S. grand strategy and the post–Cold War system have rested on American military overmatch. As that overmatch fades, U.S. strategy and the order it supports will come under rising strain.

THE FALSE PROMISE OF RETRENCHMENT

So, how should America respond? One option is reducing commitments. If the United States cannot sustain its existing global strategy, then it could pare back global obligations until they are more commensurate with available capabilities.

The United States might, for instance, embrace a twenty-first-century Nixon Doctrine, by making clear that while it will protect its Middle Eastern partners from conventional, state-based aggression, they must defend themselves against nontraditional threats such as the Islamic State.[39] Or it could simply delegate Persian Gulf security to its Arab allies in the region. Most dramatically, if the United States were really serious about slashing commitments, it could dispense with those obligations most difficult to uphold—to Taiwan and the Baltic states, for instance. In short, America would respond to overstretch through retrenchment. It would reduce commitments proactively rather than having their hollowness exposed by war.

There are historical precedents for this approach. The Nixon Doctrine and U.S. withdrawal from Vietnam helped Washington retreat to a more defensible strategic perimeter in the 1970s following strategic overstretch in the decade prior. More significantly, beginning in the late nineteenth century, the United Kingdom gradually conducted an elegant global retreat. It did so, first, by relying on rising regional powers such as the United States and Japan to maintain acceptable regional orders and, ultimately, by encouraging Washington to shoulder many of London's global burdens after World War II. Graceful retrenchment, then, is not an impossibility.[40]

It is, however, extremely problematic today. This approach—particularly the more aggressive variants—would be enormously difficult to implement. The U.S. commitment to the Baltic states is part of a larger commitment to NATO; shredding the former guarantee risks undermining the broader alliance. Even in Asia, where the United States has bilateral alliances, withdrawing the ambiguous U.S. commitment to Taipei could cause leaders in Manila, Seoul, or Tokyo to wonder if they might be abandoned next—and to hedge their strategic bets accordingly. Alliances hinge on the credibility of the patron's promises; it is difficult to revoke some guarantees without discrediting others.[41]

This dynamic underscores another liability—the likelihood of profound geopolitical instability. Retrenchment has historically worked best when the overstretched hegemon can hand off excessive responsibilities to some friendly power. But today, there is no liberal superpower waiting in the wings. Rather, the countries most sympathetic to America's view of the international order—Japan, the United Kingdom, key European allies—confront graver long-term economic and demographic challenges than the United States. The countries most likely to gain influence following U.S. retrenchment—Russia and China—have very different global visions.

In these circumstances, U.S. retrenchment seems unlikely simply to force friendly local actors to do more to defend themselves and check revisionist powers. Rather, the outcome might easily be underbalancing—in which collective action problems, internal political divisions, or resource limitations prevent timely action against a potential aggressor—or bandwagoning, in which exposed countries buy a measure of safety by aligning with, rather than against, an aggressive power.[42] Meanwhile, although writing off Taiwan or Estonia might produce a near-term improvement of relations with Beijing or Moscow, the longer-term effect would be to remove a chief constraint on the aggressive behavior these powers have increasingly been manifesting. If Moscow and Beijing seem eager to bring their "near abroads" to heel now, just wait until the United States retracts its security perimeter.

If more aggressive variants of retrenchment are thus deeply flawed, even more limited versions—such as a Middle Eastern Nixon Doctrine—have weaknesses. As Iran's military power continues to grow in the coming years—and removal of nuclear-related sanctions makes this seem likely—even the wealthy Persian Gulf kingdoms will find it increasingly difficult to deal with Tehran's advanced and asymmetric capabilities without U.S. assistance. This is all the more so because, without U.S. leadership, long-standing collective action problems between the Gulf countries are likely to worsen. Moreover, the United States essentially tried a version of this approach by withdrawing from Iraq in late 2011. But as it soon became clear, Iraq—a vital state in a key region—could not withstand challenges from nontraditional foes such as the Islamic State on its own. In fact, U.S. retrenchment actually encouraged developments that left Iraq more vulnerable to collapse, such as the increasingly sectarian nature of Nouri al-Maliki's governance and the hollowing out of the Iraqi Security Forces.[43] Retrenchment, then, may narrow the gap between capabilities and commitments in the short run, but only by inviting greater global dangers and instability.

LIVING WITH RISK

If the United States is unwilling to spend significantly more on defense, but does not wish to invite the geopolitical instability associated with retrenchment, a second option is to live with greater risk.

Living with greater risk could take two different—but not mutually exclusive—forms. First, the United States could accept higher risk with respect to its global commitments, by wagering that even exposed commitments are unlikely to be tested because U.S. adversaries are risk averse and are unwilling to start a war—even a potentially successful one—that might cause American intervention. In other words, the United States might not be able to defend Taiwan effectively, but the mere prospect that a Chinese invasion or other assault might provoke a Sino-American war would stay Beijing's hand.

Second, the United States could bridge the capabilities-commitments gap through riskier strategies substituting escalation for additional resources. Most likely, this would entail relying more heavily on nuclear warfighting and the threat of nuclear retaliation to defend vulnerable allies in East Asia or eastern Europe. (Because U.S. allies are already covered by the U.S. extended nuclear deterrent, this approach would involve making more explicit nuclear threats and guarantees, and integrating greater reliance on nuclear weapons into U.S. plans.) Similarly, this approach could entail use, or threat of use, of powerful nonnuclear capabilities such as strategic cyberattacks against an enemy's critical infrastructure for the same purpose—bolstering deterrence on the cheap, by raising the costs an aggressor would expect to pay.[44]

Lest these approaches sound ridiculous, both have a distinguished pedigree. In the late 1940s, the United States could not credibly defend western Europe from a Soviet invasion. But the Truman administration still undertook the security guarantees associated with NATO on the calculated gamble that Moscow was unlikely to risk global war by attacking U.S. allies, particularly during the period of the U.S. nuclear monopoly.[45] And in the 1950s, to control costs and address the continuing deficiency of U.S. and allied conventional forces, the Eisenhower administration relied heavily on nuclear threats to deter aggression.[46] Throughout much of the Cold War, in fact, the United States compensated for conventional inferiority—particularly in central Europe—by integrating early recourse to nuclear weapons into its war plans. Accepting greater risk would mean updating Cold War–era approaches for today's purposes.

Yet substituting risk for cost entails serious liabilities. Simply hoping that exposed commitments will not be challenged might work—for a while. But this strategy carries enormous risk of those guarantees eventually being tested and found wanting, with devastating effects on America's reputation and credibility. The United States could experience its version of the "Singapore moment"—an episode, as when the Japanese captured that supposedly impregnable British redoubt and sank much of Britain's Far Eastern battle fleet along the way, when a great power's strength and promises are revealed to be an empty shell, and its image as a strong and capable actor in a key part of the world never recovers. Meanwhile, a strategy of bluff could weaken deterrence and reassurance on the installment plan, as allies and adversaries perceive a shifting balance of power and understand that U.S. guarantees are increasingly chimerical.

The second variant of this approach—embracing more escalatory approaches—is also problematic, because it lacks credibility. Consider threatening to employ strategic cyberattacks against an aggressor in a conflict over Taiwan or the Baltic states. Such threats are potentially counterproductive, because, as President Obama acknowledged in 2016, "open societies" such as the United States are "more vulnerable" to massive cyberattacks than are authoritarian rivals such as Russia or China.[47] America may simply lack the escalation dominance needed to make a strategy of cyber retaliation believable.

So too in the nuclear realm. Threats to punish communist aggression with nuclear retaliation might have been credible in the 1950s, when China lacked nuclear weapons, Washington had a massive nuclear advantage over Moscow, and neither power could reliably target the U.S. homeland. (Even then, however, there were doubts—including within the Eisenhower administration—about whether the president would actually execute a strategy that entailed starting a nuclear war to defend commitments that were not themselves crucial to the global balance of power.)[48] But today, both rivals possess secure second-strike capabilities and could inflict horrific damage on America should nuclear escalation occur. This approach thus risks leading the United States into a trap where, if its interests are challenged, it is confronted with a choice between pursuing escalatory options that carry a potentially unacceptable cost, on the one hand, and acquiescing to aggression, on the other. Awareness of this dynamic may, in turn, make adversaries more likely to probe and push. Trading cost for risk may seem attractive in theory, but in practice the risks may prove far more dangerous than they initially seem.

REINVESTING IN PRIMACY

This leaves a final option—significantly increasing resources devoted to defense, thereby bringing capabilities back into alignment with commitments and strengthening the hard-power backbone of U.S. strategy. Given current trends, this would likely entail a sustained, multiyear buildup of magnitude roughly similar to the Carter-Reagan buildup, when real defense spending increased by around 50 percent. This buildup would require permanently lifting the BCA caps, to provide increased resources and budgetary stability. It would require not just procuring larger quantities of existing capabilities, but also investing aggressively in future capabilities geared toward defeating great-power challengers as well as middle-tier problem countries such as Iran and North Korea. And crucially, greater resources would have to be coupled with development of innovative operational concepts, streamlining Department of Defense procedures and acquisition processes, and other efforts to maximize the Pentagon's effectiveness and efficiency.

Recent proposals demonstrate the likely parameters of this approach. If the goal is to restore an authentic two MRC capability, the United States might follow the recommendations issued in 2014 by the National Defense Panel. Those recommendations call for a force consisting—at minimum—of 490,000 active-duty Army personnel and 182,000 Marines, a Navy of between 323 and 346 ships (versus 274 at the time of writing), and an Air Force of unspecified size but substantially larger than the end strength envisioned in late Obama-era budgets.[49] If, more ambitiously, the United States seeks a two-plus- or even a three-war standard, a more significant buildup would be required.

One estimate, issued by Senator John McCain in early 2017, calls for a three-theater force—a Navy of over 330 ships and nearly 900 frontline naval strike fighters, an Air Force of 60 combat squadrons and 1,500 combat aircraft, an Army of at least 490,000–500,000 active-duty soldiers, and a Marine Corps of at least 200,000 active-duty Marines. (Because McCain's budget reaches out only five years, these numbers would presumably grow further over time.)[50] Another three-theater proposal, by the American Enterprise Institute, advocates a ten-year expansion to 600,000 active-duty Army soldiers, over 200,000 active-duty Marines, a Navy of 346 ships, and an Air Force of unspecified but significantly increased end strength. The number of F-22s, for instance, would rise from 185 to 450.[51]

These proposals would, of course, require significant new investments. The McCain budget calls for US$430 billion in new money over five years compared to Obama's final defense budget, culminating in a Fiscal Year 2022 budget of roughly US$800 billion.[52] The American Enterprise Institute proposal, issued in late 2015, calls for US$1.3 trillion over ten years.[53] All of these force constructs reflect a "high-low" mix designed to enable effective operations ranging from counterterrorism, to major conventional war against Iran or North Korea, to high-end combat against a great-power adversary. All the proposals include robust recapitalization of the U.S. nuclear triad. And although these proposals differ on specifics, all are meant to enable a range of investments necessary to maintaining U.S. primacy in a more competitive environment.

If the United States were to undertake a buildup of this magnitude, it could, for instance, invest in a more survivable, multibrigade presence in eastern Europe. It could significantly increase investments in capabilities—from additional Zumwalt-class destroyers and nuclear attack submarines, to stealthy fighters and penetrating long-range bombers, to vastly enhanced stocks of precision-guided and standoff munitions, to improved air and missile defenses—that are necessary to retain air and sea control in high-end conflicts, as well as to maintain the upper hand in fights with Iran and North Korea.[54] This approach would ease the tradeoffs between critical capabilities for today's fight (and particularly for counterterrorism operations), such as the A-10, and those critical for confronting more advanced adversaries in tomorrow's fight, such as the F-35. Crucially, it would allow aggressive development and production of future technologies—in areas from hypersonics to directed energy—which are now receiving seed funding but cannot be fielded in numbers without additional resources.[55] Finally, this approach—particularly the more aggressive, three-theater options—would permit the increased force structure necessary to cover a larger number of contingencies and reduce stress on the current force.

So, how viable is this option? Critics offer four primary objections. The first is that this approach is unnecessary, because the Pentagon can maintain U.S. primacy at existing budget levels either by pursuing technological innovation and strategic offsets or by undertaking business and acquisition reforms. The second is that a sustained, multiyear buildup will overtax the U.S. economy and is unaffordable given persistent budget deficits and a debt-to-GDP ratio of 76 percent.[56] The third is that this approach will prove self-defeating, because it will spur arms races with American adversaries. The fourth is that this will incentivize continued free riding by U.S. allies and partners, by forcing Washington to continue subsidizing their defense. All of these arguments have some logic, but none is persuasive.

The first argument—about innovation, offsets, and defense reform—is alluring but unsatisfying. To be sure, repurposing existing capabilities, developing high-end future capabilities to create significant dilemmas for competitors from Iran to China, and designing innovative operational concepts—essentially, what former Secretaries Hagel and Carter termed the "Third Offset strategy"—is absolutely vital to restoring strategic solvency. Yet offsets and innovation cannot by themselves compensate for the fact that Washington simply has too few forces to cover the range of plausible contingencies. Moreover, any meaningful offset strategy is itself dependent on significantly greater resources. As senior Pentagon officials have acknowledged, right now the United States cannot currently field even promising technologies in numbers sufficient to have strategic impact. "We'll do the demo, we'll be very happy with the results, [but] we won't have the money to go on," Undersecretary of Defense Frank Kendall warned in 2016.[57] Offsets and innovation are necessary for sustaining American primacy, but they are hardly sufficient. Similarly, although virtually all experts consider defense reform essential, no one has yet identified a feasible reform program sufficient to close the capabilities-commitments gap.

The economic argument is also deceptive. Although a multiyear buildup would be very expensive, it would hardly be unmanageable. Even the most aggressive proposed buildups would push defense spending only to 4 percent of GDP. The United States has, historically, supported far higher defense burdens without compromising economic performance.[58] One cannot draw a perfect parallel with earlier eras, of course, because during the 1950s America enjoyed higher growth and lower levels of deficits and debt than it does today. But these factors do not make a major buildup economically impossible.

For one thing, defense spending increases can actually stimulate overall growth. As Martin Feldstein, a former chair of the Council of Economic Advisers, has noted, "Military procurement has the . . . advantage that almost all of the equipment and supplies that the military buys is made in the United States, creating demand and jobs here at home."[59] Moreover, defense spending simply does not drive federal spending or deficits to the extent often imagined. In Fiscal Year 2016, defense consumed 16 percent of federal spending; domestic entitlements consumed 49 percent.[60] As a result, the growth of federal debt is influenced far more by unconstrained entitlement spending and insufficient tax revenues than by defense outlays. Put differently, if Washington can make politically difficult decisions regarding tax increases and curbing entitlement growth, it can spend significantly more on defense while also getting its fiscal house in order. If, conversely, the United States is unwilling to confront such politically difficult decisions, then the deficit will explode, the debt-to-GDP ratio will skyrocket, and Social Security and Medicare/Medicaid will go bankrupt regardless of how much or how little the country spends on defense.

The third objection, regarding intensified competition with U.S. rivals, is also unpersuasive. For it is hard to see how increased U.S. defense spending could trigger an arms race with Russia or China, or Iran or North Korea, because these countries are already working very hard to build military capabilities aimed at the United States. China, for instance, has averaged double-digit annual defense spending increases for roughly two decades. Strenuous military competition is already under way, in other words; U.S. adversaries are just the ones taking the competition most seriously. Moreover, although increased U.S. defense efforts—particularly if paired with additional forward presence in eastern Europe or East Asia—might cause increased near-term tensions with Moscow or Beijing, basic deterrence theory would suggest that over the longer term, failure to counter Russian and Chinese buildups, and to limit their opportunities for successful coercion, might well prove more destabilizing.

To be sure, this is not to suggest that Russia and China, or even Iran and North Korea, are powerless to respond to U.S. capability enhancements, or that there will *never* come a time when Washington simply cannot preserve the desired level of overmatch at an acceptable cost. Yet in light of the significant internal challenges—political, economic, demographic, or all of the above—facing each of America's adversaries, neither is the passing of U.S. primacy inevitable.[61] And given how advantageous U.S. primacy and the associated grand strategy have proved over the decades, America's goal should be to push the point at which they become unsustainable as far into the future as possible.

The fourth and final objection, regarding allied free riding and the need for a collective approach, can also be answered. U.S. strategy has always been a concert strategy, and so this approach certainly requires enhanced allied efforts. Countries from Japan and Taiwan to Poland and the Baltic states will have to spend more on defense if their situation is not to become untenable; they will, in many cases, also have to adopt more cost-effective and realistic defense strategies.[62]

But because the United States cannot simply make this decision for its allies, the question is which U.S. approach is most likely to encourage constructive changes. And although advocates of retrenchment often argue that allies will do more only if the United

States does less, the United States has historically been most successful at securing increased allied contributions when it, too, has been willing to do more. In previous instances when NATO allies collectively increased military spending—as part of the Lisbon program of the early 1950s, or the long-term defense program of the Carter-Reagan years—they did so as part of a broader program in which Washington also significantly increased its contributions to European security.[63] Likewise, the United States elicited the best performance from the Iraqi military and government when the American commitment to Baghdad was greatest, during the surge of 2007–08. The performance declined rather than improved as the U.S. commitment was subsequently reduced.[64] In sum, the United States may actually get the most out of its allies and partners when those countries are reassured of the American commitment—and are thus prepared to take risks of their own.

As the principal objections to this approach fall away, the advantages and logic become clearer. This approach recognizes, for instance, how beneficial U.S. military primacy has been in shaping a relatively stable, prosperous, and congenial international order, and it makes the investments necessary to sustain as much of this order as possible. This approach is the one best geared toward maintaining deterrence and reassurance, by providing the United States with greater ability to meet aggression from a range of enemies and rivals—without recourse to dangerously escalatory strategies in the most operationally demanding scenarios. As a result, this approach is arguably best suited to *avoiding* the use of force over the long term, by averting situations in which American adversaries from Iran and North Korea to Russia and China think aggression might pay. "Peace through strength" is not a meaningless catchphrase; it is good strategy. Closing the capabilities-commitments gap by increasing the former therefore represents the best available approach.

CONCLUSION

"Without superior aggregate military strength, in being and readily mobilizable, a policy of 'containment' . . . is no more than a policy of bluff."[65] This admonition, written by the authors of NSC-68 in 1950, reflected a dawning realization that America's global commitments were endangered by insufficient military power. Today, the United States again faces a crisis of strategic solvency, as gathering international threats have combined with dwindling military resources to leave the American superpower in an increasingly perilous state. The crisis of American military primacy is arriving, with potentially severe impacts for deterrence, reassurance, and the stability of the post–Cold War order.

America thus confronts a stark choice about how to proceed. Of the options considered here, the best approach is to find the resources necessary to bring American forces back into line with the grand strategy they are meant to support. Undertaking a sustained, major military buildup will not be cheap or politically easy, but it is not unaffordable for a wealthy superpower. Indeed, the fundamental question regarding whether America can undertake this course is not an economic one. It is whether the country will politically prioritize the investments needed to sustain its primacy and all the benefits that primacy has long provided, or whether it will allow itself to slip into strategic insolvency, with all the associated dangers for the United States and global order.

SEVEN

AMERICAN GRAND STRATEGY IN THE AGE OF TRUMP

Prediction is a perilous endeavor in international politics; world events often make fools of those who claim to foresee them. It seems certain, though, that historians will someday view Donald Trump's presidency as an inflection point in the trajectory of American grand strategy and the U.S.-led international system. To be sure, "grand strategy" may not be the first phrase that comes to mind regarding Trump, whose indiscipline and outbursts, unfamiliarity with key issues, and unexpected changes of course have led many observers to conclude that his foreign policy lacks any structure whatsoever.[1] And yet it has already become clear that Trump's presidency is freighted with grand strategic significance.

In part, this is simply because grand strategic decisionmaking is unavoidable, even for leaders who scarcely realize they are doing it. All leaders make choices about their country's geopolitical orientation and relationships; all leaders affect the image their nation presents on the international stage. All statesmen have some notion—however wise or foolish, consistent or contradictory—about how the world works and what type of actions will produce security and well-being; all statesmen must formulate policies to address critical challenges. These issues are all deeply grand strategic in nature and are all inherent in governing. You may not be interested in grand strategy, as Trotsky might have said, but grand strategy is interested in you.[2]

More important still, Trump took power at a critical passage in American foreign relations. For over seventy years before his election, the United States had pursued a world-building project of great energy and ambition; for the quarter-century before 2016, America had done so on the basis of its remarkable post–Cold War primacy. Yet Trump entered office as the world was becoming progressively more difficult for the superpower and the international system it had constructed. The rise of China was increasingly testing America's economic and military predominance, as geopolitical threats and tumults—from sharpening great-power rivalry, to the return of authoritarian challenges to democracy, to the unfolding of catastrophic upheaval in the greater Middle East and beyond—were intensifying and multiplying. There were, additionally, signs of mounting world-weariness at home, evoking questions about whether Washington would continue to play its longstanding role abroad.[3] In the run-up to November 2016, then, it seemed likely that once Hillary Clinton—a reliably internationalist candidate—was elected president, her principal grand strategic challenge would be bolstering American primacy and fortifying the U.S.-centric global order.

It was Trump who triumphed, however, so events have taken a different course. Trump came to Washington promising a grand strategic revolution—the deconstruction of America's multigeneration project to shape a stable, open world. So far, the president's statecraft has proved somewhat less radical than his rhetoric portended. He has not simply pulled up the drawbridge to Fortress America; he has been drawn toward more moderate stances on several key issues. Yet it is wrong to conclude that the president has simply been tamed by the system, because Trump has nonetheless left his own distinctive, and largely destructive, mark on U.S. strategy.[4] For rather than using his nationalist credentials constructively, to strengthen America's engagement with the international system it created, Trump has, in words and deeds alike, seemed to take dead aim at many of the core ideas and practices that have made Washington such an effective—indeed, exceptional—global leader. The president surely believes that his policies will maximize American wealth, power, and independence in a remorselessly competitive global arena. In practice, however, Trump's initiatives and mannerisms are serving primarily to diminish the American superpower, and to intensify the stresses on a system that has served Washington and so many others so well for so long.

THE DOUBLE TAPROOT OF U.S. DOMINANCE

For four generations, America has led an international order that has been admirably peaceful, prosperous, and democratic, at least compared to other international orders the world has known. Its success in doing so has had a double taproot—the first branch being unequaled hard power and the second being the distinctive manner in which Washington has employed that might.

From a hard-power perspective, America has been primed to lead since World War II if not before. Even during the Cold War competition with Moscow, the world was never truly bipolar. America dramatically outstripped the Soviet Union in economic prowess; it possessed overall military superiority despite Moscow's conventional advantage in Central Europe. After the Cold War,

U.S. primacy reached new heights. America commanded global power-projection capabilities likely greater than those of the rest of the world combined; it accounted for a quarter of global GDP. "Nothing has ever existed like this disparity of power; nothing," Paul Kennedy marveled in 2002.[5] Even today, as intensifying geopolitical and geo-economic competition cuts into the U.S. lead, Washington remains far and away the world's preeminent power. Leadership rests primarily on material capability, and America's vast economic and military advantages have represented the hard-power pillars of its global role.

Yet America's run as a superpower has also rested on *how* those strengths were wielded. Washington might have elected, after World War II, to pursue a narrow conception of its own interests, or even to use its power coercively, to extract maximum unilateral advantage from its various relationships. Instead, driven by the searing memory of war and depression, American policymakers worked to transform the international environment, by fashioning institutions and arrangements meant to benefit not just the United States but also like-minded countries around the world. By anchoring military alliances that delivered security in key regions, by emphasizing international as well as national prosperity, by providing public goods such as freedom of the seas and leadership in addressing global challenges, the United States strove to create a flourishing world in which America itself could flourish.[6]

To stress this preoccupation with "global order" is not, as one critic asserts, to indulge in "teary-eyed nostalgia as cover for U.S. hegemony," much less to obscure how ruthlessly self-interested U.S. policy could be.[7] After all, America would never have sustained this strategy for so long had it not benefited handsomely from the endeavor, in the form of economic prosperity, diplomatic and military influence, and other gains. "America First?" one European diplomat said in early 2017. "We've all been marching to your tune for seventy years."[8] And as inhabitants of countries from

Vietnam to Nicaragua can attest, U.S. officials were hardly averse to practicing the dark arts of violence and intimidation in dealing with challenges to the system they sought to erect.

The point, rather, is simply that, by the often-tragic standards of world affairs, America exercised its power in *comparatively* consensual and benevolent fashion; it behaved *less* exploitatively than it might have; it permitted and even encouraged the well-being of those who accepted the U.S. concept of international order. This approach powerfully differentiated America from the Soviet Union during the Cold War and made U.S. preeminence comparatively palatable for many global actors; indeed, most U.S. partners have feared American withdrawal more than American hegemony.[9]

The style of U.S. leadership has mattered greatly in other respects, as well. Since 1945, international security has rested heavily on the credibility of American commitments; U.S. officials have thus sought to demonstrate that Washington is a reliable and competent actor, one that can carry out complex tasks effectively and serve as a source of stability in a dangerous world.[10] Numerous presidents have encouraged—with decidedly imperfect consistency—the spread of democracy and human rights, in the belief that America's moral leadership is integral to its geopolitical leadership and that the country will be safer and stronger in a more liberal world. There was a "truly profound connection" between democracy and security, George Shultz once commented. "It is no accident . . . that America's closest and most lasting relationships are its alliances with its fellow democracies."[11] Similarly, Washington has forged bonds of deep, institutionalized collaboration with its closest partners, on grounds that common geopolitical interests and political values justified going beyond purely transactional ties and forming an enduring strategic community.

Finally, U.S. influence has derived not solely from America's material might, but from its image as an attractive—if flawed—society worthy of esteem and emulation. Enviable soft power has been a force-multiplier for U.S. hard power.[12] These qualities have sometimes been more honored in the breach than the observance, of course—Iraq, Vietnam, and segregation are as central to American history as are the Marshall Plan and NATO. And by no means has U.S. policy been without its frustrations, failures, and flaws. But all of these qualities have been broadly vital to postwar American strategy, and all are being challenged today.

TRADITION, DISRUPTION, AND DONALD TRUMP

In many ways, this is unsurprising given the views Trump has long espoused. If Dean Acheson was "present at the creation" of the American-led system, Trump's campaign rhetoric frequently lent the impression he intended to be present at the destruction. Trump's geopolitical heresies were legion, from his denigration of U.S. alliances, to his advocacy of protectionism and trade wars, to his disdain for democracy-promotion and unembarrassed admiration for authoritarians such as Vladimir Putin. He pledged to restore torture and order the military to commit war crimes in the struggle against terrorism; he trafficked in an often-xenophobic nationalism. No less striking was the core intellectual impulse driving these ideas—that America had actually betrayed its own welfare by embracing economic interdependence, providing global public goods, and assuming unprecedented international burdens. The postwar foreign policy tradition, Trump argued, was not an expression of higher self-interest. It was a naïve giveaway that enriched an ungrateful world at America's expense.[13]

These ideas were sufficiently radical that they provoked an unprecedented revolt by GOP foreign policy experts, while leaving many observers to wonder whether Trump really meant what he said. Yet as Thomas Wright has noted, Trump's bedrock views on international affairs—particularly his belief that America has gotten a bum deal from the world—have remained stable for decades.[14] The attacks Trump launched against allegedly parasitic allies and trade partners such as Japan and Kuwait in the 1980s were essentially those he leveled against Germany and Mexico in 2015–16. It seems prudent, then, to assume that the ideas Trump espoused during the campaign represented his true convictions.

Nonetheless, there were always reasons to think that Trump's conduct in office might be somewhat less revolutionary than his rhetoric foretold. The president was sure to face resistance from a Congress and professional bureaucracy that remained deeply internationalist, and many of his proposals—tearing up NAFTA, for instance—would actually harm his political base if implemented. Moreover, Trump's views on foreign affairs were strongly held but often poorly informed, raising the possibility that his position might change as he learned more. There was also the simple fact that drastic change is difficult—that displacing policies and institutions deeply embedded in American practice invariably proves harder than presidents expect. Not least, the unorthodoxy of Trump's views made it inherently challenging to staff an administration with true-believing "America Firsters," and made it likely he would appoint somewhat more moderate officials—as indeed he did, by naming individuals such as James Mattis, John Kelly, H. R. McMaster, Nikki Haley, and Gary Cohn to key positions.

There have consequently been several respects in which Candidate Trump's bark proved to be worse than President Trump's bite. Trump has not—so far—reinstated torture or directed the killing of suspected terrorists' families; he has not ordered indiscriminate aerial attacks against the Islamic State. He has not slapped 45 percent industrial tariffs on Beijing or declared China a currency manipulator; he has not withdrawn U.S. forces from Europe or consummated a diplomatic rapprochement with Russia. After much deliberation, Trump neither ordered a withdrawal from Afghanistan nor turned that mission over to mercenaries, choosing instead to modestly increase troop levels in a war he had previously derided as pointless.[15] Nor has Trump begun construction of a great wall along the U.S.-Mexican border or imposed sanctions meant to make Mexico pay for it.[16] Some of these things could easily change, but to date Trump's conduct has been more restrained than many observers might have predicted.

On other issues, too, Trump's policy has remained fairly close to the mainstream. Despite a deeply problematic stance toward NATO, Trump has continued augmenting U.S. military capabilities in Europe.[17] On counterterrorism, he has largely adopted—while incrementally intensifying—Obama's medium-footprint approach to defeating the Islamic State and other jihadist groups.[18] Perhaps most notably, although Trump had previously advocated making Syria's Bashar al-Assad a partner in the war on terror, as president he ordered a cruise missile strike against Assad's forces after the Syrian regime carried out a horrific chemical weapons attack against civilians in April 2017—thereby vindicating President Obama's red line from five years prior.[19] These shifts were largely welcomed by the bipartisan foreign policy elite, and they were mirrored in internal staffing shake-ups, as some of the America First firebrands that did initially advise Trump—Steve Bannon, most notably—were fired or marginalized over the course of 2017.

Some GOP observers have therefore argued that Trump has adopted "a fairly familiar Republican approach to foreign policy," and that his statecraft has been largely constructive and sober.[20] This, unfortunately, goes too far. For one thing, Trump has frequently *tried* to enact sharper and sometimes more dangerous policy departures, and has simply been prevented or, at the last minute, dissuaded from doing so. Trump did seek to lift sanctions and undertake a diplomatic rapprochement with Russia, but was checked by fierce resistance from the State Department bureaucracy and Congress.[21] The White House did reportedly draft an executive order laying the groundwork for the return of torture and CIA "black sites," only to be blocked by internal opposition here, too.[22] Trump nearly terminated NAFTA in April 2017—and may still do so—but pulled back after key advisers unified against the proposal.[23] Finally, Trump did apparently seek a tacit reconciliation with Assad in early 2017, by dropping the previous U.S. insistence that he leave office, only to execute a U-turn when Assad apparently interpreted this policy shift as a green light for chemical attacks.[24]

Trump, in other words, has often sought to act in just the fashion he advertised on the campaign trail; insofar as he has moved toward the mainstream, he has often been dragged there unwillingly. This, in turn, points to a more fundamental issue. Trump may not have pursued the wholesale deconstruction of U.S. foreign policy, but by no means has he simply accepted the conventions of postwar statecraft. Rather, the president has shaped his administration as much as his administration has shaped him; he has undertaken a number of innovations that are proving quite disruptive.

ZERO-SUM WORLD

Consider, first, how Trump has reframed the basic U.S view of world order. The commitment to building a broadly beneficial, positive-sum system has been a defining theme of U.S. statecraft since World War II, and it has served as a fount of the considerable international legitimacy that Washington has managed to generate. It is this project, however, that President Trump has scorned and sought to revise. Indeed, the central organizing principle of Trump's statecraft has been the idea that America is systematically exploited as a result of the arrangements it has constructed—free trade pacts, alliances, international organizations—and that the country will only become prosperous and powerful again if it accepts that global affairs are fundamentally a zero-sum game.

Trump's inaugural address was zero-sum at its core, a paean to a narrowly exclusive view of national self-interest. "We've made other countries rich while the wealth, strength, and confidence of our country has disappeared over the horizon," he declared; a more ruthless ethos was required for America to start "winning again, winning like never before."[25] The president expressed similar views in his address to the United Nations in September, complaining that America was too often exploited by, or "gets nothing in return" from other nations that "gamed the system."[26] In this and other speeches, Trump emphasized a return to nationalism and sovereignty as indispensable bulwarks against the depredations of a hostile world, in sharp contrast to the allegedly pernicious internationalism and openness of America's postwar project. "The nationstate remains the true foundation for happiness and harmony," Trump has repeatedly declared; the "false song of globalism" will lead America to ruin.[27] Finally, this perspective suffused the most explicit statement of the administration's worldview to date—a *Wall Street Journal* op-ed published by McMaster and Cohn in May 2017.

"The world," they argued, "is not a 'global community,' but an arena where nations, nongovernmental actors, and businesses engage and compete for advantage. We bring to this forum unmatched military, political, economic, cultural, and moral strength. Rather than deny this elemental nature of international affairs, we embrace it."[28] The language here was telling. In a "community," mutually beneficial outcomes are possible. In an "arena," there are only winners and losers.

These ideas have driven Trump's approach to numerous issues, most notably foreign economic policy. Whereas recent administrations broadly sought to deepen the international trade regime, Trump is taking a more mercantilist approach. He has instituted some protectionist measures—against Canadian airplanes and softwood lumber, for instance—and begun positioning the administration to do likewise in other cases.[29] The administration has been consistently hostile to the World Trade Organization and insisted on removing anti-protectionist language from statements issued by the Group of 20.[30] The president has flirted with imposing high tariffs on steel from countries such as China, South Korea, Japan, and Germany—potentially the opening shot in a trade war—and several times threatened to terminate agreements such as NAFTA and the U.S.-South Korea (KORUS) free trade pact.[31] Throughout, Trump has shown an abiding preoccupation with bilateral trade deficits, seemingly insisting that America run surpluses with all its major trade partners simultaneously.

Not all of these measures are unprecedented in recent history; previous administrations sometimes imposed targeted sanctions to generate leverage in ongoing trade negotiations. For Trump, however, these measures are all informed not by a desire to strengthen or deepen an international trade system that has delivered so much prosperity for America and the world, but by a desire to fortify U.S. economic sovereignty and freedom of action *at the expense* of that system. To drive home the point, Trump withdrew from two major international agreements of the Obama era—the Trans-Pacific Partnership (TPP) and the Paris climate change accords—because these deals allegedly privileged the interests of others to the detriment of American prosperity and economic independence. The president prioritizes, as he put it, the interests of "Pittsburgh, not Paris," and he often frames those interests as conflicting, not complementary.[32] Foreign policy is not missionary work, as Henry Kissinger might have said, and any president would agree that America must look out for itself. What Trump has done, however, is to pit his strident nationalism *against* the American internationalist tradition.

AMBIVALENT ALLY

In doing so, Trump is challenging a second tenet of U.S. statecraft—the idea that there is a group of like-minded nations to which America is bound by more than a transitory alignment of interests. Lord

Palmerston famously remarked that countries have no eternal allies and no perpetual enemies, only eternal and perpetual interests. Since World War II, however, Washington *has* had eternal and perpetual allies—the "free world" community of (mostly) democratic nations that constitute the core of U.S. alliance structures in Europe and the Asia-Pacific region.

These nations have been tied to America by what Acheson called "a common faith" in democratic values and a broadly shared vision of international order; those bonds have been reinforced by decades of institutionalized collaboration in addressing the world's greatest security challenges.[33] U.S. leadership of this bloc has therefore ensured that Washington can muster a vast *over*balance of power on key issues of global order.[34] Trump, however, has often behaved in ways that seem almost calculated to sunder the ties between America and its closest partners.

Trump has berated NATO allies for alleged free riding, telling Paris that America "wants our money back" and demanding that Berlin cough up "vast sums of money."[35] He has chastised allies at their most difficult moments—following terrorist attacks in the United Kingdom, for instance—and declared that he trusts Germany's Angela Merkel no more than Russia's Vladimir Putin.[36] In fact, Trump has more energetically criticized the European allies than the country—Russia—that most threatens them, and he initially pursued a rapprochement with Putin absent any apparent coordination with NATO. Not least, Trump has talked down America's defense obligations by deliberately refusing to endorse the U.S. commitment to NATO's Article 5 guarantee during his first European visit (in addition to behaving in a generally abrasive manner throughout that episode).[37] Trump's aides have insisted that this is all "tough love" designed to elicit better burden sharing, and the administration—led by Secretary of Defense Mattis—has continued NATO's Enhanced Forward Presence program and the European Reassurance Initiative.[38] Yet the decidedly unreassuring fact remains that America's president has shown more animosity than amity toward America's oldest partners.[39]

Other allies have suffered similar treatment. Amid a worsening nuclear crisis on the Korean peninsula, Trump has repeatedly attacked *South* Korea, by inveighing against the KORUS agreement, demanding that Seoul offer greater payments for U.S. protection, and lambasting President Moon Jae-in for "appeasement" of Pyongyang.[40] Trump has also taken a cavalier attitude toward the prospect of a war that could devastate South Korea, on grounds that "if thousands die, they're going to die over there."[41] Washington has historically taken pains to reassure allies of U.S. support and reliability; Trump seems to be doing just the opposite.

This conduct flows from two core premises of Trump's worldview: first, that U.S. alliances are bad deals because Washington bears the costs and risks while allies reap the benefits; and second, that America should therefore take a more transactional, ad hoc approach to relationships even with its closest friends. These ideas are seriously flawed; scholarship demonstrates that the cost-benefit assessment of U.S. alliances is strongly positive, even if some free riding does inevitably occur, and that the highly institutionalized nature of those alliances produces much of their utility.[42] Yet these concepts have nonetheless permeated official thinking. "Simply put, America will treat others as they treat us," wrote McMaster and Cohn. "Where our interests align, we are open to working together to solve problems and explore opportunities."[43]

This innocuous-sounding statement is, one imagines, actually quite ominous for America's allies. For it implies that special, enduring relationships are passé—that goodwill or past cooperation cannot be banked with Trump's America, and that transactional dealings on the basis of temporarily convergent interests are the new order of things. America has benefited greatly from leading a strategic community bound together with hoops of steel, but Trump often acts as though Washington desires no permanent friends.

POWER AND PURPOSE

Trump is simultaneously undermining the "free world" in another way, by diminishing America's role as global champion of democracy and human rights. The belief that America should act in this capacity—which has influenced policy for generations and been particularly strong since the 1970s—is not merely ideological zealotry.[44] Rather, America's commitment to promoting democratic ideals has helped it amass tremendous power with comparatively little global resistance; it has endowed Washington with moral appeal that neither Moscow nor any other authoritarian rival could match. Likewise, America's active support for human rights and political reform played a contributing—if hardly all-determining—role in the dramatic democratic gains of the 1970s and after, thereby rendering the international environment more favorable to U.S. ideals and interests alike.[45] Excessive evangelism can be dangerous, of course, and U.S. presidents have not always steered clear of that danger. On the whole, though, a foreign policy attentive to the spread of freedom has paid strategic dividends.

Trump, however, has distanced himself from this heritage. He has argued that America lacks the competence to promote democracy abroad, and framed "values" issues as distractions from the real business of advancing U.S. security and prosperity. He has also evinced undisguised admiration for authoritarians and claimed that a society as flawed as America has no business meddling in others' affairs.[46] The upshot has been a presidency in which issues of human rights and democracy are more marginalized than at any time in decades.

Start with something as mundane as body language: Trump's dealings with dictators have often been as comfortable and fluid as his dealings with democratic leaders have been awkward and confrontational.[47] The president has refused to "lecture" Arab regimes—or even authoritarian rivals Russia and China—on their political repression, but has eagerly chided Germany and other democratic allies for their supposed failings.[48] Likewise, Trump has praised backsliding democracies for blatantly illiberal behavior—commending Rodrigo Duterte for his campaign of extrajudicial executions in the Philippines, for instance, or congratulating Turkey's Recep Tayyip Erdogan for winning a rigged referendum in April 2017.[49] Secretary of State Rex Tillerson explicitly cast values issues as "obstacles" to American statecraft in early remarks to U.S. diplomats, while also downgrading human rights initiatives and attempting to excise democracy promotion from his department's mission statement.[50] And just as Trump has advocated a more transactional geopolitics, he has embraced a sort of amoral transactionalism—a willingness to cooperate with any regime, no matter how repressive—on issues such as counterterrorism. "We will make common cause with any nation that chooses to stand and fight alongside us against this global threat," Trump remarked.[51]

Admittedly, the president has criticized human rights abuses by adversaries Venezuela, Iran, Syria, and North Korea, but any broader or more systematic concern with these issues seems absent.[52] Trump's presidency thus features not just skepticism regarding military nation-building—an understandable sentiment in light of long wars in Iraq and Afghanistan—but a larger ambivalence about integrating American values into U.S. statecraft.

This shift has been piercingly clear at the intellectual level. In Warsaw in July 2017, Trump did emphasize the role of values in a supposed civilizational clash between the West and radical Islam. Yet in doing so he implied that democratic values were the peculiar province of the West, rather than being—as his predecessors often argued—universal in nature. Moreover, Trump delivered this speech in Poland, but declined to note the undeniable authoritarian resurgence in that country—or the role of Russia in undermining democratic institutions in Europe and beyond.[53] At the United Nations in September, Trump disclaimed any intention to promote

America's form of government abroad, and stressed the overriding importance of strengthening national sovereignty amid geopolitical turmoil. All states, he argued, must "respect . . . the rights of every other sovereign nation."[54] Sovereignty, of course, is the crutch on which authoritarians lean to shield internal repression from external scrutiny; promoting liberal values inevitably requires sometimes subordinating issues of sovereignty to concerns of legitimacy.[55] Trump's speech—and policies—were thus surely pleasing to autocrats in the Middle East and elsewhere. They were just as surely disconcerting to those who believe the prudent promotion of political freedom remains an important U.S. objective.

DISPENSABLE NATION

Trump's statecraft is likewise testing a fourth strategic tradition: America's reputation for taking the helm in confronting key global threats and challenges, and its corresponding ability to reap the benefits that accompany that role. Make no mistake: Washington has *always* demanded special privileges and deference from its partners, on issues from intra-alliance diplomacy to international monetary relations.[56] But America's friends have tolerated these impositions because Washington has also borne special burdens. The United States has, for decades, been the first responder running toward the fire; it has organized and catalyzed collective action in addressing critical global problems from rebuilding Europe and creating a flourishing international economy after World War II, to confronting aggressors such as Kim-Il Sung, Saddam Hussein, and the Islamic State. Under Trump, however, the "indispensable nation" is becoming less indispensable by absenting itself from the vanguard on several issues of global concern.

Globalization is under fire as protectionist pressures surge—yet the message conveyed by Trump's withdrawal from the TPP and attacks on other free trade agreements is that America is retreating from efforts to keep the international economy open. Climate change represents a stark long-term threat to international security and prosperity—but by making the United States one of just two nations to reject the Paris accords, Trump has effectively walked away from multilateral efforts to meet the challenge. Refugee flows constitute a grave humanitarian crisis and a growing peril to social and political stability in many countries—but Trump is reducing the already-small number of refugees America accepts and seeking mainly to insulate the country from the problem.[57]

To be sure, Trump has urged that the international community rally to confront the threats of greatest concern to his administration, namely terrorism, Iran, and North Korea.[58] But Trump has simultaneously exalted nationalism and sovereignty in a way that seems ill-suited to addressing key transnational challenges, and adopted a *sauve qui peut* manner on issues that matter greatly to many others.

This approach corresponds with Trump's belief that bearing the costs of global leadership is a losing proposition for America. But it risks rupturing the generations-old bargain between Washington and its partners, and so it is unsurprising that foreign leaders have registered their dismay and begun to adjust policies accordingly. Merkel publicly "deplored" the U.S. withdrawal from Paris; even before that, she had called for Europeans "truly . . . to take our fate into our own hands."[59] Major trade initiatives excluding the United States—a rump TPP and an European Union–Japan deal— have emerged or accelerated during the Trump era; the international community is proceeding on Paris without America.[60] And although one might hope that Japan, Germany, and other allies would fill the leadership vacuum created by Trump, more dangerous actors are also maneuvering to do so.

Since Trump's election, China's leaders have cast their nation as a responsible global leader on climate change, trade, and other issues, in unsubtle contrast to U.S. conduct. Beijing is playing a greater role, one foreign ministry official remarked, "because the original front-runners suddenly fell back and pushed China to the front."[61] It is remarkable to see China—an illiberal, mercantilist nation whose increasingly revisionist behavior represents perhaps the greatest long-term threat to the existing international order—styling itself as champion of the liberal, cooperative system America forged. Yet in such ways are global arrangements shifting under Trump.

UNSTEADY AS SHE GOES

Equally disruptive is a fifth aspect of Trump's presidency: his weakening of America's reputation for diplomatic steadiness and reliability. Past presidents occasionally embraced the idea of deliberately behaving erratically to discomfit adversaries, the classic—if mostly unsuccessful—example being Richard Nixon's "madman strategy."[62] By and large, though, U.S. officials have understood that superpowers lack the luxury of being fundamentally unpredictable.

After all, the international order ultimately rests on the credibility of U.S. commitments; America's leadership hinges on its partners believing that Washington will use its power responsibly and act as a source of global stability. This is precisely why international observers have been so dismayed by episodes such as the Iraq war, in which America has seemed to behave dangerously or erratically—in which "great power was being wielded without great responsibility."[63] Trump, however, has shown little interest in global order, and has often argued that unpredictability will enable America better to manipulate adversaries and allies alike.[64] And so, whether as a matter of strategy or his own combustible temperament, Trump has cultivated a reputation for just the volatility and unreliability that system leaders typically seek to avoid.

He has done so by abandoning the Paris accords and the TPP, two major multilateral agreements that Washington had spear-headed and prodded numerous others to join. "For America's friends and partners, ratifying [the TPP] is a litmus test for your credibility and seriousness of purpose," Prime Minister Lee Hsien Loong of Singapore had commented. Trump's abrupt withdrawal presumably indicated that Washington had failed that test.[65] Like-wise, by repeatedly threatening to end NAFTA and KORUS, Trump injected uncertainty and no little animosity into these key relation-ships. In the Middle East, U.S. officials touted the formation of an "Arab NATO" to confront Iran and other threats—only for Trump to abruptly shift course by reportedly encouraging Saudi Arabia and the United Arab Emirates (UAE) to provoke a showdown with one of America's key partners in the region, Qatar.[66] And, of course, Trump's evident ambivalence about NATO's Article 5 has unavoidably cast doubt on his commitment to upholding Ameri-ca's most fundamental international obligations.

Indeed, Trump's tenure has raised disturbing questions about whether the U.S. president—the most powerful person in the world—can be trusted to handle critical issues of war and peace. America now has a leader who has casually threatened to attack Venezuela.[67] Trump has also decertified and appeared bent on undermining the Iran nuclear deal that Washington and several other countries spent years negotiating—despite a near-consensus judgment that Iran is not violating the accord, despite fears that doing so could precipitate a new nuclear crisis in the Gulf, despite the availabil-ity of options that would allow Washington to better compete with Tehran without triggering such a crisis, and despite the fact that reneging on or simply weakening the Iran agreement would surely further decrease any possibility of successful nuclear diplo-macy with North Korea.[68] Regarding North Korea itself, Trump has seemingly sought to match Kim Jong Un in threat and bluster. He has engaged in personal name calling (ignoring his advisers' counsel not to do so), promised to "totally destroy" North Korea with "fire and fury," publicly contradicted aides who argue that diplomacy remains the preferred course, and casually drawn red lines—against the testing of a North Korean ICBM, for instance, or against even the issuance of further rhetorical threats from Pyongyang—that America probably cannot enforce at acceptable cost.[69]

In fairness, in the cases of both Iran and North Korea, Trump inherited serious problems—an imperfect Iran deal that did little to constrain Tehran's regional expansionism, a rapidly maturing North Korean ICBM capability—and his policies have so far been less radical than his rhetoric. It also remained possible, as of this writing, that Trump's break with the Iran deal might ultimately prove more symbolic than substantive.[70] And, of course, there remained the possibility—albeit a seemingly remote one—that Trump's confrontational posture might sufficiently discombobulate America's adversaries to produce a breakthrough on one or both of these issues.

What seemed likelier, however, was that Trump's behavior would have a series of more problematic outcomes: fostering global perceptions that America is now fueling rather than dampening instability, undermining confidence that he can steer the country—and the world—through the military and diplomatic crises that inevitably mark any presidency, and perhaps even leading the United States into a trap where it must choose between escalation and the humiliating acknowledgment that Trump has been making threats he cannot carry out. The former choice would risk potentially catastrophic consequences, particularly with respect to North Korea; the latter would seriously undercut the geopolitical credibility U.S. leaders have long sought to build and encourage greater uncertainty about which of America's many red lines are truly red. Senator Bob Corker, the Republican chairman of the Senate Foreign Relations Committee, has said he worries Trump might put the country "on the path to World War III"; one allied official has reportedly remarked that "Washington, D.C., is now the epicenter of instability in the world." Hyperbole aside, both statements are revealing commentaries on how America's hard-won reputation for steadiness and reliability is dissipating under Trump.[71]

THE COMPETENCE GAP

So are perceptions of basic U.S. competence in global affairs. "For much of the postwar period," writes Stephen Walt, "the United States benefitted greatly from an overarching aura of competence."[72] U.S. policy featured its share of bungles, the mishandled occupation of Iraq being the most prominent recent example. In general, however, the country that successfully oversaw the Marshall Plan, the reunification of Germany, and the Persian Gulf War, and that helped mitigate—if not entirely solve—seemingly intractable problems from the proliferation of nuclear weapons to Europe's propensity for catastrophic violence, earned a reputation for being able to handle itself capably. "The leadership, determination, diplomatic skill, and military efficiency displayed by the U.S. stunned many Japanese," American officials in Tokyo reported following the Persian Gulf War.[73] Unfortunately, Trump's presidency is encouraging the opposite conclusion, because persistent diplomatic incompetence has marked his tenure.

The first unforced error came before Trump was inaugurated, when he threatened to revisit America's longstanding one-China policy in order to pressure Beijing—only to retreat after Beijing responded by reportedly freezing the entire diplomatic relationship.[74] The administration then issued its executive order temporarily banning refugees and the issuance of visas to travelers from several Muslim-majority countries. That policy was seriously flawed in conception, because it seemed certain to undermine rather than advance the struggle against terrorism by alienating

Muslims overseas; it was equally flawed in execution, as a hasty drafting process produced chaos at American airports and made the affair a high-profile fiasco. (That flawed process also invited repeated judicial interventions that forced the redrafting of the measure, vindicating one prominent critic's description of the episode as "malevolence tempered by incompetence.")[75]

Then, in dealing with Syria in early 2017, the administration stumbled by abandoning—without gaining any apparent concession or, evidently, without anticipating the likely consequences—the "Assad must go" policy, a departure that may have encouraged Assad to resume large-scale chemical weapons attacks.[76] Whatever leverage the subsequent airstrikes against Assad's forces may have yielded was quickly dissipated by the administration's evident confusion regarding what strategic effects the strikes were meant to produce, whether they were a prelude to additional military action, and whether they represented a reversal of Trump's earlier positions on Syria and Assad.[77] It was unsurprising, then, that when Tillerson sought to capitalize on the airstrikes by demanding that Putin's Russia cease aiding Assad, he failed.[78]

There followed, the next month, Trump's apparent decision to give Saudi Arabia and the United Arab Emirates the green light to confront Qatar—a move that provoked a potentially dangerous crisis amid the counter-Islamic State campaign, put the president publicly at odds with top advisers (Mattis and Tillerson) working to defuse regional tensions, and had the predictable if undesired effect of pushing Doha closer to Tehran.[79] Throughout this period, moreover, Trump repeatedly disrupted his administration's own coercive diplomacy strategy toward North Korea—by haranguing Seoul as well as Pyongyang, giving conflicting signals about U.S. objectives, and issuing ultimatums that Pyongyang was certain to ignore. Finally, the president's apparently improvised threats of military action against Venezuela served mainly to blind-side regional critics of the Maduro government (and distract attention from that government's own failings) by raising the prospect of unwanted U.S. intervention.[80] Added to this list might be additional missteps, including rapid-fire shifts of rhetoric and policy on numerous issues, repeated instances in which Trump has publicly contradicted his secretary of state and other advisers, and even angry tweets about Iranian missile tests that did not occur.[81] Every administration stumbles, particularly during its first year, but Trump has done so repeatedly and across an array of issues.

The reasons for this are not difficult to discern. Trump took office with a long list of unrealistic policy proposals, meager knowledge about many essential issues, an ingrained tendency to improvise and resist systematic policy development, and—not least of all—an unstable and often volcanic personality. These characteristics virtually ensured habitual errors and were substantially reinforced by another factor—Trump's undisguised hostility toward a professional bureaucracy that has traditionally lent competence and expertise to American policy.

The president's erstwhile chief political adviser, Steve Bannon, promised early in 2017 that Trump would undertake the "deconstruction of the administrative state." Indeed, the president has frequently seemed to be at war with the executive branch.[82] He compared CIA officials to Nazis, proposed crippling budget cuts for the State Department, and left hundreds of high and mid-level national security posts unfilled through much of his first year. The White House repeatedly bypassed State and other departments on important policy issues; Trump publicly accused the "deep state" of subverting his presidency.[83] The upshot has been the striking demoralization and marginalization of America's policy professionals—a phenomenon that may well have negative long-term implications for U.S. security, and one that is undoubtedly impairing the administration's ability to conduct competent statecraft today.[84]

THE SOFT POWER DEFICIT

These issues all relate to a final way Trump is jeopardizing U.S. influence—by depleting America's formidable soft power. Soft power refers to several things: the esteem foreigners have for U.S. culture, politics, and society; the perception that America stands for something more than its own self-interest in global affairs; the use of non-coercive tools to accomplish geopolitical objectives.[85] The United States has derived enormous advantages from each of these elements of soft power. Goodwill generated by the Marshall Plan and Peace Corps were crucial weapons in the Cold War; the power of America's democratic ideals has given Washington veritable ideological fifth columns in countries around the world. Indeed, the imperatives of soft power have sometimes pushed U.S. leaders not simply to carry out good works abroad but to face the flaws of American society at home. Federal government support for desegregation in the 1950s and 1960s, for instance, was understood to be a critical campaign in the Cold War propaganda struggle.[86] Yet Trump—despite episodically invoking America's moral example—has impaired U.S. soft power in multiple ways.

The first way is by attacking the bureaucratic institutions through which America exerts nonmilitary influence. Trump's first budget submission coupled a largely symbolic elevation of U.S. hard power—a proposed 3 percent increase in military spending—with a painfully tangible denigration of U.S. soft power—roughly 30 percent cuts for the State Department and U.S. Agency for International Development. "This is a hard-power budget," said Mick Mulvaney, director of the White House Office of Management and Budget. "It is not a soft-power budget."[87] If enacted, this proposal would have severely constrained the civilian activities—diplomacy, development, humanitarian assistance—that Pentagon officials have deemed critical to sustaining any gains by U.S. forces in the counter–Islamic State campaign, Afghanistan, and other areas.[88]

Congressional leaders quickly made clear that Trump's budget was therefore "dead on arrival," but White House disdain for soft-power tools was nonetheless evident.[89]

Meanwhile, the president was tarnishing other aspects of American soft power. Trump's continuing appeals to bigotry and nativism; his evident dishonesty and his contempt for democratic norms; the pervasive conflicts of interest and appearance of official corruption; the entire spectacle of the Trump presidency: These issues were already diminishing global esteem for America, even *before* Trump refused forcefully and consistently to condemn white supremacists responsible for tragic violence in Charlottesville, Virginia, in August 2017.[90] Likewise, if Thomas Jefferson wrote of paying "a decent respect to the opinions of mankind," the administration's pursuit of policies widely deemed offensive overseas (such as its persistent efforts to restrict immigration and refugees from Muslim-majority countries), along with its flaunting of an America First agenda that, by definition, places everyone else second, hardly cast the country in a favorable global light. When the president's own defense secretary says America must "get the power of inspiration back," there is undoubtedly a soft-power problem at work.[91]

Global polling reveals the extent of that problem. Just months into Trump's presidency, America's global favorability rating had dropped from 64 percent to 49 percent. Large global majorities described Trump as "intolerant" (65 percent), "arrogant" (75 percent), and "dangerous" (62 percent); even the world's leading dictators—Xi Jinping and Vladimir Putin—had higher favorability ratings. "Confidence in the U.S. president's ability to do the right thing . . . has plummeted," the Pew Research Center noted, "back to levels . . . similar to or lower than" George W. Bush's ratings after the invasion of Iraq.[92] Hard power is certainly indispensable in the rougher geopolitical environment now merging. But one suspects the soft-power deficit Trump is creating will prove quite damaging.

THE UNEXCEPTIONAL SUPERPOWER

Change is not inherently a bad thing in U.S. foreign policy, and to assert that Trump's statecraft is flawed is not to claim that America's postwar performance has been flawless. Today, as at any point over the past seventy years, the United States must address difficult questions about how to optimize burden sharing within alliances, how hard to press for the spread of democracy and human rights, and myriad other issues. And today, perhaps more so than at any time in a quarter-century, America faces the challenge of fortifying its own power and the international system that power underwrites amid growing geopolitical dangers. It was not inconceivable, then, that a somewhat sharper, more nationalistic approach to grand strategy could have paid dividends in the current circumstances—that a foreign policy that deftly blended a clear commitment to preserving the postwar internationalist tradition, on the one hand, with a harder-edged approach to enhancing U.S. power and interests, on the other, might actually shore up America's geopolitical position and thus bolster the system itself. This was, in some measure, the approach taken by Richard Nixon in the late 1960s and early 1970s—another time of great strain on American power and the international system—and there was some hopeful speculation following the 2016 election that Trump might attempt a similar feat.[93]

Nearly a year into his presidency, unfortunately, Trump has shown few signs of any personal commitment to—or even an understanding of—the virtues of America's postwar grand strategy. He has shown fewer signs still of possessing the discipline and shrewdness necessary to productively interweave an appreciation of internationalism with his own stridently nationalist instincts. As a result, Trump has too often pursued policies that have undercut, rather than updated, the most productive characteristics of America's postwar engagement with the world. The president may have been thus far constrained from implementing an undiluted

America First agenda; he has not wholly demolished the pillars of U.S. foreign policy and the postwar international order. But even so, it is a profound mistake to think that the "axis of adults" has triumphed, or that Trump has been thoroughly mainstreamed, because the president has nonetheless been weakening those pillars in meaningful ways.[94]

Breathlessness should be avoided in considering the ramifications here: Trump's behavior will not cause U.S. power and leadership to collapse overnight, nor does his presidency spell imminent doom for the system America has done so much to create. America's core alliances are institutionalized enough that they will surely outlast Trump; the international trade system has sufficient resiliency and support from other leading members that it, too, will likely endure, even though it will come under far greater pressure. America's international image may recover once Trump departs the scene (as it did after George W. Bush's presidency), and the United States will retain, for many years to come, ample hard-power capacity to influence global affairs. The silver lining, then, is that America is simply too powerful, and the international order it has underwritten too robust and successful, for Trump to squander this strategic inheritance entirely. The dark cloud, however, is that Trump can still cause real damage over the course of a four-year or perhaps eight-year presidency—and the damage will only accumulate the longer this approach to foreign policy persists.

After all, actions have consequences, even for a superpower, and the consequences of Trump's actions are unlikely to be benign. If Washington no longer acts as leader of first resort in tackling transnational issues of global concern and global consequence, then those issues will become harder to resolve—and other countries will become less solicitous of American preferences in devising responses of their own. Just look, for instance, at how actors from China to the European Union have responded to Trump's presidency—and particularly his protectionist impulses—by accelerating the negotiation of regional and bilateral trade agreements that may well prove detrimental to the interests of American firms and exporters.[95] If the United States is seen as a less competent and reliable actor, then fewer countries will be willing to run political or geopolitical risks at American behest. In this regard, the memory of the TPP, the Paris accords, and perhaps—it increasingly seems—the Iran nuclear deal will be prominent in the minds of America's partners the next time U.S. officials try to organize some difficult multilateral endeavor.[96] Moreover, if the United States ceases to advocate—even by diplomatic as opposed to military methods—for democratic freedoms and human rights, those principles will surely be at a disadvantage in an increasingly competitive global ideological climate.

Likewise, if Trump tarnishes America's image as an estimable society that stands for universal values, he will diminish the moral prestige and unparalleled soft power that have traditionally facilitated the exercise of U.S. hard power. Not least, if Washington derides and devalues its alliances in favor of a more transactional geopolitics, it may unnerve and enervate the strategic community of democracies that has so greatly augmented American influence over the decades, precisely as that community confronts worsening dangers. Frontline allies and partners may begin to doubt the strength of American commitment; accordingly, they may begin considering geopolitical backup plans or even exploring greater accommodation with the countries—namely Russia and China—that threaten them. "Were I to be in office right now," Toomas Hendrik Ilves, the former president of Estonia, has said, "the concern would be trying to [determine] what is exactly the [U.S.] policy that we're going to have to count on."[97]

There are signs, in fact, that countries such as Vietnam are already recalibrating their statecraft in response to Trump's rise; strategic debates about how Australia should position itself between America and China are taking on new urgency.[98] To be sure, most American allies and partners will, for the time being, simply keep their heads down and hope that U.S. policy soon returns to normal. But geopolitical commitment is, in the end, a two-way street, and if America is persistently standoffish toward its friends then that attitude will eventually be repaid in kind. In the meantime, the general uncertainty, ambivalence, and volatility of U.S. policy will certainly not contribute to stability in an era of intensified global competition. On numerous dimensions, then, Trump's words and actions seem likely to exacerbate—rather than ameliorate—the geopolitical difficulties and strains of the present moment, and to weaken—rather than enhance—America's effectiveness in global affairs. And although there are many aspects of Trump's presidency that are encouraging this outcome, his zero-sum worldview has the potential to prove particularly damaging.

Great power can easily be seen as threatening, rather than reassuring, by other actors in the international system, and America still commands impressive hard-power advantages. It follows, then, that if Washington pursues policies rooted in the idea that international relations is a Hobbesian struggle for unilateral advantage, and that America can thrive only by being significantly less attentive to other countries' interests, it will corrode its reputation as a comparatively benign superpower and take on the image of a more selfish, even dangerous hegemon. That change, in turn, would undermine America's longstanding effort to foster a global environment in which a degree of restraint, stability, and cooperation prevails and incentives for unmitigated competition are dampened. Moreover, given that U.S. leadership has long rested on the consent of friends and partners who view that leadership as less threatening than the probable alternatives, this change would likely occasion more global objections and even diplomatic resistance to the use of U.S. power.[99] As the authors of the 1992 Defense Planning Guidance, perhaps the most candid statement of American geopolitical ambition, acknowledged, "We must account sufficiently for the interests of the advanced industrial nations to discourage them from challenging our leadership or seeking to overturn the established political and economic order."[100] The durability of U.S. preeminence, in other words, depends not just on how much power America possesses but on how benign and broadly beneficial that preeminence is seen to be.

Herein lies the greatest and furthest-reaching peril of Trump's foreign policy—that it will leave the American superpower looking far less exceptional than before. U.S. policy may never have been particularly altruistic or self-effacing, as analysts such as Andrew Bacevich have rightly noted.[101] What *has* made the United States exceptional compared to many other great powers is something subtler but nonetheless crucial—its willingness to occasionally de-emphasize the pursuit of near-term, unilateral advantage so as to attain the higher self-interest of fostering an environment in which the well-being of so many others contributes to the well-being of America itself. In the age of Trump, unfortunately, the United States seems to be embracing a darker calculus, as it distances itself from some of the key ideas and policies that have enabled the country's run as an ambitious and relatively effective superpower. Should this approach persist over time, one fears, that American superpower will appear more ordinary and perhaps menacing to much of the world—and it will be far less successful in advancing U.S. interests.

Notes

CHAPTER ONE

1. For works expressing some or all of these ideas, see Stephen Walt, "The End of the American Era," *National Interest* (November/December 2011), pp. 6–16; John Mearsheimer, "Imperial by Design," *National Interest* (January/February 2011), pp. 16–34; Michael Mandelbaum, *Mission Failure: America and the World in the Post–Cold War Era* (Oxford University Press, 2016); Christopher Layne, "The Unipolar Illusion Revisited: The Coming End of the United States' Unipolar Moment," *International Security* 31, no. 2 (Fall 2006), pp. 7–41.

2. This is a view with which I concurred in an earlier book: Hal Brands, *From Berlin to Baghdad: America's Search for Purpose in the Post–Cold War World* (University Press of Kentucky, 2008).

3. See Melvyn Leffler, *A Preponderance of Power: National Security, the Truman Administration, and the Cold War* (Stanford University Press, 1992); G. John Ikenberry, *Liberal Leviathan: The Origins, Crisis, and Transformation of the American World Order* (Princeton University Press, 2011).

4. On post–Cold War grand strategy, see Hal Brands, *Making the Unipolar Moment: U.S. Foreign Policy and the Rise of the Post–Cold War*

Order (Cornell University Press, 2016); Peter Feaver and Stephen Biddle, "Assessing Strategic Choices in the War on Terror," in *How 9/11 Changed Our Ways of War*, edited by James Burk (Stanford University Press, 2014), esp. pp. 29–31; Barton Gellman, "Keeping the U.S. First: Pentagon Would Preclude a Rival Superpower," *Washington Post*, March 11, 1992.

5. On the long legacy of democracy promotion in U.S. foreign policy, see Tony Smith, *America's Mission: The United States and the Worldwide Struggle for Democracy in the Twentieth Century* (Princeton University Press, 1994).

6. NSC-68, "United States Objectives and Programs for National Security," April 14, 1950 (http://fas.org/irp/offdocs/nsc-hst/nsc-68.htm).

7. Mearsheimer, "Imperial by Design"; also Barry Posen, "Pull Back: The Case for a Less Activist Foreign Policy," *Foreign Affairs* 92, no. 1 (January/February 2013), pp. 116–29.

8. See Donald Trump, "Trump on Foreign Policy," *National Interest*, April 27, 2016.

9. Francis Fukuyama, "The End of History?," *National Interest* (Summer 1989), pp. 3–18.

10. Kenneth Waltz, "The Emerging Structure of International Politics," *International Security* 18, no. 2 (Fall 1993), pp. 44–79; Christopher Layne, "The Unipolar Illusion: Why New Great Powers Will Rise," *International Security* 17, no. 4 (Spring 1993), pp. 5–51.

11. See John Mearsheimer, "Why We Will Soon Miss the Cold War," *The Atlantic* (August 1990), pp. 35–50.

12. See Freedom House, *Freedom in the World 2013: Democratic Breakthroughs in the Balance*, 2013, 29 (www.freedomhouse.org/sites/default/files/FIW%202013%20Booklet.pdf).

13. On this dynamic, see Zachary Selden, "Balancing against or Balancing With? The Spectrum of Alignment and the Endurance of American Hegemony," *Security Studies* 22, no. 3 (May 2013), pp. 330–63.

14. This is a point sometimes conceded by some leading critics of U.S. policy. See John Mearsheimer, "Why Is Europe Peaceful Today?," *European Political Science* 9, no. 3 (September 2010), pp. 387–97, esp. p. 388.

15. See Mark Kramer, "Neorealism, Nuclear Proliferation, and East-Central European Strategies," in *Unipolar Politics: Realism and State Strategies after the Cold War*, edited by Ethan Kapstein and Michael Mastanduno (Columbia University Press, 1999), pp. 385–463.

16. Ashton Carter and William Perry, *Preventive Defense: A New Security Strategy for America* (Brookings Institution Press, 2000), 3–7, 65–91.

17. Paul Miller, "American Grand Strategy and the Democratic Peace," *Survival* 52, no. 2 (March/April 2012), pp. 49–76; John Dumbrell, *Clinton's Foreign Policy: Between the Bushes, 1992–2000* (New York: Routledge, 2009), pp. 41–61.

18. Christopher Layne, "This Time It's Real: The End of Unipolarity and the *Pax Americana*," *International Studies Quarterly* 56, no. 1 (March 2012), pp. 203–13.

19. Unless otherwise noted, all figures on percentages of military spending used in this chapter are derived from the Stockholm International Peace Research Institute (SIPRI) Military Expenditure Database (www.sipri.org/databases/milex), last accessed May 2017. Unless otherwise noted, all figures on percentages of global GDP are derived from the Economic Research Service of the U.S. Department of Agriculture, "GDP Shares by Country and Region Historical" (www.ers/usda.gov/data-products /international-macroeconomic-data-set/aspx), last accessed January 2017. Figures on U.S. allies include the NATO countries plus U.S. treaty allies in Asia and Taiwan (thanks to its quasi-ally status, as enshrined in the Taiwan Relations Act). The data used here is also available in Hal Brands, *Dealing with Allies in Decline: Alliance Management and U.S. Strategy in an Era of Global Power Shifts* (Washington, D.C.: Center for Strategic and Budgetary Assessments, 2017).

20. For a good overview, see Walter Russell Mead, "The Return of Geopolitics: The Revenge of the Revisionist Powers," *Foreign Affairs* 93, no. 3 (May/June 2014), pp. 69–79.

21. For reports on North Korean ICBM capability, see Barbara Staff and Ryan Browne, "Intel Officials: North Korea 'Probably' Has Miniaturized Nuke," CNN, March 25, 2016.

22. Larry Diamond, "Facing Up to the Democratic Recession," *Journal of Democracy* 26, no. 1 (January 2015), pp. 141–55; William J. Dobson, *The Dictator's Learning Curve: Inside the Global Battle for Democracy* (New York: Doubleday, 2012).

23. See chapter 6 in this volume for a more thorough description of these challenges.

24. Paul Lewis, "Most Americans Think U.S. Should 'Mind Its Own Business' Abroad, Survey Finds," *Guardian*, December 3, 2013.

25. For these figures, see World Bank, "GDP (Current US$)" (http://data.worldbank.org/indicator/NY.GDP.MKTP.CD); "GDP per Capita, PPP (Current International $)" (http://data.worldbank.org/indicator/NY.GDP.PCAP.PP.CD); also the SIPRI military spending data referenced above. The World Bank information was accessed in August 2017.

26. Stephen Brooks and William Wohlforth, "The Rise and Fall of the Great Powers in the Twenty-First Century," *International Security* 40, no. 3 (Winter 2015/2016), pp. 7–53, esp. pp. 31–32.

27. Stephen Brooks and William Wohlforth, "The Once and Future Superpower: Why China Won't Overtake the United States," *Foreign Affairs* 95, no. 3 (May/June 2016), pp. 91–92.

28. See John Lewis Gaddis, *Strategies of Containment: A Critical Appraisal of American National Security Policy during the Cold War* (Oxford University Press, 2005), p. 393; World Bank, "Military Expenditure (% of GDP)" (http://data.worldbank.org/indicator/MS.MIL.XPND.GD.ZS?locations=US).

29. See Loren Thompson, "Pentagon Budget Headed below 3% of GDP as Warfighting Edge Wanes," *Forbes*, February 2, 2015; also David Ochmanek and others, *America's Security Deficit: Addressing the Imbalance between Strategy and Resources in a Turbulent World* (Santa Monica, Calif.: RAND Corporation, 2015).

30. Bernard Brodie, *Strategy in the Missile Age* (Santa Monica, Calif: RAND Corporation, 1959), p. 358.

31. See Hal Brands and Eric Edelman, *Avoiding a Strategy of Bluff: The Crisis of American Military Primacy* (Washington, D.C.: Center for Strategic and Budgetary Assessments, 2017).

32. Chicago Council on Global Affairs, *America Divided: Political Partisanship and U.S. Foreign Policy* (October 2015) (www.thechicagocouncil.org/sites/default/files/CCGA_PublicSurvey2015.pdf); also Craig Kafura and Dina Smeltz, "On Eve of NATO Summit, Majority of Americans Say Alliance Is Essential," Chicago Council on Global Affairs, July 6, 2016 (www.thechicagocouncil.org/publication/eve-nato-summit-majority-americans-say-alliance-essential).

33. See the subsequent discussion of American internationalism in chapter 4 of this volume.

34. A good example would be the recent efforts of Republican senator Ben Sasse of Nebraska. See "Ben Sasse: Automation, Not Free Trade or Immigration, Responsible for Economic Turmoil," *Washington Times*, May 26, 2016.

CHAPTER TWO

1. Major texts on offshore balancing include Christopher Layne, *The Peace of Illusions: American Grand Strategy from 1940 to the Present* (Cornell University Press, 2006), pp. 159–92; Christopher Layne, "From Preponderance to Offshore Balancing: America's Future Grand Strategy," *International Security* 22, no. 1 (Summer 1997), pp. 86–124; Christopher Layne, "Offshore Balancing Revisited," *Washington Quarterly* 25, no. 2 (Spring 2002), pp. 233–48; Benjamin Schwartz and Christopher Layne, "A New Grand Strategy," *The Atlantic* (January 2002), pp. 36–42; John Mearsheimer, "Imperial by Design," *National Interest* (January/February 2011), pp. 16–34; Eugene Gholz and Daryl Press, "Footprints in the Sand," *American Interest* (March/April 2010), pp. 59–67; Barry Posen, "The Case for Restraint," *American Interest* (November/December 2007), pp. 7–17; Barry Posen, "Pull Back: The Case for a Less Activist Foreign Policy," *Foreign Affairs* 92, no. 1 (January/February 2013), pp. 116–29; Barry Posen, *Restraint: A New Foundation for U.S. Grand Strategy* (Cornell University Press, 2014); Robert Pape, *Dying to Win: The Strategic Logic of Suicide Terrorism* (University of Chicago Press, 2005), esp. pp. 237–50; Stephen Walt, "The End of the American Era," *National Interest* (November/December 2011), pp. 6–16; Stephen Walt, "In the National Interest: A New Grand Strategy for U.S. Foreign Policy," *Boston Review* (February/March 2005) (http://bostonreview.net/BR30.1/walt .php); Stephen Walt, *Taming American Power: The Global Response to U.S. Primacy* (New York: Norton, 2006). See also the sources cited subsequently. While some of these scholars do not explicitly embrace the term "offshore balancing," and there is occasionally disagreement on specific policy prescriptions, in a broad sense all argue for the same basic grand strategy.

2. Stephen Walt, "Offshore Balancing: An Idea Whose Time Has Come," *Foreign Policy*, November 2, 2011; Christopher Layne, "The (Almost) Triumph of Offshore Balancing," *National Interest*, January 27, 2012; also Peter Beinart, "Obama's Foreign Policy Doctrine Finally Emerges with 'Offshore Balancing,'" *Daily Beast*, November 28, 2011.

3. For the most thorough exception, see Robert Art, *A Grand Strategy for America* (Cornell University Press, 2003), esp. pp. 176–77, 181–222. For a theater-specific critique, see James Holmes and Toshi Yoshihara, "An Ocean Too Far: Offshore Balancing in the Indian Ocean," *Asian Security* 8, no. 1 (March 2012), pp. 1–26. For a strong defense of the existing U.S. grand strategy, see Stephen Brooks and William Wohlforth,

America Abroad: The United States' Global Role in the 21st Century (Oxford University Press, 2016).

4. Walt, "In the National Interest."

5. U.S. leaders have also long considered Latin America a region of crucial interest to the United States, but Washington's dominance in that region has been so pronounced that a large-scale, permanent presence has generally not been necessary.

6. The quote and basic description of postwar strategy are from Stephen G. Brooks, G. John Ikenberry, and William Wohlforth, "Don't Come Home, America: The Case against Retrenchment," *International Security* 37, no. 3 (Winter 2012/13), pp. 7–51, esp. p. 11; also Robert Kagan, *The World America Made* (New York: Vintage, 2012), pp. 16–68.

7. On the origins, rationale, and effects of the United States' postwar strategy, see Melvyn Leffler, *A Preponderance of Power: National Security, the Truman Administration, and the Cold War* (Stanford University Press, 1992); G. John Ikenberry, *After Victory: Institutions, Strategic Restraint, and the Rebuilding of Order after Major Wars* (Princeton University Press, 2001), pp. 163–214; Michael Mandelbaum, *The Case for Goliath: How America Acts as the World's Government in the 21st Century* (New York: PublicAffairs, 2006).

8. See Eugene Gholz, Daryl Press, and Harvey Sapolsky, "Come Home, America: The Strategy of Restraint in the Face of Temptation," *International Security* 21, no. 4 (Spring 1997), pp. 5–48.

9. This description of offshore balancing's key tenets draws on the sources cited in note 1 above. Where it refers to specific arguments made by particular authors, those sources are cited directly.

10. See, for instance, Layne, *Peace of Illusions*; Walt, "End of the American Era"; Posen, *Restraint*.

11. See Stephen Walt, "A Bandwagon for Offshore Balancing?," *Foreign Policy*, December 1, 2011; Layne, *Peace of Illusions*, pp. 186–88; John Mearsheimer, "America Unhinged," *National Interest* (January/February 2014), pp. 22–23. As Peter Feaver has noted, however, one of the confusing aspects of offshore balancing is that its proponents applaud partnerships with dictators and other unsavory measures in theory, but sometimes criticize them when undertaken in practice. See Peter Feaver, "Not Even One Cheer for Offshore Balancing?," *Foreign Policy*, April 30, 2013.

12. See Schwartz and Layne, "A New Grand Strategy"; Mearsheimer, "Why the Ukraine Crisis Is the West's Fault: The Liberal Delusions That

Provoked Putin," *Foreign Affairs* 93, no. 5 (September/October 2014), pp. 77–89; Layne, "China's Challenge to U.S. Hegemony," *Current History* (January 2008), esp. pp. 17–18.

13. See particularly Posen, *Restraint*; Mearsheimer, "Imperial by Design"; Walt, "End of the American Era."

14. John Mearsheimer, *The Tragedy of Great Power Politics* (New York: Norton, 2003), pp. 234–66. But see also Galen Jackson, "The Offshore Balancing Thesis Reconsidered: Realism, the Balance of Power in Europe, and America's Decision for War in 1917," *Security Studies* 21, no. 3 (August 2012), pp. 455–89.

15. Following World War II and the Persian Gulf War, of course, the United States abandoned its offshore balancing approach in favor of onshore presence.

16. Posen, "Pull Back," pp. 118, 121–23; also Walt, "In the National Interest"; Walt, "End of the American Era." As noted, however, offshore balancers are sometimes ambiguous or conflicted regarding whether local powers will be able to contain China by themselves. See, for instance, John Mearsheimer and Stephen Walt, "The Case for Offshore Balancing: A Superior U.S. Grand Strategy," *Foreign Affairs* 95, no. 4 (July/August 2016), pp. 70–83; for a critique, see Hal Brands and Peter Feaver, "Risks of Retreat," *Foreign Affairs* 95, no. 6 (November/December 2016), pp. 164–69.

17. See, for instance, Mearsheimer, "Why the Ukraine Crisis Is the West's Fault"; Posen, *Restraint*, pp. 31–32; Layne, "China's Role in American Grand Strategy: Partner, Regional Power, or Great Power Rival?," in *The Asia-Pacific: A Region of Transitions*, edited by Jim Rolfe (Honolulu: Asia-Pacific Center for Security Studies, 2004), pp. 54–80.

18. See Pape, *Dying to Win*; Gholz and Press, "Footprints in the Sand," esp. pp. 63–65; Mearsheimer, "Imperial by Design," pp. 29–30; Harvey Sapolsky and others, "Restraining Order: For Strategic Modesty," *World Affairs* (Fall 2009), esp. pp. 88–91.

19. Layne, "Offshore Balancing Revisited," pp. 245–46.

20. Posen, "Pull Back," p. 127; Christopher Preble, *The Power Problem: How American Military Dominance Makes Us Less Safe, Less Prosperous, and Less Free* (Cornell University Press, 2009), esp. pp. 151–56.

21. For instance, Joshua Shifrinson and Sameer Lalwani, "It's a Common Misunderstanding: The Limited Threat to American Command of the Commons," in Christopher Preble and John Mueller, *A Dangerous World? Threat Perception and U.S. National Security* (Washington, D.C.: Cato Institute, 2014), esp. p. 241; Christopher Layne, "China

and America: Sleepwalking to War?," *National Interest* (May/June 2015), pp. 37–45.

22. Pape, *Dying to Win*, pp. 237–50; Gholz and Press, "Footprints in the Sand," pp. 63–65.

23. Mearsheimer, "Imperial by Design," pp. 30, 32–33.

24. How much money is not entirely clear. If one assumes that the United States would otherwise fight another Iraq War every decade, then the savings from offshore balancing would be fairly substantial. If one takes the 1990s or the period since 2011 as a baseline, the savings would be much smaller.

25. For Cold War figures, see John Lewis Gaddis, *Strategies of Containment: A Critical Appraisal of American National Security Policy during the Cold War* (Oxford University Press, 2005), p. 393. For post–Cold War figures, see data in World Bank, "Military Expenditure (% of GDP)" (http://data.worldbank.org/indicator/MS.MIL.XPND.GD.ZS?page=3).

26. See Hal Brands and Eric Edelman, *Avoiding a Strategy of Bluff: The Crisis of American Military Primacy* (Washington, D.C.: Center for Strategic and Budgetary Assessments, 2017), 25; Marilyn Ware Center for Security Studies, *To Rebuild America's Military* (Washington, D.C.: American Enterprise Institute, 2015), p. 2.

27. Evan Montgomery, "Contested Primacy in the Western Pacific: China's Rise and the Future of U.S. Power Projection," *International Security* 38, no. 4 (Spring 2014), esp. p. 121. For all their emphasis on retrenchment, Montgomery writes, offshore balancers believe that U.S. military power must "remain sufficient to prevent any nation from dominating its neighbors through aggression or coercion."

28. Elbridge Colby, *Grand Strategy: Contending Contemporary Analyst Views and Implications for the U.S. Navy* (Alexandria, Va.: Center for Naval Analyses, November 2011), p. 29.

29. Patrick Mills and others, "The Costs of Commitment: Cost Analysis of Overseas Air Force Basing," Working Paper (Santa Monica, Calif.: RAND Corporation, April 2012), pp. 13, 21–22. The CBO study is cited in the working paper.

30. Department of Defense, *Nuclear Posture Review Report* (U.S. Government Printing Office, 2010), p. 33.

31. On the costs of nuclear modernization, see William Broad and David Sanger, "U.S. Ramping Up Major Renewal in Nuclear Arms," *New York Times*, September 21, 2014.

32. Posen, *Restraint*, pp. 135–63, estimate on p. 135.

33. Compare Posen's analysis to the force structure and posture discussed in Holmes and Yoshihara, "An Ocean Too Far," pp. 15–19.

34. For 1999 military spending figures and more recent trends, see "Military Expenditure (% of GDP)" (http://data.worldbank.org/indicator /MS.MIL.XPND.GD.ZS?page=3).

35. For shares of federal budget, see Center on Budget and Policy Priorities, "Policy Basics: Where Do Our Federal Tax Dollars Go?," March 4, 2016 (www.cbpp.org/research/federal-budget/policy-basics -where-do-our-federal-tax-dollars-go). For annual deficits in recent years (and for out-year deficit and spending projections), see the various charts available at Office of Management and Budget, The White House, "Historical Tables" (www.whitehouse.gov/omb/budget/Historicals), last accessed August 2017. The range of US$484 billion to US$1.41 trillion reflects annual deficits from 2009 to 2016.

36. Pape, *Dying to Win*; Robert Pape and James K. Feldman, *Cutting the Fuse: The Explosion of Global Suicide Terrorism and How to Stop It* (University of Chicago Press, 2010).

37. Adam Gadahn quoted in Robert Art, "Selective Engagement in the Era of Austerity," in *America's Path: Grand Strategy for the Next Administration*, edited by Richard Fontaine and Kristin Lord (Washington, D.C.: Center for a New American Security, 2012), p. 27; also World Islamic Front Statement, "Jihad against Jews and Crusaders," February 23, 1998 (fas.org /irp/world/para/docs/980223-fatwa.htm); Daniel Byman, "A U.S. Military Withdrawal from the Greater Middle East: Impact on Terrorism," in Stephen van Evera and Sidharth Shah, *The Prudent Use of Power in American National Security Strategy* (Cambridge, Mass.: Tobin Project, 2010), esp. pp. 160–62, quoted on p. 164.

38. Colin Kahl and Marc Lynch, "U.S. Strategy after the Arab Uprisings: Toward Progressive Engagement," *Washington Quarterly* 36, no. 2 (2013), pp. 39–60, esp. p. 52.

39. Rick Brennan, "Withdrawal Symptoms: The Bungling of the Iraq Exit," *Foreign Affairs* 93, no. 6 (November/December 2014), pp. 34–35.

40. Art, *Grand Strategy for America*, pp. 201–2.

41. "Theory Talk #40—Kenneth Waltz," Theory Talks, June 3, 2011 (www.theory-talks.org/2011/06/theory-talk-40.html); Nuno Monteiro, "Unrest Assured: Why Unipolarity Is Not Peaceful," *International Security* 36, no. 3 (Winter 2011/2012), p. 26.

42. See M. Taylor Fravel and Evan Medeiros, "China's Search for Assured Retaliation: The Evolution of Chinese Nuclear Strategy and Force

Structure," *International Security* 35, no. 2 (Fall 2010), esp. pp. 58–61. For predictions that a U.S. invasion of Iraq would catalyze other states' nuclear programs, see National Intelligence Council, "Regional Consequences of Regime Change in Iraq," ICA-2003-03, in Senate Select Committee on Intelligence, *Report on Prewar Intelligence Assessments about Post-war Iraq* (U.S. Government Printing Office, 2007).

43. Scott D. Sagan, "Why Do States Build Nuclear Weapons? Three Models in Search of a Bomb," *International Security* 21, no. 3 (Winter 1996/97), pp. 54–86; Hal Brands and David Palkki, "Saddam, Israel, and the Bomb: Nuclear Alarmism Justified?," *International Security* 36, no. 1 (Summer 2011), pp. 133–66.

44. Department of Defense, *Nuclear Posture Review Report*, p. xii. This page of the report also notes that such arrangements limit proliferation by demonstrating to nonallies that "their pursuit of nuclear weapons will only undermine their goal of achieving military or political advantages."

45. See Francis Gavin, "Strategies of Inhibition: U.S. Grand Strategy and the Nuclear Revolution," *International Security* 40, no. 1 (Summer 2015), pp. 9–46; Gene Gerzhoy, "Alliance Coercion and Nuclear Restraint: How the United States Thwarted West Germany's Nuclear Ambitions," *International Security* 39, no. 4 (Spring 2015), pp. 91–129.

46. As Mark Kramer has written, the promise of NATO membership and robust security guarantees were key reasons why Poland and other former Warsaw Pact states did not seek nuclear weapons after the Cold War. Were those security guarantees weakened by U.S. retrenchment, the nuclear option might be revisited. See Mark Kramer, "Neorealism, Nuclear Proliferation, and East-Central European Strategies," in *Unipolar Politics: Realism and State Strategies after the Cold War*, edited by Ethan Kapstein and Michael Mastanduno (Columbia University Press, 1999), pp. 385–463.

47. Walt, "In the National Interest."

48. See Jordan Becker, "Offshore Balancing or Overbalancing? A Preliminary Empirical Analysis of the Effect of U.S. Troop Presence on the Political Behavior of Regional Partners," in *American Grand Strategy and the Future of Landpower*, edited by Joseph da Silva, Hugh Liebert, and Isaiah Wilson III (Carlisle, Penn.: Strategic Studies Institute, 2014), pp. 261–86; also Nigel Thalakada, *Unipolarity and the Evolution of America's Cold War Alliances* (New York: Palgrave Macmillan, 2012), esp. pp. 12–13, 17–19.

49. In 1963, for instance, the United States used its security leverage to help force Konrad Adenauer from office after he sought to reorient

West German policy away from Washington. See Marc Trachtenberg, *A Constructed Peace: The Making of the European Settlement, 1945–1963* (Princeton University Press, 1999), pp. 370–79. On economic negotiating advantages, see Francis Gavin, *Gold, Dollars, and Power: The Politics of International Monetary Relations, 1958–1971* (University of North Carolina Press, 2004), esp. pp. 30–31, 113–14, 165–66; Brooks, Ikenberry, and Wohlforth, "Don't Come Home, America," pp. 43–45.

50. John Mearsheimer, "Why Is Europe Peaceful Today?," *European Political Science* 9, no. 2 (September 2010), pp. 387–97, esp. p. 388. See also Trachtenberg, *Constructed Peace*; and Mandelbaum, *Case for Goliath*, esp. pp. 31–87.

51. Mearsheimer, "Why Is Europe Peaceful Today?," p. 389. Indeed, Mearsheimer has (somewhat ironically) long predicted increased instability following a U.S. withdrawal from key regions. See John Mearsheimer, "Back to the Future: Instability in Europe after the Cold War," *International Security* 15, no. 1 (Summer 1990), pp. 5–56.

52. Mandelbaum, *Case for Goliath*, pp. 88–140.

53. Mearsheimer, "Imperial by Design," p. 33. On the rise of Chinese power, see also Aaron Friedberg, *A Contest for Supremacy: China, America, and the Struggle for Mastery in Asia* (New York: Norton, 2011).

54. Robert Gilpin, *War and Change in World Politics* (Cambridge University Press, 1983), p. 194.

55. On this general tendency, see Zachary Selden, "Balancing Against or Balancing With? The Spectrum of Alignment and the Endurance of American Hegemony," *Security Studies* 22, no. 3 (May 2013), pp. 330–63, esp. pp. 331, 338–39. The Thai commentator is quoted here. It might be objected that offshore balancing cannot cause East Asian countries *simultaneously* to engage in nuclear proliferation while also causing them to "under-balance" or otherwise acquiesce in Chinese expansion. That may be true. But even if these scenarios are considered to be mutually exclusive, from a U.S. perspective either one would be quite damaging.

56. Bruce Jentleson, "Strategic Recalibration: Framework for a 21st-Century National Security Strategy," *Washington Quarterly* 37, no. 1 (2014), pp. 115–36.

CHAPTER THREE

1. Derek Chollet, *The Long Game: How Obama Defied Washington and Redefined America's Role in the World* (New York: PublicAffairs, 2016); Jeffrey Goldberg, "The Obama Doctrine," *The Atlantic* (April 2016).

2. Colin Dueck, *The Obama Doctrine: American Grand Strategy Today* (Oxford University Press, 2015), p. 2.

3. Leslie Gelb, "The Elusive Obama Doctrine," *National Interest* (September/October 2012), pp. 18–28.

4. David Remnick, "Going the Distance: On and Off the Road with Barack Obama," *New Yorker*, January 27, 2014.

5. Some ideas expressed in this chapter were first developed in Hal Brands, "Breaking Down Obama's Grand Strategy," *National Interest*, June 23, 2014.

6. Hal Brands, *What Good Is Grand Strategy? Power and Purpose in American Statecraft from Harry S. Truman to George W. Bush* (Cornell University Press, 2014).

7. Robert Kagan, *The World America Made* (New York: Vintage, 2012); Peter Feaver, "American Grand Strategy at the Crossroads: Leading from the Front, Leading from Behind, or Not Leading At All," in *America's Path: Grand Strategy for the Next Administration,* edited by Richard Fontaine and Kristin Lord (Washington, D.C.: Center for a New American Security, May 2012), pp. 59–70.

8. *National Security Strategy*, May 2010 (The White House, 2010); Department of Defense, *Sustaining U.S. Global Leadership: Priorities for 21st Century Defense*, January 2012 (http://archive.defense.gov/news /Defense_Strategic_Guidance.pdf); *National Security Strategy*, February 2015 (The White House, 2015).

9. The White House, Office of the Press Secretary, "Remarks by the President at the United States Military Academy Commencement Ceremony," May 28, 2014 (www.whitehouse.gov/the-press-office/2014/05/28 /remarks-president-united-states-military-academy-commencement -ceremony); Aaron Mehta, "Global Military Spending Grows for First Time since 2011," *Defense News*, April 4, 2016.

10. See David Sanger, *The Inheritance: The World Obama Confronts and the Challenges to American Power* (New York: Broadway Books, 2010).

11. David Rothkopf, *National Insecurity: American Leadership in an Age of Fear* (New York: PublicAffairs, 2014).

12. The White House, Office of the Press Secretary, "Remarks by the President to the United Nations General Assembly," September 23, 2010 (www.whitehouse.gov/the-press-office/2010/09/23/remarks-president -united-nations-general-assembly).

13. *Politico Playbook*, June 1, 2014; also Goldberg, "The Obama Doctrine."

14. Department of Defense, *Sustaining U.S. Global Leadership*. See also Jack Goldsmith and Matthew Waxman, "The Legal Legacy of Light-Footprint Warfare," *Washington Quarterly* 39, no. 2 (Summer 2016), pp. 7–21.

15. Military spending statistics are drawn from the Stockholm International Peace Research Institute (SIPRI) Military Expenditure Database (www.sipri.org/databases/milex), last accessed May 2017.

16. Department of Defense, *Sustaining U.S. Global Leadership*.

17. Eric Rosenbach and Aki Peritz, *Find, Fix, Finish: Inside the Counterterrorism Campaigns That Killed bin Laden and Devastated al-Qaeda* (New York: PublicAffairs, 2013).

18. Ivo Daalder and James Stavridis, "NATO's Victory in Libya: The Right Way to Run an Intervention," *Foreign Affairs* 91, no. 2 (March/April 2012), pp. 2–7.

19. The White House, Office of the Press Secretary, "Remarks by the President in Address to the Nation on the Way Forward in Afghanistan and Pakistan," December 1, 2009 (www.whitehouse.gov/the-press-office/remarks-president-address-nation-way-forward-afghanistan-and-pakistan).

20. Mark Mazzetti, Robert Worth, and Michael Gordon, "Obama's Uncertain Path amid Syria Bloodshed," *New York Times*, October 22, 2013.

21. Ashton Carter, "Statement on the Counter-ISIL Campaign before the Senate Armed Services Committee," December 9, 2015 (www.defense.gov/News/Speeches/Speech-View/Article/633510/statement-on-the-counter-isil-campaign-before-the-senate-armed-services-committ).

22. *National Security Strategy*, May 2010, esp. p. 11.

23. Chollet, *The Long Game*, pp. 65–68; Ian Traynor, "Barack Obama Launches Doctrine for Nuclear-Free World," *Guardian*, April 5, 2009.

24. Hillary Clinton, *Hard Choices* (New York: Simon and Schuster, 2014), pp. 201–10; Arthur Rachwald, "A 'Reset' of NATO-Russia Relations: Real or Imaginary?," *European Security* 20, no. 1 (April 2011), pp. 117–26. Although Obama canceled the particular missile defense system that was planned to be deployed in 2009, the administration soon announced plans to replace that system with another, scaled-down variant.

25. Obama quoted in Peter Baker, "Obama's Iran Deal Pits His Faith in Diplomacy against Skepticism," *New York Times*, July 15, 2015; also David Sanger, "Obama Order Sped Up Wave of Cyberattacks against Iran," *New York Times*, June 1, 2012; The White House, Office of the Press Secretary, "Fact Sheet: Sanctions Related to Iran," July 31, 2012.

26. On Bush and Asia, see Michael Green, "The Iraq War and Asia: Assessing the Legacy," *Washington Quarterly* 31, no. 2 (Spring 2008), pp. 181–200; Christopher Twomey, "Missing Strategic Opportunity in U.S. China Policy since 9/11: Grasping Tactical Success," *Asian Survey* 47, no. 4 (July/August 2007), pp. 536–59.

27. Hillary Clinton, "America's Pacific Century," *Foreign Policy* (November 2011), pp. 56–63.

28. Ashton Carter, "Remarks on the Next Phase of the U.S. Rebalance to the Asia-Pacific," April 6, 2015 (www.defense.gov/News/Speeches/Speech-View/Article/606660/remarks-on-the-next-phase-of-the-us-rebalance-to-the-asia-pacific-mccain-instit); Carter, "Remarks on America's Growing Security Network in the Asia-Pacific," April 8, 2016 (www.defense.gov/News/Speeches/Speech-View/Article/716909/remarks-on-americas-growing-security-network-in-the-asia-pacific-council-on-for).

29. "The Obama Administration's Pivot to Asia: A Conversation with Assistant Secretary Kurt Campbell," Foreign Policy Initiative, undated (www.foreignpolicyi.org/files/uploads/images/Asia%20Pivot.pdf); Kurt Campbell, *The Pivot: The Future of U.S. Statecraft in Asia* (New York: Grand Central Publishing, 2016).

30. Obama quoted in Steven Mufson and Joby Warrick, "Obama Urges World Action on Climate Change: No Nation 'Immune' to Global Warming," *Washington Post*, November 30, 2015.

31. Clinton, *Hard Choices*, pp. 207–8; Chollet, *The Long Game*, pp. 159–62; Ruth Deyermond, "Assessing the Reset: Successes and Failures in the Obama Administration's Russia Policy, 2009–12," *European Security* 22, no. 4 (2013), pp. 500–23.

32. "Partially" because Assad retained some undeclared weapons, some of which he later used in another major chemical weapons attack in early 2017. Colum Lynch and David Kenner, "U.S. and Europe Say Assad May Have Kept Some Chemical Weapons," *Foreign Policy*, August 23, 2016.

33. For balanced analysis, see Robert Jervis, "Turn Down for What? The Iran Deal and What Will Follow," *Foreign Affairs*, July 15, 2015.

34. F. Gregory Gause, "Why the Iran Deal Scares Saudi Arabia," *New Yorker*, November 26, 2013; Jay Solomon, *The Iran Wars: Spy Games, Bank Battles, and the Secret Deals That Reshaped the Middle East* (New York: Random House, 2016), esp. chaps. 9 and 10; Ilan Goldenberg, "A Strategy to Push Back Iran in Syria," Center for a New American Security, September 24, 2015.

35. David Kirkpatrick, "As U.S. and Iran Seek Nuclear Deal, Saudi Arabia Makes Its Own Moves," *New York Times*, March 30, 2015; Yaroslav Trofimov, "Like Israel, U.S. Arab Allies Fear Obama's Iran Nuclear Deal," *Wall Street Journal*, March 4, 2015; "Senior Saudi Prince Condemns Obama Comments on Middle East," Reuters, March 14, 2015; Paul Shinkman, "The Obama Doctrine: Let the Mideast Fights Its Own Wars," *U.S. News and World Report*, April 2, 2015.

36. Daniel Byman, "Why Drones Work: The Case for Washington's Weapon of Choice," *Foreign Affairs* 92, no. 4 (July/August 2013), pp. 32–43, esp. pp. 32–33.

37. Mark Thompson, "Former U.S. Commanders Take Increasingly Dim View of War on ISIS," *Time*, August 31, 2016; Jim Garamone, "Carter Convenes Counter-ISIL Coalition Meeting at Andrews," *DoD News*, July 20, 2016 (www.defense.gov/News/Article/Article/850782/carter-convenes -counter-isil-coalition-meeting-at-andrews); Brett McGurk, "Global Efforts to Defeat ISIS," testimony before Senate Foreign Relations Committee, June 28, 2016 (www.foreign.senate.gov/imo/media/doc/062816_McGurk _Testimony.pdf). See also Hal Brands and Peter Feaver, "Trump and Terrorism: U.S. Strategy after ISIS," *Foreign Affairs* 96, no. 2 (March/April 2017), pp. 28–36.

38. Sean Naylor, "Yemen Was Washington's Counter-Terrorism Success Story. Not Anymore," *Foreign Policy*, March 23, 2015; Mark Mazzetti and Scott Shane, "For U.S., Killing Terrorists Is a Means to an Elusive End," *New York Times*, June 16, 2015.

39. Daalder and Stavridis, "NATO's Victory in Libya."

40. Alan Kuperman, "Obama's Libya Debacle: How a Well-Meaning Intervention Ended in Failure," *Foreign Affairs* 94, no. 2 (March/April 2015), pp. 66–77.

41. Bob Woodward, *Obama's Wars* (New York: Simon and Schuster, 2010).

42. Michael Gordon and Bernard Trainor, *The Endgame: The Inside Story of the Struggle for Iraq, from George W. Bush to Barack Obama* (New York: Pantheon Books, 2012), pp. 560–684; Rick Brennan, "Withdrawal

Symptoms: The Bungling of the Iraq Exit," *Foreign Affairs* 93, no. 6 (November/December 2014), pp. 25–36; Leon Panetta, "How the White House Misplayed Iraqi Troop Talks," *Time*, October 1, 2014.

43. For one interpretation, see Hal Brands and Peter Feaver, "Was the Rise of ISIS Inevitable?," *Survival* 59, no. 3 (May/June 2017), pp. 18–30.

44. For such a critique, see Simon Shuster, "A Failed Russia 'Reset' Haunts Obama in Europe," *Time*, June 3, 2014.

45. Ashton Carter, "Remarks at EUCOM Change of Command," U.S. Department of Defense, May 3, 2016 (www.defense.gov/News /Speeches/Speech-View/Article/750946/remarks-at-eucom-change-of -command); Robin Emmott and Phil Stewart, "NATO to Send Troops to Deter Russia, Putin Orders Snap Checks," Reuters, June 14, 2016; Alec Luhn, "Russia's GDP Falls 3.7% as Sanctions and Low Oil Price Take Effect," *Guardian*, January 25, 2016.

46. David Shlapak and Michael Johnson, *Reinforcing Deterrence on NATO's Eastern Flank: Wargaming the Defense of the Baltics*, RAND Corporation, January 2016 (www.rand.org/pubs/research_reports/RR1253.html).

47. On these activities, see Alexander Lanoszka, "Russian Hybrid Warfare and Extended Deterrence in Eastern Europe," *International Affairs* 92, no. 1 (January 2016), pp. 175–95.

48. Mark Landler and David Sanger, "Obama Says He Told Putin: 'Cut It Out' on Hacking," *New York Times*, December 16, 2016.

49. Department of Defense, *Sustaining U.S. Global Leadership*, esp. p. 3.

50. On these initiatives, see "Remarks by Secretary Carter and Q&A at the Shangri-La Dialogue, Singapore," U.S. Department of Defense, June 5, 2016 (www.defense.gov/News/Transcripts/Transcript-View/Article /791472/remarks-by-secretary-carter-and-qa-at-the-shangri-la-dialogue -singapore); Department of Defense, *Asia-Pacific Maritime Security Strategy*, 2015 (www.defense.gov/Portals/1/Documents/pubs/NDAA%20A-P _Maritime_SecuritY_Strategy-08142015-1300-FINALFORMAT.PDF).

51. Ely Ratner, "The False Cry of the Pivot Deniers," *Foreign Policy*, April 25, 2014.

52. Department of Defense, *Annual Report to Congress: Military and Security Developments Involving the People's Republic of China 2016* (www .defense.gov/Portals/1/Documents/pubs/2016%20China%20Military%20 Power%20Report.pdf).

53. U.S. diplomatic missteps may have contributed to this problem. In 2009, the Obama administration pledged to respect China's "core in-

terests," and in 2013, it broadly affirmed Beijing's concept of a "new model of great power relations." These innocuous-sounding phrases were often used by Chinese officials to connote a situation in which Washington would be more deferential to Chinese prerogatives, and so it is possible that their endorsement was interpreted as giving Beijing greater license to push those prerogatives more assertively.

54. Eric Heginbotham and others, *The U.S.-China Military Scorecard: Forces, Geography, and the Evolving Balance of Power, 1996–2017* (Santa Monica, Calif.: RAND Corporation, 2015), esp. p. xxxi.

55. On Chinese gray-zone activities, see Andrew Erickson and Conor Kennedy, "China's Maritime Militia: What It Is and How to Deal with It," *Foreign Affairs*, June 23, 2016.

56. *National Security Strategy*, February 2015; The White House, Office of the Press Secretary, "Remarks by the President at the United States Military Academy Commencement Ceremony," May 28, 2014.

57. Condoleezza Rice, *No Higher Honor: A Memoir of My Years in Washington* (New York: Crown, 2011), 568.

58. David Rohde and Warren Strobel, "The Micromanager in Chief: How Syria Overwhelmed an Overcentralized White House," *The Atlantic*, October 9, 2014; Adam Entous, "Obama Blocked Rebel Arms," *Wall Street Journal*, February 12, 2013.

59. Anne Applebaum, "The Disastrous Non-intervention in Syria," *Washington Post*, August 29, 2016.

60. Mitchel Wallerstein, "The Price of Inattention: A Survivable North Korean Nuclear Threat?," *Washington Quarterly* 38, no. 3 (Fall 2015), pp. 21–35; Institute for Economics and Peace, *Global Terrorism Index 2015* (economicsandpeace.org/wp-content/uploads/2015/11/Global-Terrorism -Index-2015.pdf).

61. Robert Kaplan, *The Revenge of Geography* (New York: Random House, 2012), p. 20. As Kaplan writes, "Realism is not exciting. It is respected only after the seeming lack of it has made a situation demonstrably worse."

CHAPTER FOUR

1. Alastair Jamieson and Richie Duchon, "World Reacts to Trump's Election Win: 'It's the End of an Era,'" *NBC News*, November 9, 2016.

2. Robert Kagan, "Trump Marks the End of America as the World's 'Indispensable Nation,'" *Financial Times*, November 19, 2016.

3. Quoted in George Herring, *From Colony to Superpower: U.S. Foreign Relations since 1776* (Oxford University Press, 2008), p. 598.

4. Quoted in Hal Brands, *Making the Unipolar Moment: U.S. Foreign Policy and the Rise of the Post–Cold War Order* (Cornell University Press, 2016), p. 15; also Robert Kagan, *The World America Made* (New York: Vintage, 2012); Melvyn Leffler, *A Preponderance of Power: National Security, the Truman Administration, and the Cold War* (Stanford University Press, 1992).

5. See Kagan, *The World America Made*; also Robert Johnson, *Congress and the Cold War* (Cambridge University Press, 2006).

6. Daniel Deudney and G. John Ikenberry, "Unraveling America the Great," *American Interest* (May/June 2016), p. 11.

7. Cassandra Vinograd, "Donald Trump Remarks on NATO Trigger Alarm Bells in Europe," *NBC News*, July 21, 2016.

8. Stephanie Condon, "Donald Trump: Japan, South Korea Might Need Nuclear Weapons," *CBS News*, March 29, 2016.

9. Maggie Severns, "Trump Pins NAFTA, 'Worst Trade Deal Ever,' on Clinton," *Politico*, September 26, 2016; Christiano Lima, "Trump Calls Trade Deal 'a Rape of Our Country,'" *Politico*, June 28, 2016.

10. Eugene Scott, "Trump: My Muslim Friends Don't Support My Immigration Ban," CNN, December 13, 2015; Miriam Valverde, "How Trump Plans to Build, and Pay for, a Wall along U.S.-Mexico Border," *Politifact*, July 26, 2016 (www.politifact.com/truth-o-meter/article/2016/jul/26/how-trump-plans-build-wall-along-us-mexico-border/).

11. See Thomas Carothers, "Prospects for U.S. Democracy Promotion under Trump," Carnegie Endowment for International Peace, January 5, 2017 (http://carnegieendowment.org/2017/01/05/prospects-for-u.s.-democracy-promotion-under-trump-pub-66588); Anna Nemtsova, "Why Russia Is Rejoicing over Trump," *Politico*, July 20, 2016.

12. Chris Cillizza, "Donald Trump Gave a Doozy of a Speech at the National Prayer Breakfast," *Washington Post*, February 2, 2017.

13. See, for instance, Jeet Heer, "Donald Trump's Foreign Policy Revolution," *New Republic*, March 25, 2016.

14. "Read Donald Trump's Speech on Trade," *Time*, June 28, 2016.

15. Julian Borger, "Trump's Plan to Seize Iraq's Oil: 'It's Not Stealing, We're Reimbursing Ourselves,'" *Guardian*, September 21, 2016.

16. See Clinton's comments in Zack Beauchamp, "Hillary Clinton Just Made Her Best Case against Donald Trump," *Vox*, June 2, 2016.

17. Carol Morello, "Former GOP National Security Officials: Trump Would Be 'Most Reckless' American President in History," *Washington Post*, August 8, 2016.

18. See Trump's tweet from January 24, 2016 (https://twitter.com/real donaldtrump/status/691276412666261504?lang=en); also Pamela Engel, "Donald Trump: 'I Would Bomb the S— out of' ISIS," *Business Insider*, November 13, 2015; Yeganeh Torbati, "Trump Election Puts Iran Nuclear Deal on Shaky Ground," Reuters, November 9, 2016.

19. On Jacksonianism, see Walter Russell Mead, "The Jacksonian Tradition and American Foreign Policy," *National Interest* (Winter 1999/2000), pp. 5–29.

20. See "Open Letter on Donald Trump from GOP National Security Leaders," *War on the Rocks*, March 2, 2016; Morello, "Former GOP National Security Officials."

21. See David Wright, "Poll: Trump, Clinton Score Historic Unfavorable Ratings," CNN, March 22, 2016.

22. "Clinton Maintains Double-Digit Lead over Trump," *PRRI*, October 19, 2016 (www.prri.org/research/prri-brookings-oct-19-poll-politics -election-clinton-double-digit-lead-trump/); Nate Silver, "The Comey Letter Probably Cost Clinton the Election," *FiveThirtyEight*, May 3, 2017.

23. James Goldgeier, "The Next Clinton Doctrine," *National Interest* (May/June 2015), pp. 22–30.

24. Allan Smith, "Poll: Majority of Americans Support the Trans-Pacific Partnership and Globalization," *Business Insider*, September 7, 2016.

25. Ibid.

26. Pew Research Center, "Public Sees U.S. Power Declining as Support for Global Engagement Slips," December 3, 2013 (www.people-press .org/2013/12/03/public-sees-u-s-power-declining-as-support-for-global -engagement-slips/).

27. Bruce Drake and Carroll Doherty, "Key Findings on How Americans View the U.S. Role in the World," Pew Research Center, May 5, 2016 (www.pewresearch.org/fact-tank/2016/05/05/key-findings-on-how -americans-view-the-u-s-role-in-the-world/); Chicago Council on Global Affairs, *America in the Age of Uncertainty: American Public Opinion and U.S. Foreign Policy* (Chicago: Chicago Council on Global Affairs, 2016), p. 29.

28. Pew Research Center, "Public Uncertain, Divided over America's Place in the World," May 5, 2016 (www.people-press.org/2016/05/05/public -uncertain-divided-over-americas-place-in-the-world/).

29. Craig Kafura, "Public Opinion and the U.S.-Japan Alliance at the Outset of the Trump Administration," Chicago Council on Global Affairs, February 8, 2017 (www.thechicagocouncil.org/publication/public -opinion-and-us-japan-alliance-outset-trump-administration).

30. Pew Research Center, "Public Uncertain, Divided"; also Carrie Dann, "Not Worth It: Huge Majority Regret Iraq War, Exclusive Poll Shows," *NBC News*, June 24, 2014; Gallup, "More Americans Now View Afghanistan War as a Mistake," February 19, 2014 (www.gallup.com/poll /167471/americans-view-afghanistan-war-mistake.aspx).

31. Pew Research Center, "Public Uncertain, Divided," pt. 6, "NATO, U.S. Allies, the EU and UN," May 5, 2016 (www.people-press.org/2016/05 /05/6-nato-u-s-allies-the-eu-and-un/); Dina Smeltz, Craig Kafura, and Kelhan Martin, "Growing Support in U.S. for Some Climate Change Action," Chicago Council on Global Affairs, November 21, 2016 (www.the chicagocouncil.org/publication/growing-support-us-some-climate-change -action).

32. Drake and Doherty, "Key Findings on How Americans View the U.S. Role in the World."

33. Ibid.

34. Chicago Council on Global Affairs, *America in the Age of Uncertainty*, p. 26.

35. Ibid., p. 32.

36. Theodore Schleifer, "Graham Ridicules 'Mucho Sad' Border Tax Proposal," CNN, January 26, 2017; Ryan Kilpatrick, "Republican Senators Warn Trump against Withdrawing from NAFTA," *Time*, April 26, 2017.

37. Austin Wright, "McCain Looks to Assure Australia after Trump Call," *Politico*, February 2, 2017.

38. Josh Rogin, "Congress Wants Trump to Pressure North Korea, Rather Than U.S. Allies," *Washington Post*, May 1, 2017.

39. See, for instance, Trevor Thrall and John Glaser, "America First? Not So Fast! What We've Learned from 100 Days of Trump Foreign Policy," *War on the Rocks*, April 27, 2017.

40. See, for instance, Walter Isaacson and Evan Thomas, *The Wise Men: Six Friends and the World They Made* (New York: Simon and Schuster, 1986); also Ted Galen Carpenter, "Trump Chases the NATO Burden Sharing Unicorn," *National Interest*, May 4, 2016.

41. See James A. Johnson, "The New Generation of Isolationists," *Foreign Affairs* 49, no. 1 (October 1970), pp. 136–46; Connally quoted in

Francis Gavin, *Gold, Dollars, and Power: The Politics of International Monetary Relations, 1958–1971* (University of North Carolina Press, 2004), p. 194.

42. George Herring, *America's Longest War: The United States and Vietnam, 1950–1975* (New York: McGraw-Hill, 1985), p. 274.

43. See Leffler, *Preponderance of Power*; Robert Kagan, "Superpowers Don't Get to Retire," *New Republic*, May 26, 2014.

44. Quoted in D. Quentin Miller, *John Updike and the Cold War: Drawing the Iron Curtain* (University of Missouri Press, 2001), p. 164.

45. Tim Alberta, " 'The Ideas Made It, but I Didn't,' " *Politico Magazine* (May/June 2017).

46. Stephen Brooks and William Wohlforth, *America Abroad: The United States' Global Role in the 21st Century* (Oxford University Press, 2016).

47. Thom Shanker, "Defense Secretary Warns NATO of 'Dim' Future," *New York Times*, June 10, 2011.

48. "Obama's Weekly Address: Time to 'Focus on Nation-Building Here at Home,' " *ABC News*, May 5, 2012.

49. Bruce Drake, "Americans Put Low Priority on Promoting Democracy Abroad," Pew Research Center, December 4, 2013 (www.pew research.org/fact-tank/2013/12/04/americans-put-low-priority-on-promot ing-democracy-abroad/).

50. "Open Letter on Donald Trump."

51. Tim Nichols, *The Death of Expertise: The Campaign against Established Knowledge and Why It Matters* (Oxford University Press, 2017).

52. Daniel Bessner and Stephen Wertheim, "Democratizing U.S. Foreign Policy: Bringing Experts and the Public Back Together," *Foreign Affairs*, April 5, 2017; Ivan Eland, "In the 2016 Campaign, the U.S. Foreign Policy Establishment Is Not Doing Well Either," *Huffington Post,* February 1, 2016.

53. Deudney and Ikenberry, "Unraveling America the Great"; also John Gerard Ruggie, "International Regimes, Transactions, and Change: Embedded Liberalism in the Postwar Economic Order," *International Organization* 36, no. 2 (Spring 1982), pp. 397–415.

54. Jeff Colgan and Robert Keohane, "The Liberal Order Is Rigged," *Foreign Affairs* 96, no. 3 (May/June 2017), p. 38.

55. Nicholas Eberstadt, "Our Miserable 21st Century," *Commentary*, February 15, 2017.

56. See, variously, Barry Bluestone and Bennett Harrison, *The Deindustrialization of America: Plant Closings, Community Abandonment, and the Dismantling of Basic Industry* (New York: Basic Books, 1992); Jefferson Cowie, *Stayin' Alive: The 1970s and the Last Days of the Working Class* (New York: New Press, 2012); Judith Stein, *Pivotal Decade: How the United States Traded Factories for Finance in the Seventies* (Yale University Press, 2011).

57. Dani Rodrik, "Has Globalization Gone Too Far?," *California Management Review* 39, no. 3 (Spring 1997), pp. 29–53.

58. Colgan and Keohane, "The Liberal Order Is Rigged."

59. Daron Acemoglu and others, "Import Competition and the Great U.S. Employment Sag of the 2000s," *Journal of Labor Economics* 34, no. S1 (January 2016), pp. S141–98; also David Autor, David Dorn, and Gordon Hanson, "The China Shock: Learning from Labor Market Adjustment to Large Changes in Trade," Working Paper 21906 (Cambridge, Mass.: National Bureau of Economic Research, 2016) (www.nber.org/papers/w21906.pdf).

60. Pew Research Center, "Public Uncertain, Divided."

61. Drake and Doherty, "Key Findings on How Americans View the U.S. Role in the World"; Jordan Weissmann, "Did Donald Trump Win the Election Because of Trade? A New Study Suggests It Helped," *Slate*, December 2, 2016; Autor, Dorn, and Hanson, "The China Shock."

62. James Surowiecki, "Economic Populism at the Primaries," *New Yorker*, February 22, 2016.

63. Pew Research Center, "Public Sees U.S. Power Declining"; Drake and Doherty, "Key Findings on How Americans View the U.S. Role in the World."

64. For example, Gabor Steingart, "A Superpower in Decline: America's Middle Class Has Become Globalization's Loser," *Der Spiegel*, October 24, 2006; Peter Trubowitz, "Trump's Victory Will Fuel the Growing Backlash against Globalization in the West," London School of Economics, November 28, 2016 (http://blogs.lse.ac.uk/usappblog/2016/11/28/trumps-victory-will-fuel-the-growing-backlash-against-globalization-in-the-west/).

65. See George Borjas, "Immigration and the American Worker: A Review of the Academic Literature," Center for Immigration Studies, April 2013 (www.hks.harvard.edu/fs/gborjas/publications/popular/CIS 2013.pdf); Walter Russell Mead, "The Jacksonian Revolt," *Foreign Affairs* 96, no. 2 (March/April 2017), pp. 4–6.

66. Mead, "The Jacksonian Revolt," p. 4.

67. Chicago Council on Global Affairs, *America in the Age of Uncertainty*, p. 2; Drake and Doherty, "Key Findings on How Americans View the U.S. Role in the World"; Pew Research Center, "Beyond Distrust: How Americans View Their Government," November 23, 2015 (www.people -press.org/2015/11/23/beyond-distrust-how-americans-view-their-gov ernment/).

68. Daniel Cox, Rachel Lienesch, and Robert Jones, "Beyond Economics: Fears of Cultural Displacement Pushed the White Working Class to Trump," *PRRI*, May 9, 2017 (www.prri.org/research/white-working-class -attitudes-economy-trade-immigration-election-donald-trump/).

69. Bret Stephens, *America in Retreat: The New Isolationism and the Coming Global Disorder* (New York: Penguin, 2015); Robert Kagan, "The Twilight of the Liberal World Order," Brookings Institution, January 24, 2017 (www.brookings.edu/research/the-twilight-of-the-liberal-world -order/).

70. Pew Research Center, "Public Uncertain, Divided."

71. Charles Krauthammer, "Beyond the Cold War," *New Republic*, December 19, 1988, pp. 14–19.

72. See, for instance, Daniel Sargent, *A Superpower Transformed: The Remaking of American Foreign Relations in the 1970s* (Oxford University Press, 2014).

CHAPTER FIVE

1. This section draws particularly on G. John Ikenberry, *Liberal Leviathan: The Origins, Crisis, and Transformation of the American World Order* (Princeton University Press, 2011).

2. See, variously, Stephen Brooks and William Wohlforth, *America Abroad: The United States' Global Role in the 21st Century* (Oxford University Press, 2016); Robert Gilpin, *The Challenge of Global Capitalism: The World Economy in the 21st Century* (Princeton University Press, 2000); Douglas Irwin, *Free Trade under Fire* (Princeton University Press, 2000); Alfred Eckes and Thomas Zeiler, *Globalization and the American Century* (Cambridge University Press, 2003).

3. See James Goldgeier, "The Next Clinton Doctrine," *National Interest* (May/June 2015), pp. 22–30.

4. See Pew Research Center, "Public Uncertain, Divided over America's Place in the World," May 5, 2016 (www.people-press.org/2016 /05/05/6-nato-u-s-allies-the-eu-and-un/); Allan Smith, "Poll: Majority of

Americans Support the Trans-Pacific Partnership and Globalization," *Business Insider,* September 7, 2016.

5. See Irwin, *Free Trade under Fire;* also Pew Research Center, "Public Uncertain, Divided."

6. Thom Shanker, "Blunt U.S. Warning Reveals Deep Strains in NATO," *New York Times,* June 10, 2011.

7. Paul Lewis, "Most Americans Think U.S. Should 'Mind Its Own Business' Abroad, Survey Finds," *Guardian,* December 3, 2013.

8. Bruce Drake and Carroll Doherty, "Key Findings on How Americans View the U.S. Role in the World," Pew Research Center, May 5, 2016 (www.pewresearch.org/fact-tank/2016/05/05/key-findings-on-how-americans-view-the-u-s-role-in-the-world/).

9. James Surowiecki, "Economic Populism at the Primaries," *New Yorker,* February 22, 2016.

10. Cristiano Lima, "Trump Calls Trade Deal 'a Rape of Our Country,'" *Politico,* June 28, 2016.

11. Aaron Eglitis, Toluse Olorunnipa, and Andy Sharp, "Trump's NATO Skepticism Raises Alarm for Allies near Russia," Bloomberg, July 21, 2016.

12. Donald Trump, "Trump on Foreign Policy," *National Interest,* April 27, 2016; also Thomas Wright, "Trump's 19th Century Foreign Policy," *Politico,* January 20, 2016.

13. The discussion in this section expands on Hal Brands, *American Grand Strategy and the Liberal Order: Continuity, Change, and Options for the Future* (Santa Monica, Calif.: RAND Corporation, 2016), pp. 22–25.

14. "Inaugural Address: Trump's Full Speech," CNN, January 21, 2017.

15. Ibid.

16. This idea was sometimes proposed in the years since 9/11. See, for instance, Thomas Friedman, "Dancing Alone," *New York Times,* May 13, 2014.

17. The term is used by Barry Posen, "Pull Back: The Case for a Less Activist Foreign Policy," *Foreign Affairs* 92, no. 1 (January/February 2013), pp. 116–29.

18. Phrase borrowed from Colin Kahl and Hal Brands, "Trump's Grand Strategic Train Wreck," *Foreign Policy,* January 31, 2017.

19. Trump broached this idea in 2016. See Stephanie Condon, "Donald Trump: Japan, South Korea Might Need Nuclear Weapons," *CBS News,* March 29, 2016. He subsequently denied having raised the idea.

20. During the campaign, Trump often expressed ideas similar to this pillar and the previous pillar of Fortress America. See Thomas Carothers, "Prospects for U.S. Democracy Promotion under Trump," Carnegie Endowment for International Peace, January 5, 2017 (http://carnegieendow ment.org/2017/01/05/prospects-for-u.s.-democracy-promotion-under -trump-pub-66588).

21. For hints of such an approach, see Max Fischer, "Trump Prepares Orders Aiming at Global Funding and Treaties," *New York Times*, January 25, 2017.

22. The White House, Office of the Press Secretary, "Remarks by President Trump at National Prayer Breakfast," February 2, 2017 (www .whitehouse.gov/the-press-office/2017/02/02/remarks-president-trump -national-prayer-breakfast); also "Inaugural Address."

23. On these various issues, see the sources cited previously, as well as Wright, "Trump's 19th Century Foreign Policy"; Thomas Wright, "Trump's Team of Rivals, Riven by Distrust," *Foreign Policy*, December 14, 2016; Abby Phillip and Abigail Hauslohner, "Trump on the Future of Proposed Muslim Ban, Registry: 'You Know My Plans,'" *Washington Post*, December 22, 2016.

24. On this point, see Jim Tankersley, "What Republicans Did 15 Years Ago That Helped Create Donald Trump Today," *Washington Post*, March 21, 2016.

25. George Borjas, "Immigration and the American Worker: A Review of the Academic Literature," Center for Immigration Studies, April 2013 (http://cis.org/immigration-and-the-american-worker-review-aca demic-literature).

26. See Christopher Layne, "Sleepwalking with Beijing," *National Interest* (May/June 2015), pp. 37–45.

27. See, for instance, Brooks and Wohlforth, *America Abroad*.

28. This paragraph and the previous paragraph draw on Robert Kagan, *The World America Made* (New York: Vintage, 2012); Ikenberry, *Liberal Leviathan*; Brooks and Wohlforth, *America Abroad*; Tony Smith, *America's Mission: The United States and the Global Struggle for Democracy in the Twentieth Century* (Princeton University Press, 1994); Bruce Russett, *Grasping the Democratic Peace: Principles for a Post–Cold War World* (Princeton University Press, 1994); Henry Nau, *At Home Abroad* (Cornell University Press, 2002); Gilpin, *The Challenge of Global Capitalism*; Irwin, *Free Trade under Fire*; Ambassador Samantha Power, "The Future of United Nations Peacekeeping," Testimony to Senate Foreign

Relations Committee, December 9, 2015 (www.foreign.senate.gov/imo /media/doc/120915_Power_Testimony.pdf).

29. On the illusion of energy independence, as well as the real benefits of greater U.S. energy production, see Meghan O'Sullivan, " 'Energy Independence' Alone Won't Boost U.S. Power," *Bloomberg View*, February 14, 2013.

30. Ikenberry, *Liberal Leviathan*.

31. For a cogent analysis that emphasizes the deal-cutting aspect of this strategy, see Philip Zelikow, "The Art of the Global Deal," *American Interest*, December 13, 2016.

32. Francis Gavin, *Gold, Dollars, and Power: The Politics of International Monetary Relations, 1958–1971* (University of North Carolina Press, 2004), pp. 187–97.

33. See Document #29, "Editorial Note," in *Foreign Relations of the United States, 1969–1976*, vol. 1: *Foundations of Foreign Policy, 1969–1972* (https://history.state.gov/historicaldocuments/frus1969-76v01/d29).

34. Economic Policy Committee Meeting Minutes, September 9, 1985, CREST Archival Database, U.S. National Archives and Records Administration II, College Park, Md.

35. "301" sanctions are so named because they were originally created by section 301 of the Trade Act of 1974. The sanctions were later amended by the "Super 301" provisions of the Omnibus Trade and Competitiveness Act of 1988.

36. Along similar lines, see Robert Atkinson and Stephen Ezell, "Time for Constructive Confrontation with China," *The Hill*, September 25, 2015.

37. Many of the challenges and initiatives discussed in this paragraph are covered in greater length in Hal Brands, *Dealing with Allies in Decline: Alliance Management and U.S. Strategy in an Era of Global Power Shifts* (Washington, D.C.: Center for Strategic and Budgetary Assessments, 2017).

38. This was true, for instance, of increased NATO defense spending in the 1950s. See, generally, Richard L. Kugler, *Laying the Foundations: The Evolution of NATO in the 1950s*, Research Note (Santa Monica, Calif.: RAND Corporation, June 1990).

39. Aspects of such an approach are broached in Efraim Karsh and Eitan Shamir, "What after Counter-Insurgency? Raiding in Zones of Turmoil," *International Affairs* 92, no. 6 (2016), pp. 1427–41; Max Boot, "De-

feating ISIS," Council on Foreign Relations, Policy Innovation Memorandum No. 51, November 2014 (www.cfr.org/iraq/defeating-isis/p33773).

40. Daniel Byman, "What Trump Should Do about Terrorism (but Probably Won't)," *Lawfare* (blog), February 16, 2017 (https://lawfareblog .com/what-trump-should-do-about-terrorism-probably-wont).

41. See Larry Diamond, "Democracy in Decline: How Washington Can Reverse the Tide," *Foreign Affairs* 95, no. 4 (July/August 2016), pp. 151–60.

42. On Roosevelt, see Frederick Marks III, *Velvet on Iron: The Diplomacy of Theodore Roosevelt* (University of Nebraska Press, 1979).

43. Donovan Slack, "Building a Wall Not Enough to Secure Border, DHS Nominee John Kelly Says," *USA Today*, January 10, 2017.

44. See, for instance, Geoffrey Gertz, "What Will Trump's Embrace of Bilateralism Mean for America's Trade Partners?," Brookings Institution, February 8, 2017 (www.brookings.edu/blog/future-development/2017 /02/08/what-will-trumps-embrace-of-bilateralism-mean-for-americas -trade-partners/).

45. Jim Townsend, "Can Mattis Back Up His NATO Threat?," *Foreign Policy*, February 16, 2017.

46. The point is made in Zelikow, "The Art of the Global Deal."

47. See Michael Mastanduno, "System Maker and Privilege Taker: U.S. Power and the International Political Economy," *World Politics* 61, no. 1 (January 2009), pp. 121–54. Mastanduno argues that this power is in decline, in part due to the relative dearth of international security threats today, but this analysis was written prior to the significant increase in international *in*security in recent years.

48. For assessments of U.S. public opinion, see Dina Smeltz and others, *America Divided: Political Partisanship and U.S. Foreign Policy* (Chicago: Chicago Council on Global Affairs, October 2015); Pew Research Center, "Public Uncertain, Divided over America's Place in the World."

49. See Daniel Sargent, *A Superpower Transformed: The Remaking of American Foreign Relations in the 1970s* (Oxford University Press, 2014).

50. "Inaugural Address"; also James Crabtree, "Steve Bannon's War on India's High-Tech Economy," *Foreign Policy*, February 8, 2017.

51. Trump quoted in Tara Palmieri and others, "Trump's Faux Pas Diplomacy," *Politico*, February 8, 2017.

52. See Wright, "Trump's 19th Century Foreign Policy."

53. Gregory Hellman, "Flynn Calls Alliances 'One of the Greatest Tools We Have," *Politico*, January 10, 2017.

54. Dan Lamothe and Michael Birnbaum, "Defense Secretary Mattis Issues New Ultimatum to NATO Allies on Defense Spending," *Washington Post*, February 15, 2017.

55. Theodore Schleifer, "Graham Ridicules 'Mucho Sad' Border Tax Proposal," CNN, January 26, 2017; Ryan Kilpatrick, "Republican Senators Warn Trump against Withdrawing from NAFTA," *Time*, April 26, 2017; Austin Wright, "McCain Looks to Assure Australia after Trump Call," *Politico*, February 2, 2017.

56. See Nancy Cook and Josh Dawsey, "Businesses Grow Concerned about Trump after Early Excitement," *Politico*, February 3, 2017; Brian Heater, "New York's Tech Community Pens Letter Condemning Trump's Immigration Ban," *TechCrunch*, January 30, 2017 (https://tech crunch.com/2017/01/30/tech-nyc-trump/); Bess Levin, "Why Goldman Sachs Is Suddenly Worried about Donald Trump," *Vanity Fair*, February 6, 2017.

57. See, for instance, Trevor Thrall and John Glaser, "America First? Not So Fast! What We've Learned from 100 Days of Trump Foreign Policy," *War on the Rocks*, April 27, 2017.

CHAPTER SIX

1. As noted in the acknowledgments, this chapter is derived from an article that was originally coauthored with Eric Edelman. I am grateful to Eric for allowing me to republish this piece here.

2. Chuck Hagel, "Defense Innovation Days" Keynote Address, Newport, Rhode Island, September 3, 2014.

3. Walter Lippmann, *U.S. Foreign Policy: Shield of the Republic* (Boston: Little, Brown, 1943), pp. 9–10.

4. In practice, these options are not mutually exclusive—one could conceivably pursue a hybrid approach. But here I treat these options as distinct, to better flesh out their respective risks and merits.

5. Michael Mazarr, "The Risks of Ignoring Strategic Insolvency," *Washington Quarterly* 35, no. 4 (Fall 2012), pp. 7–22.

6. "Commencement Address at the United States Military Academy in West Point, New York," June 1, 2002 (www. presidency.ucsb.edu/ws /index.php?pid=62730&st=&st1=); Eric Edelman, "The Strange Career of the 1992 Defense Planning Guidance," in *In Uncertain Times: American*

Foreign Policy after the Berlin Wall and 9/11, edited by Melvyn P. Leffler and Jeffrey W. Legro (Cornell University Press, 2011), pp. 63–77.

7. Unless otherwise noted, military spending statistics are drawn from the Stockholm International Peace Research Institute (SIPRI) Military Expenditure Database (www.sipri.org/databases/milex), accessed May 2017.

8. John Lewis Gaddis, *Strategies of Containment: A Critical Appraisal of American National Security Policy during the Cold War* (Oxford University Press, 2005), p. 393; World Bank, "Military Expenditure (% of GDP)" (http://data.worldbank.org/indicator/MS.MIL.XPND.GD.ZS?locations=US&page=3).

9. Department of Defense, *Report of the Quadrennial Defense Review*, May 1997 (www.dod.gov/pubs/qdr/).

10. International Institute for Strategic Studies, *The Military Balance 2015* (London: International Institute for Strategic Studies, 2016), pp. 159–67; Catrin Einhorn, Hannah Fairfield, and Tim Wallace, "Russia Rearms for a New Era," *New York Times*, December 24, 2015.

11. SIPRI database, accessed May 2017.

12. Barbara Staff and Ryan Browne, "Intel Officials: North Korea 'Probably' Has Miniaturized Nuke," CNN, March 25, 2016; David Albright, "Future Directions in the DPRK's Nuclear Weapons Program: Three Scenarios for 2020," U.S.-Korea Institute, Johns Hopkins School of Advanced International Studies, Washington, D.C., November 2015.

13. See General David Goldfein, Chief of Staff of the U.S. Air Force, Statement to Senate Armed Services Committee, September 15, 2016 (www.armed-services.senate.gov/imo/media/doc/Goldfein_09-15-16 .pdf).

14. "DNI Clapper Provides Series of Threat Assessments on Capitol Hill," Office of the Director of National Intelligence, February 29, 2016 (www.dni.gov/index.php/newsroom/featured-articles/223-featured -articles-2016/1334-dni-clapper-provides-series-of-threat-assessments -on-capitol-hill).

15. SIPRI database, accessed May 2017.

16. World Bank, "Military Expenditure (% of GDP)"; Loren Thompson, "Pentagon Budget Headed below 3% of GDP as Warfighting Edge Wanes," *Forbes*, February 2, 2015.

17. Alex Daugherty, William Douglas, and Vera Bergengruen, "Budget Fights Imperils Trump's Military Spending Demands," *Miami Herald*,

May 1, 2017; Jeremy Herb, "Sources: Mattis Tells Hill Trump Budget Won't Fully Rebuild Military," CNN, April 21, 2017.

18. Robert Zarate, "Obama's FY2014 Defense Budget & the Sequestration Standoff," Foreign Policy Initiative, April 11, 2013 (http://www .foreignpolicyi.org/content/fpi-analysis-obama%E2%80%99s-fy2014 -defense-budget-sequestration-standoff); Todd Harrison, *Analysis of the FY 2013 Defense Budget and Sequestration* (Washington, D.C.: Center for Strategic and Budgetary Assessments, August 2012).

19. Quoted in Dave Majumdar, "The Pentagon's Readiness Crisis: Why the 2017 Defense Bill Will Make Things Worse," *National Interest,* July 13, 2016.

20. Travis Tritten, "Service Chiefs Paint Bleak Picture ahead of Defense Budget," *Stars and Stripes,* September 15, 2016; General Mark Milley, Chief of Staff, United States Army, Statement to Senate Armed Services Committee, September 15, 2016 (www.armed-services.senate.gov/imo /media/doc/Milley_09-15-16.pdf).

21. Cheryl Pellerin, "Service Chiefs: Budget Uncertainty, Funding Levels Are Biggest Challenges," *DoD News,* September 15, 2016.

22. Todd Harrison and Evan Montgomery, *The Cost of U.S. Nuclear Forces: From BCA to Bow Wave and Beyond* (Washington, D.C.: Center for Strategic and Budgetary Assessments, August 2015).

23. Jim Tice, "Army Shrinks to Smallest Level since before World War II," *Army Times,* May 7, 2016; Tony Capaccio and Gopal Ratnam, "Hagel Seeks Smallest U.S. Army since before 2001 Attack," Bloomberg, February 24, 2014.

24. Mark Gunzinger, *Shaping America's Future Military: Toward a New Force Planning Construct* (Washington, D.C.: Center for Strategic and Budgetary Assessments, 2013), pp. 2–3.

25. On Chinese spending, see SIPRI database.

26. Eric Heginbotham and others, *The U.S.-China Military Scorecard: Forces, Geography, and the Evolving Balance of Power, 1996–2017* (Santa Monica, Calif.: RAND Corporation, 2015), p. 342.

27. David Shlapak and Michael Johnson, "Outnumbered, Outranged, and Outgunned: How Russia Defeats NATO," *War on the Rocks,* April 21, 2016; David Shlapak and Michael Johnson, *Reinforcing Deterrence on NATO's Eastern Flank: Wargaming the Defense of the Baltics* (Santa Monica, Calif.: RAND Corporation, January 2016) (www.rand.org/pubs /research_reports/RR1253.html).

28. Mark Gunzinger with Chris Dougherty, *Outside-In: Operating from Range to Defeat Iran's Anti-Access and Area-Denial Threats* (Washington, D.C.: Center for Strategic and Budgetary Assessments, 2011), pp. 21–52.

29. Sydney Freedberg, "Army $40B Short on Modernization vs. Russia, China: CSA Milley," *Breaking Defense*, October 3, 2016.

30. Shlapak and Johnson, *Reinforcing Deterrence on NATO's Eastern Flank*.

31. Heginbotham and others, *U.S.-China Military Scorecard*, pp. xxx, 338, 342.

32. Statement of Admiral John Richardson, Chief of Naval Operations, to Senate Armed Services Committee, September 15, 2016 (www .armed-services.senate.gov/imo/media/doc/Richardson_09-15-16 .pdf).

33. Department of Defense, *Report of the Quadrennial Defense Review*, section 3, "Defense Strategy" (www.dod.gov/pubs/qdr/sec3.html).

34. Department of Defense, *Sustaining U.S. Global Leadership: Priorities for 21st Century Defense* (Department of Defense, 2012), p. 4.

35. National Defense Panel, *Ensuring a Strong U.S. Defense for the Future: The National Defense Panel Review of the 2014 Quadrennial Defense Review*, July 2014, p. 23 (www.usip.org/sites/default/files/Ensuring-a -Strong-U.S.-Defense-for-the-Future-NDP-Review-of-the-QDR_0.pdf).

36. Ben Blanchard, "Duterte Aligns Philippines with China, Says U.S. Has Lost," Reuters, October 20, 2016.

37. Heginbotham and others, *U.S.-China Military Scorecard*, p. xxxi.

38. See Bret Stephens, "Yes, America Should Be the World's Policeman," *Wall Street Journal*, November 15, 2014.

39. Under the Nixon Doctrine, Washington would keep existing treaty commitments in Asia and defend allies against aggression by a nuclear power, but it would provide only military and economic assistance to allies and partners facing other threats, such as insurgencies.

40. See, generally, Paul MacDonald and Joseph Parent, "Graceful Decline? The Surprising Success of Great Power Retrenchment," *International Security* 35, no. 4 (Spring 2011), pp. 7–44.

41. On credibility and reputation, see Keren Yarhi-Milo and Alexander Weisiger, "Revisiting Reputation: How Past Actions Matter in International Politics," *International Organization* 69, no. 2 (March 2015), pp. 473–95.

42. On these phenomena, see Randall Schweller, *Unanswered Threats: Political Constraints on the Balance of Power* (Princeton University Press, 2008); Schweller, "Bandwagoning for Profit: Bringing the Revisionist State Back In," *International Security* 19, no. 1 (Summer 1994), pp. 72–107.

43. Rick Brennan, "Withdrawal Symptoms: The Bungling of the Iraq Exit," *Foreign Affairs* 93, no. 6 (2014), pp. 25–34; Dexter Filkins, "What We Left Behind," *New Yorker*, April 28, 2014.

44. To clarify, this would entail more than simply using cyber as part of a U.S. conventional defense of Taiwan or the Baltic. Rather, it would entail using strategic cyberattacks against strategic targets—economic, infrastructural, or military—not directly associated with the aggression.

45. Marc Trachtenberg, *A Constructed Peace: The Making of the European Settlement, 1945–1963* (Princeton University Press, 1999), pp. 87–90.

46. H. W. Brands, "The Age of Vulnerability: Eisenhower and the National Insecurity State," *American Historical Review* 94, no. 4 (October 1989), pp. 963–89.

47. Ron Synovitz, "Europe Bracing against Risk of Russian 'Influence Operations,'" *Radio Free Europe/Radio Liberty*, January 16, 2017.

48. Brands, "Age of Vulnerability"; also Campbell Craig, *Destroying the Village: Eisenhower and Thermonuclear War* (Columbia University Press, 1998).

49. National Defense Panel, *Ensuring a Strong U.S. Defense for the Future*.

50. Senator John McCain, *Restoring American Power: Recommendations for the FY 2018–FY2022 Defense Budget*, January 2017 (www.mccain .senate.gov/public/_cache/files/25bff0ec-481e-466a-843f-68ba5619e6d8 /restoring-american-power-7.pdf), esp. pp. 9–14.

51. Marilyn Ware Center for Security Studies, *To Rebuild America's Military* (Washington, D.C.: American Enterprise Institute, 2015), esp. p. 25.

52. McCain, *Restoring American Power*, p. 20.

53. Thomas Donnelly, "Great Powers Don't Pivot," in *How Much Is Enough? Alternative Defense Strategies*, edited by Jacob Cohn, Ryan Boone, and Thomas Mahnken (Washington, D.C.: Center for Strategic and Budgetary Assessments, 2016), p. 7; also Ware Center, *To Rebuild America's Military*, p. 70.

54. On the importance of these various capabilities, see Evan Braden Montgomery, "Contested Primacy in the Western Pacific: China's Rise and the Future of U.S. Power Projection," *International Security* 38, no. 4

(Spring 2014), pp. 140–43; Timothy Walton, "Securing the Third Offset Strategy: Priorities for the Next Secretary of Defense," *Joint Force Quarterly* 82 (3rd Quarter 2016), pp. 6–15; Gunzinger with Dougherty, *Outside-In.*

55. Sydney Freedberg, "Pentagon Can't Afford to Field 3rd Offset Tech under BCA: Frank Kendall," *Breaking Defense,* October 31, 2016.

56. On debt-to-GDP ratio, see Congressional Budget Office, *The Budget and Economic Outlook: 2016 to 2026* (Congressional Budget Office, 2016), p. 3.

57. Freedberg, "Pentagon Can't Afford to Field 3rd Offset Tech under BCA."

58. Ware Center, *To Rebuild America's Military,* p. 2.

59. Martin Feldstein, "Defense Spending Would Be Great Stimulus," *Wall Street Journal,* December 24, 2008.

60. Center on Budget and Policy Priorities, "Policy Basics: Where Do Our Federal Tax Dollars Go?," March 4, 2016 (www.cbpp.org/research /federal-budget/policy-basics-where-do-our-federal-tax-dollars-go).

61. See, for instance, Robert Kaplan, "Eurasia's Coming Anarchy: The Risks of Chinese and Russian Weakness," *Foreign Affairs* 95, no. 2 (March/April 2016), pp. 33–41.

62. See, for instance, Jim Thomas, John Stillion, and Iskander Rehman, *Hard ROC 2.0: Taiwan and Deterrence through Protraction* (Washington, D.C.: Center for Strategic and Budgetary Assessments, 2014).

63. See Richard L. Kugler, *Laying the Foundations: The Evolution of NATO in the 1950s,* Research Note (Santa Monica, Calif.: RAND Corporation, June 1990).

64. Stephen Biddle, Michael O'Hanlon, and Kenneth Pollack, "How to Leave a Stable Iraq," *Foreign Affairs* 87, no. 5 (2008), pp. 40–58; also Peter Mansoor, *Surge: My Journey with General David Petraeus and the Remaking of the Iraq War* (Yale University Press, 2013).

65. NSC-68, "United States Objectives and Programs for National Security," April 14, 1950 (http://fas.org/irp/offdocs/nsc-hst/nsc-68.htm).

CHAPTER SEVEN

1. Rebecca Lissner and Micah Zenko, "There Is No Trump Doctrine, and There Will Never Be One," *Foreign Policy,* July 21, 2017. Other early analyses include Stephen Sestanovich, "The Brilliant Incoherence of Trump's Foreign Policy," *The Atlantic* (May 2017); Peter Dombrowski and Simon Reich, "Does Donald Trump Have a Grand Strategy?," *In-*

ternational Affairs 93, no. 5 (September 2017), pp. 1013–37; Reinhard Wolf, "Donald Trump's Status-Driven Foreign Policy," *Survival* 59, no. 5 (August–September 2017), pp. 99–116; Eliot Cohen, "How Trump Is Ending the America Era," *The Atlantic* (October 2017); Matthew Kroenig, "The Case for Trump's Foreign Policy: The Right People, the Right Positions," *Foreign Affairs* 96, no. 3 (May/June 2017), pp. 30–35; G. John Ikenberry, "The Plot against American Foreign Policy: Can the Liberal Order Survive?," *Foreign Affairs* 96, no. 3 (May/June 2017), pp. 2–9; Elliott Abrams, "Trump the Traditionalist: A Surprisingly Standard Foreign Policy," *Foreign Affairs* 96, no. 4 (July/August 2017), pp. 10–16.

2. Hal Brands, *What Good Is Grand Strategy? Power and Purpose in American Statecraft from Harry S. Truman to George W. Bush* (Cornell University Press, 2014).

3. Kori Schake, "Republican Foreign Policy after Trump," *Survival* 58, no. 5 (October–November 2016), pp. 33–52.

4. For a version of the argument that Trump has been tamed, see Trevor Thrall and John Glaser, "America First? Not so Fast! What We've Learned from 100 Days of Trump Foreign Policy," *War on the Rocks,* April 27, 2017.

5. Paul Kennedy, "The Eagle Has Landed," *Financial Times,* February 2, 2002; Stephen Brooks and William Wohlforth, "American Primacy in Perspective," *Foreign Affairs* 81, no. 4 (July/August 2002), pp. 20–33; Stephen Brooks and William Wohlforth, "The Rise and Fall of the Great Powers in the Twenty-First Century: China's Rise and the Fate of America's Global Position," *International Security* 40, no. 3 (Winter 2015/2016), pp. 7–53.

6. G. John Ikenberry, *Liberal Leviathan: The Origins, Crisis, and Transformation of the American World Order* (Princeton University Press, 2011); Melvyn Leffler, *A Preponderance of Power: National Security, the Truman Administration, and the Cold War* (Stanford University Press, 1992).

7. Andrew Bacevich, "The 'Global Order' Myth," *American Conservative,* June 15, 2017.

8. Author's conversation with European diplomat, February 2017.

9. John Lewis Gaddis, *We Now Know: Rethinking Cold War History* (Oxford University Press, 1997).

10. Robert McMahon, "Credibility and World Power: Exploring the Psychological Dimension in Postwar American Diplomacy," *Diplomatic History* 15, no. 4 (October 1991), pp. 455–72.

11. Tony Smith, *America's Mission: The United States and the World-wide Struggle for Democracy* (Princeton University Press, 2012), esp. p. 270.

12. Joseph Nye, *Soft Power: The Means to Success in World Politics* (New York: PublicAffairs, 2004).

13. See Jeet Heer, "Donald Trump's Foreign Policy Revolution," *New Republic,* March 25, 2016; Cassandra Vinograd, "Donald Trump Remarks on NATO Trigger Alarm Bells in Europe," *NBC News,* July 21, 2016; "Trump on Foreign Policy," *National Interest,* April 27, 2016; Victor Morton, "Trump Says He'd Force U.S. Military to Commit War Crimes," *Washington Times,* March 3, 2016.

14. Thomas Wright, "Trump's 19th Century Foreign Policy," *Politico,* January 20, 2016.

15. Peter Feaver, "Trump Is Right about Afghanistan," *Foreign Policy,* August 22, 2017.

16. He did, however, continue to harangue Mexican officials, thereby scotching an early summit with his Mexican counterpart. Daniela Diaz, "Mexican President Cancels Meeting with Trump," CNN, January 27, 2017.

17. Cheryl Pellerin, "2018 Budget Request for European Reassurance Initiative Grows to $4.7 Billion," *DoD News,* June 1, 2017.

18. Brian McKeon, "Trump's 'Secret Plan' to Defeat ISIS Looks a Lot Like Obama's," *Foreign Policy,* May 31, 2017.

19. Michael R. Gordon, Helene Cooper, and Michael Shear, "Dozens of U.S. Missiles Hit Air Base in Syria," *New York Times,* April 6, 2017.

20. Abrams, "Trump the Traditionalist," p. 10; Kroenig, "The Case for Trump's Foreign Policy."

21. Michael Isikoff, "How the Trump Administration's Secret Efforts to Ease Russia Sanctions Fell Short," Yahoo News, June 1, 2017.

22. Charlie Savage, "Trump Poised to Lift Ban on CIA 'Black Site' Prisons," *New York Times,* January 25, 2017.

23. Ashely Parker and others, "'I Was All Set to Terminate': Inside Trump's Sudden Shift on NAFTA," *Washington Post,* April 27, 2017.

24. Michelle Nichols, "U.S. Priority on Syria No Longer Focused on 'Getting Assad Out': Haley," Reuters, March 30, 2017.

25. "Inaugural Address: Trump's Full Speech," CNN, January 21, 2017.

26. "Full Text: Trump's 2017 U.N. Speech Transcript," *Politico,* September 19, 2017.

27. Julian Hattem, "Trump Warns against 'False Song of Globalism,'" *The Hill*, April 27, 2016; "Trump's 2017 U.N. Speech Transcript."

28. H. R. McMaster and Gary Cohn, "America First Doesn't Mean America Alone," *Wall Street Journal*, May 30, 2017.

29. Ana Swanson and Ian Austen, "Trump Talks Tough on China and Mexico, but Trade Actions Hit Canada," *New York Times*, September 27, 2017.

30. Claire Jones and Sam Fleming, "G20 Drops Vow to Resist All Forms of Protectionism," *Financial Times*, March 18, 2017.

31. Maytaal Angel and David Lawder, "Despite Delay, U.S. Expected to Impose Steel Tariffs," Reuters, August 15, 2017; Damien Paletta, "Trump Preparing Withdrawal from South Korea Trade Deal, a Move Opposed by Top Aides," *Washington Post*, September 2, 2017.

32. "Transcript: President Trump's Remarks on Leaving the Paris Climate Deal, Annotated," *Washington Post*, June 1, 2017; Robert Blackwill and Theodore Rappleye, "Trump's Five Mistaken Reasons for Withdrawing from the Trans-Pacific Partnership," *Foreign Policy*, June 22, 2017.

33. Robert McMahon, *Dean Acheson and the Creation of an American World Order* (Washington, D.C.: Potomac Books, 2008), p. 74.

34. On the idea of an "overbalance," see Richard Rosecrance, "The Emerging Overbalance of Power," *American Interest*, August 22, 2014.

35. Jon Sharman, "Donald Trump Says Germany Owes U.S. and NATO 'Vast Sums of Money' for Defence," *Independent*, March 18, 2017; Tara Palmieri, Kenneth Vogel, Josh Dawsey, and Nahal Toosi, "Trump's Faux Pas Diplomacy," *Politico*, February 8, 2017.

36. Samuel Osborne, "Donald Trump Avoids Saying Who He Trusts More—Vladimir Putin or Angela Merkel," *Independent*, January 16, 2017; Nolan McCaskill, "Trump's Tweet on London Attack Draws Ire from U.K. Officials," *Politico*, September 15, 2017.

37. Isikoff, "How the Trump Administration's Secret Efforts to Ease Russia Sanctions Fell Short"; Rosie Gray, "Trump Declines to Affirm NATO's Article 5," *The Atlantic*, May 25, 2017.

38. Greg Jaffe, "National Security Adviser McMaster Defends Trump's Approach with Allies as "Tough Love,'" *Washington Post*, June 28, 2017.

39. Trump has also overclaimed credit for increases in European defense spending, given that NATO outlays had already begun to increase in 2015 and 2016. See Robbie Gramer, "Thank Putin, Not Trump, for NATO's New Defense Spending Boost," *Foreign Policy*, June 28, 2017.

40. Max Greenwood, "Trump Threatens to Scrap 'Horrible' South Korea Trade Deal," *The Hill*, April 27, 2017; Glenn Thrush and Mark Landler, "Why Trump, after North Korea's Test, Aimed His Sharpest Fire at the South," *New York Times*, September 3, 2017.

41. Uri Friedman, "Lindsey Graham Reveals the Dark Calculus of Striking North Korea," *The Atlantic*, August 1, 2017; Ryan Struyk, "Trump: There is 'Absolutely' a Chance of 'Major, Major Conflict' with North Korea," *ABC News*, April 27, 2017.

42. See Hal Brands and Colin Kahl, "Trump's Grand Strategic Train Wreck," *Foreign Policy*, January 30, 2017; Hal Brands and Peter Feaver, "What Are America's Alliances Good For?," *Parameters* 47, no. 2 (Summer 2017), pp. 15–30.

43. McMaster and Cohn, "America First Doesn't Mean America Alone."

44. Smith, *America's Mission*; also Elliott Abrams, *Realism and Democracy: American Foreign Policy after the Arab Spring* (Yale University Press, 2017), pp. 1–91.

45. Abrams, *Realism and Democracy*, pp. 1–91; Paul Miller, "American Grand Strategy and the Democratic Peace," *Survival* 52, no. 2 (April–May 2012), pp. 49–76; Ikenberry, *Liberal Leviathan*.

46. Thomas Carothers, "Prospects for U.S. Democracy Promotion under Trump," Carnegie Endowment for International Peace, January 5, 2017 (http://carnegieendowment.org/2017/01/05/prospects-for-u.s.-democracy-promotion-under-trump-pub-66588); Brooke Seipel, "Trump Defends Putin: 'You Think Our Country Is So Innocent?,'" *The Hill*, February 4, 2017.

47. Anne Applebaum, "Don't Forget Those Smiling Images of Trump and the Russians," *Washington Post*, May 11, 2017.

48. Abby Philip and David Nakamura, "Autocrats Hear a Clear Message during Trump Trip: U.S. Will Not 'Lecture' on Human Rights," *Washington Post*, May 22, 2017; Eugene Scott, "Trump Keeps Up Criticism of Germany," CNN, May 30, 2017.

49. Joshua Berlinger and Elise Labott, "Trump Praises Duterte's Deadly Drug War in Leaked Transcript," CNN, May 24, 2017; Carol Morello, "Trump Calls Erdogan to Congratulate Him on Contested Referendum, Turkey Says," *Washington Post*, April 17, 2017.

50. Josh Rogin, "State Department Considers Scrubbing Democracy Promotion from Its Mission," *Washington Post*, August 1, 2017; Conor

Finnegan, "Tillerson: Pushing Human Rights Abroad 'Creates Obstacles' to U.S. Interests," *ABC News,* May 3, 2017.

51. The White House, Office of the Press Secretary, "Remarks by President Trump on the Strategy in Afghanistan and South Asia," August 21, 2017 (www.whitehouse.gov/the-press-office/2017/08/21/remarks-president-trump-strategy-afghanistan-and-south-asia).

52. The Trump administration did freeze or delay roughly $300 in military aid to Egypt in mid-2017, but that decision was apparently driven mostly by concern over Egyptian ties to North Korea. Joby Warrick, "A North Korean Ship Was Seized off Egypt with a Huge Cache of Weapons Destined for a Surprising Buyer," *Washington Post,* October 1, 2017.

53. The White House, Office of the Press Secretary, "Remarks by President Trump to the People of Poland," July 6, 2017 (www.whitehouse.gov/the-press-office/2017/07/06/remarks-president-trump-people-poland-july-6-2017).

54. "Trump's 2017 U.N. Speech Transcript."

55. Thomas Donnelly and William Kristol, "An Empire for Liberty," *Weekly Standard,* October 2, 2017.

56. Stephen Brooks and William Wohlforth, *America Abroad: The United States' Global Role in the 21st Century* (Oxford University Press, 2016).

57. Laura Koran, "Trump Administration Dramatically Scales Back Refugee Admissions," CNN, September 27, 2017.

58. "Trump's 2017 U.N. Speech Transcript."

59. Angela Dewan and Stephanie Halasz, "G20 Closes with Rebuke to Trump's Climate Change Stance," CNN, July 9, 2017; Krishnadev Calamur, "Merkel Urges 'Europe to Take Our Fate into Our Own Hands,'" *The Atlantic,* May 30, 2017.

60. James Kanter, "The E.U.-Japan Trade Deal: What's in It and Why It Matters," *New York Times,* July 6, 2017; Motoko Rich, "TPP, The Trade Deal Trump Killed, Is Back in Talks without U.S.," *New York Times,* July 14, 2017.

61. Josh Chin, "China Says Prepared to Lead Global Economy if Necessary," *Wall Street Journal,* January 23, 2017.

62. Scott Sagan and Jeremi Suri, "The Madman Nuclear Alert: Secrecy, Signaling, and Safety in October 1969," *International Security* 27, no. 4 (Spring 2003), pp. 150–83.

63. John Lewis Gaddis, "Grand Strategy in the Second Term," *Foreign Affairs* 84, no. 1 (January/February 2005), p. 6.

64. Jonathan Swan, "Scoop: Trump Urges Staff to Portray Him as 'Crazy Guy,'" *Axios,* October 1, 2017.

65. Navan Chanda, "Doubts Grow over TPP," *Straits Times,* September 21, 2016.

66. Josh Rogin, "Trump to Unveil Plans for an 'Arab NATO' in Saudi Arabia," *Washington Post,* May 17, 2017; Mark Landler, "Trump Takes Credit for Saudi Move against Qatar, a U.S. Military Partner," *New York Times,* June 6, 2017.

67. "Trump Alarms Venezuela with Talk of a 'Military Option,'" *New York Times,* August 12, 2017.

68. See Colin Kahl, "The Myth of a 'Better' Iran Deal," *Foreign Policy,* September 26, 2017; Murtaza Hussain, "How Trump Is Trying to Blow Up the Iran Nuclear Deal," *Intercept,* September 10, 2017; Andrew Exum, "If Trump Undermines the Iran Deal," *The Atlantic,* July 22, 2017.

69. Brian Bennett, "Aides Warned Trump Not to Attack North Korea's Leader Personally before His Fiery U.N. Address," *Los Angeles Times,* September 22, 2017; Vipin Narang and Ankit Panda, "War of the Words: North Korea, Trump, and Strategic Stability," *War on the Rocks,* August 10, 2017.

70. It appeared, as of mid-October 2017, that Trump would decertify the deal but not encourage Congress to reimpose unilateral sanctions on Iran. Anne Gearn and Karoun Demirjian, "Trump Plans to Declare that Iran Nuclear Deal Is Not in the National Interest," *Washington Post,* October 5, 2017. How competently this gambit would be implemented and how well it would work remained to be seen.

71. Jonathan Martin, "Bob Corker Says Trump's Recklessness Threatens 'World War III,'" *New York Times,* October 8, 2017; Susan Glasser, "Trump National Security Team Blindsided by NATO Speech," *Politico,* June 5, 2017.

72. Stephen Walt, "The Global Consequences of Trump's Incompetence," *Foreign Policy,* July 18, 2017.

73. Tokyo to State and Other Posts, March 14, 1991, Electronic Briefing Book 175, National Security Archive (http://nsarchive2.gwu.edu/NSAEBB/NSAEBB175/japan2-13.pdf).

74. Mark Landler and Michael Forsythe, "Trump Tells Xi Jinping U.S. Will Honor 'One China' Policy," *New York Times,* February 9, 2017.

75. Benjamin Wittes, "Malevolence Tempered by Incompetence: Trump's Horrifying Executive Order on Refugees and Visas," *Lawfare*

(blog), January 28, 2017; Wilson Fache, "In Mosul, Iraqi Soldiers Decry Trump's Travel Restrictions," *Yahoo News,* January 28, 2017.

76. Helene Cooper, "After Chemical Attack, Asking if U.S. Remarks Emboldened Assad," *New York Times,* April 7, 2007.

77. J. Dana Stuster, "Trump Administration Sends Mixed Messages about Syria Strike, Christians Targeted in Egypt, and a New Proposal for Libya," *Lawfare* (blog), April 11, 2017.

78. Carol Morello and David Filipov, "Tillerson Meets with Putin amid Deepening Tensions over U.S. Missile Strikes in Syria," *Washington Post,* April 12, 2017.

79. Josh Rogin, "Inside the Trump-Tillerson Divide over Qatar," *Washington Post,* June 14, 2017; "Qatar Foreign Minister: Blockade Pushing It Closer to Iran Economically," Reuters, September 25, 2017.

80. Ben Jacobs, "Trump Threatens 'Military Option' in Venezuela as Crisis Escalates," *Guardian,* August 11, 2017.

81. Alex Ward, "Trump Tweeted about a New Iran Missile Test That Didn't Happen," *Vox,* September 26, 2017; Karen DeYoung, "Trump Contradicts Tillerson on North Korea, the Latest in a Series of Put-Downs," *Washington Post,* October 1, 2017.

82. Max Fisher, "Stephen K. Bannon's CPAC Comments, Annotated and Explained," *New York Times,* February 24, 2017.

83. Massimo Calabresi, "Inside Donald Trump's War against the State," *Time,* March 9, 2017; Elana Schor, "Trump Administration Still Riddled with Key Vacancies," *Politico,* August 11, 2017; Jon Michaels, "Trump and the 'Deep State': The Government Strikes Back," *Foreign Affairs* 96, no. 5 (September/October 2017), pp. 52–56.

84. Robbie Gramer, Dan de Luce, and Colum Lynch, "How the Trump Administration Broke the State Department," *Foreign Policy,* July 31, 2017.

85. Nye, *Soft Power.*

86. Mary Dudziak, "Brown as a Cold War Case," *Journal of American History* 91, no. 1 (June 2004), pp. 32–42.

87. Gregory Hellman, "Trump White House Unveils a 'Hard-Power Budget,'" *Politico,* March 16, 2017. Although Trump claimed that the Pentagon's budget would rise by nearly 10 percent under his submission, the true growth—compared to Obama's final budget—would have been significantly less.

88. Gayle Tzemach Lemon, "Want to Win Wars? Fund Soft Power, Trump's Generals Says," *Defense One,* March 2, 2017.

89. Russell Berman, "President Trump's 'Hard Power' Budget," *The Atlantic,* March 16, 2017; Robbie Gramer, "Senate Panel Rejects Trump Plan for Cutting Foreign Assistance," *Foreign Policy,* September 7, 2017.

90. James Gibney, "The U.S. Will Pay a Price for Trump's Global Unpopularity," *Bloomberg View,* June 28, 2017; also the Pew data cited subsequently.

91. Amber Phillips, "Are Some of Trump's Key Cabinet Members Thinking about Abandoning Him?," *Washington Post,* August 28, 2017.

92. Richard Wike, Bruce Stokes, Jacob Poushter, and Janell Fetterolf, "U.S. Image Suffers as Publics around World Question Trump's Leadership," Pew Research Center, June 26, 2017 (www.pewglobal.org/2017 /06/26/u-s-image-suffers-as-publics-around-world-question-trumps -leadership/).

93. See Niall Ferguson, "Donald Trump's New World Order," *American Interest,* November 21, 2016, and chapter 5 of this volume.

94. Kimberly Dozier, "New Power Center in Trumpland: The "Axis of Adults,'" *Daily Beast,* April 16, 2017.

95. Adam Behsudi, "Trump's Trade Pullout Roils Rural America," *Politico,* August 7, 2017.

96. Marc Champion, "Trump's 'America First' May Be Bigger Threat to Asia than Europe," *Bloomberg News,* June 2, 2017.

97. Uri Friedman, "The Testing Ground for Trump's Russia Policy," *The Atlantic,* July 30, 2017.

98. Bill Hayton, "The Week Donald Trump Lost the South China Sea," *Foreign Policy,* July 31, 2017; James Bowen, "Trump–Turnbull Meeting Comes Amid Increasing Debate over Australia's U.S. Ties," *The Diplomat,* May 5, 2017.

99. On the basic phenomenon of diplomatic resistance to an aggressive hegemonic power, see Robert Pape, "Soft Balancing against the United States," *International Security* 30, no. 1 (Summer 2005), pp. 7–45.

100. "Excerpts from Pentagon's Plan: 'Prevent the Re-Emergence of a New Rival,'" *New York Times,* March 8, 1992.

101. Andrew Bacevich, *American Empire: The Realities and Consequences of U.S. Diplomacy* (Harvard University Press, 2002).

Index

balancing and, 30; Philippine relations with, 139; potential war with, 136–37; regional primacy of, 45–46, 59; Taiwan crisis (1995–96), 129; tariffs on, 163; trade with, 95, 111, 115; Trump policy and, 159, 169–70, 173; U.S. primacy and, 14–15; U.S. relations with, 32–33, 55, 61; U.S.-China Strategic and Economic Dialogue, 60

Clapper, James, 133

Climate change: Obama grand strategy and, 51, 58; Paris Agreement on, 88, 110, 123, 163, 169; Trump policy and, 169; U.S.-China relations and, 61

Clinton, Bill, 5

Clinton, Hillary, 59, 86–87, 105, 106, 154

Cohn, Gary, 159, 162, 165

Cold War, 90, 91, 143, 155, 176. *See also* Post–Cold War era

Colgan, Jeff, 94

Comey, James, 86

Congress: defense spending and, 92; internationalism, bipartisan support for, 82; Iran relations and, 58; on Trans-Pacific Partnership, 72; on Trump budget, 176–77; Trump relations with, 84–85, 105, 124, 159, 160

Connally, John, 90

Continentalism, 84

Corker, Bob, 172–73

Counterinsurgencies, 30, 70, 134

Crimea, Russian annexation of, 68

Cuba, U.S. relations with, 58, 61

Cyberattacks: as alternative to war, 142; as coercion short of war, 69; democratization of technology and, 132; against Iran, 58; retaliation for, 144; Russia and, 135; vulnerability to, 143–44

Defense spending: budget for, 34–36; internationalism and, 103; ISIS threat and, 98; Obama grand strategy, 53–56, 134–35, 137–38; offshore balancing and, 31, 34–37; as percentage of GDP, 14–15, 18–19, 34–36, 130, 133; as percentage of global total, 129; post–Vietnam War, 90; primacy, reinvesting in, 144–50; public opinion on, 87–88; reductions in, 53–54, 133–35; requirements for, 128–29; sustainability of, 147–48; for three-theater force, 145–47; Trump budget for, 176

Democracy: benefits of, 113; as common value of allies, 164; Fortress America model and, 109; grand strategy and, 27; ideological challenges to, 13; National Endowment for Democracy, 21; nonmilitary promotion of, 118; post–Cold War advancement of, 8; post–World War II grand strategy and, 3, 81; promotion of, 4–6, 21, 30, 53–54, 92; security and, 157; Trump on promotion of, 83, 166–68

Democratic recession, 13

Deudney, Daniel, 83

Discriminatory trade practices, 115–16, 173

Drones, 56, 64, 71

Duterte, Rodrigo, 71, 138, 167

East Asia Summit, 71

Eberstadt, Nicholas, 94

Economic nationalism, 107

Educational attainment, 94

Eisenhower, Dwight, 85, 90, 143, 144

Employment: globalization and, 93–95, 105, 111, 115; postindustrial economy and, 94–95; wages depressed by migrants, 97, 110–11